Iran and Nuclear Weapons

This book investigates what is driving Iran's nuclear weapons program in a less-hostile regional environment, using a theory of protracted conflicts to explicate proliferation.

Iran's nuclear weapons program has alarmed the international community since the 1990s, but has come to the forefront of international security concerns since 2000. This book argues that Iran's hostility with the United States remains the major causal factor for its proliferation activities. With the US administration pursuing aggressive foreign policies towards Iran since 2000, the latter's security threat intensified. A society that is split on many important domestic issues remained united on the issue of nuclear weapons acquisition after the US war in Iraq. Consequently, Iran became determined in its drive to acquire nuclear weapons and boldly announced its decision to enrich uranium, leaving the US in no doubt about its nuclear status.

This book underscores the importance of protracted conflicts in proliferation decisions, and underpinning this is the assumption that non-proliferation may be achieved through the termination of intractable conflicts. The aims of this work are to demonstrate that a state's decision to acquire nuclear weapons depends largely on its engagement in protracted conflicts, which shows not only that the presence of nuclear rivals intensifies the nuclear ambition, but also that non-nuclear status of rival states can promote non-proliferation incentives in conflicting states inclined to proliferate.

This study will be of great interest to students of Iran, Middle Eastern politics, nuclear proliferation and international relations theory.

Saira Khan is a Research Associate at McGill-University of Montreal Joint Research Group in International Security (REGIS).

Routledge global security studies
Series editors: Aaron Karp, Regina Karp and Terry Teriff

Nuclear Proliferation and International Security
Sverre Lodgaard and Morten Bremer Maerli

Global Insurgency and the Future of Armed Conflict
Debating fourth-generation warfare
Terry Terriff, Aaron Karp and Regina Karp

Terrorism and Weapons of Mass Destruction
Responding to the challenge
Edited by Ian Bellany

Globalization and WMD Proliferation
Edited by James A. Russell and Jim J. Wirtz

Power Shifts, Strategy and War
Declining states and international conflict
Dong Sun Lee

Energy Security and Global Politics
The militarization of resource management
Edited by Daniel Moran and James A. Russell

US Nuclear Weapons Policy After the Cold War
Russians, 'rogues' and domestic division
Nick Ritchie

Security and Post-Conflict Reconstruction
Dealing with fighters in the aftermath of war
Edited by Robert Muggah

Network Centric Warfare and Coalition Operations
The new military operating system
Paul T. Mitchell

American Foreign Policy and the Politics of Fear
Threat inflation since 9/11
Edited by A. Trevor Thrall and Jane K. Cramer

Risk, Global Governance and Security
The other war on terror
Yee-Kuang Heng and Kenneth McDonagh

Nuclear Weapons and Cooperative Security in the 21st Century
The new disorder
Stephen J. Cimbala

Political Economy and Grand Strategy
A neoclassical realist view
Mark R. Brawley

Iran and Nuclear Weapons
Protracted conflict and proliferation
Saira Khan

Iran and Nuclear Weapons
Protracted conflict and proliferation

Saira Khan

LONDON AND NEW YORK

First published 2010
by Routledge
2 Park Square, Milton Park, Abingdon, Oxon, OX14 4RN

Simultaneously published in the USA and Canada
by Routledge
711 Third Avenue, New York, NY 10017

Routledge is an imprint of the Taylor & Francis Group, an informa business

First issued in paperback 2011

© 2010 Saira Khan

Typeset in Times New Roman by Swales and Willis Ltd, Exeter, Devon

All rights reserved. No part of this book may be reprinted or reproduced or utilised in any form or by any electronic, mechanical, or other means, now known or hereafter invented, including photocopying and recording, or in any information storage or retrieval system, without permission in writing from the publishers.

The publisher has no responsibility for the persistence or accuracy of URLs for external or third-party internet websites referred to in this book, and does not guarantee that any content on such websites is, or will remain, accurate or appropriate.

British Library Cataloguing in Publication Data
A catalogue record for this book is available from the British Library

Library of Congress Cataloging in Publication Data
Khan, Saira.
 Iran and nuclear weapons: protracted conflict and proliferation / Saira Khan
 p. cm.
 1. Nuclear arms control—Iran. 2. Nuclear weapons—Iran. 3. Nuclear nonproliferation—Case studies. 4. United States—Foreign relations—Iran. 5. Iran—Foreign relations—United States. I. Title.
 JZ5665.K49 2009
 355.02'170955—dc22
 2009013231

ISBN10: 0–415–45307–0 (hbk)
ISBN10: 0–415–66454–3 (pbk)
ISBN10: 0–203–86942–7 (ebk)

ISBN13: 978–0–415–45307–3 (hbk)
ISBN13: 978–0–415–66454–7 (pbk)
ISBN13: 978–0–203–86942–0 (ebk)

To my dearest mother, Nargis Khan

Contents

Acknowledgments		xi
Introduction		1

PART I
Causes of proliferation — 9

1. Factors utilized to comprehend Iran's nuclear weapons aspiration — 11

PART II
Theory — 25

2. Proliferation proclivities of protracted conflict states — 27

PART III
Case study: Iran — 45

3. Iran's nuclear ambition and twin protracted conflicts between 1947 and 1979 — 47

4. Iran's nuclear program and triple protracted conflicts from 1979 onwards — 63

5. The ramifications of the asymmetric Iran–US protracted conflict from 1990 to 2000 in Iran's nuclear domain — 77

6. Iran's fast-paced proliferation activity and hostile US policy since 2000 — 89

Conclusion — 110

Notes	120
Bibliography	138
Index	152

Acknowledgments

This book could not have been written without considerable support from a great number of people. Throughout this endeavor, my colleagues, professional acquaintances, friends and family have supported and assisted me in a variety of ways. I am deeply indebted to all of them for their contributions in the making of this book.

During the research work I received enormous help from a number of people. Special thanks to Leonard Spector for giving me his precious time and his insightful thoughts on the subject. I would like to thank Charles D. Ferguson, Michael Levi, Shaul Bakhash, Farideh Fardi, and Meir Javedanfar for enlightening me with their views on the issue. Thanks also to Vali Nasr and Michael Brecher for helping me with primary research. Sincere thanks are for George Perkovich and Richard Betts for encouraging me to read their perspectives on the matter. Thanks to Shahram Chubin and Trita Parsi for agreeing to be interviewed, which I could not follow through due to unavoidable situations. I have relied on their publications instead. Very special thanks go to Akbar Ganji for giving me his precious time and his views about the issue. His thoughts have helped me in better understanding the Iranian perspective on the matter.

I have benefited a great deal from many colleagues and friends during the process of my research work. I thank my colleagues at the University of British Columbia who had to bear with my frequent loud conversations when I was conducting interviews from my office. I cannot thank Juliet Prasad enough for her help with regard to using the library facilities at McGill University. I sincerely thank T.V. Paul for always supporting me in my research endeavors. Thanks to the University of Montreal-McGill Joint Research Group in International Security (REGIS) for providing the research position as I was working on this project.

I would like to thank Andrew Humphrys, the editor of Routledge, for his assistance in publishing the book. He saw the potential in my work, which even I did not see, at an early stage of the research process. It was a pleasure having him as the editor of my book. I also want to thank the editorial staff of Routledge for assisting me in bringing this book to press.

At an early stage of the research work, I received a grant from the International Studies Association to present a paper entitled "Iran–US Protracted Conflict and Iran's Nuclear Ambition" at the ISA Convention in Chicago in 2007, which was the starting point of this book work. A generous grant was also provided by Carleton University for the research work.

Finally, I would like to thank my family. My spouse, Jalal, and son, Andaleeb, have always given me the environment at home that a researcher needs in pursuing research goals effectively. Without their encouragement and support it would not have been possible to spend so many months in researching for and writing the book. While I cannot name so many family members who have always cared for my work, although I greatly appreciate their support towards my endeavor, I would like to mention my 10-year-old nephew, Fadl Khan, as a note of appreciation for showing special interest at his age in understanding the value of writing such a book. The acknowledgment section will remain incomplete without mentioning my parents and their contributions in my life. My late father Shafiullah Khan's life and human qualities inspire me to find a "silver lining" in every difficult situation and persevere all the time. Thus, no difficult situation was able to get in the way of this endeavor. During my college years my mother, Nargis Khan, used to call me her "prize child," the impact of which I did not realize then. Today I know how much those words impacted in boosting my spirit and confidence in every realm. I dedicate this book to my mother – who has dedicated all her life in balancing between teaching, social work, and family responsibilities and received the Best College Teacher's Award of Dhaka Metropolitan area in Bangladesh in 1994 – for being my life's role-model.

Introduction

Iran's nuclear program had alarmed the international community in the 1990s, but it came to the forefront of international security concerns in 2000. Although Tehran still maintains that its nuclear program is for peaceful purposes, in the recent past it has admitted to possessing enriched uranium as part of its uranium enrichment program, which has unnerved the international community in general and the United States in particular. Iran's nuclear drive has been probed by scholars and policy-makers and although there is controversy on whether or not Iran is aiming to build nuclear weapons, most scholars who believe that Iran's nuclear program has dual purpose argue that the country has been motivated to acquire nuclear weapons for security purposes, as has been the case with almost all regional proliferators. The general understanding is that regional proliferators proliferate for regional security determinants. While this remains the primary driving force, no one has examined why Iran, in the absence of a hostile Iraq after Saddam Hussein's rule since 2003, still chooses to keep its nuclear weapons option alive and, in fact, remains more focused on the nuclear program. This deficiency begs a salient question which this study investigates: What drives Iran to acquire nuclear weapons and relentlessly move on with its nuclear weapons program in a less-hostile regional environment? The objective is to demonstrate that Iran's nuclear ambition is related to both regional and global environment due to its regional and global conflict engagements, which means that both regional and global security threats for Iran need to be absent before Tehran can give up its nuclear ambition. It is argued that Iran's hostility with the US remains the major causal factor for its serious proliferation activities since the 1990s and unrelenting effort in that realm since 2000. Iran's protracted conflict with the US started at the end of the Shah period and the beginning of the Islamic Revolution in the country in 1979. Although the development of the conflict almost coincided with the beginning of the Iran–Iraq War in 1980 which kept Iran focused on Iraq and the war, since 1979 Iran's leaders have perceived the US as the principal enemy of the Islamic states which supported their enemy, Israel, in the Middle Eastern region. Thus, in addition to having two protracted conflicts since the late 1940s and early 1950s with Israel and Iraq respectively, Iran developed a new intractable conflict with the US in 1979. From then Iran had three enemies – Iraq, Israel, and the US – to worry about for the next 30 years. Initially, Iraq was Iran's principal enemy in the region due to the territorial conflict that they were engaged in and for fighting one of the bloodiest and protracted wars in the region from 1980 to 1988. The two major regional rivals also strived for regional dominance and, consequently, this was also a structurally-determined rivalry. Israel, on the other hand, was an enemy state since its creation in 1947, but became Iran's important rival in the region since the 1980s due to the war in Lebanon and the creation of *Hezbollah* by Tehran which fights Iran's proxy wars in Lebanon against Israel. In the nuclear realm, Iraq and Israel's nuclear weapons programs alarmed Iran and the Islamic Republic became anxious to develop a deterrent capability against Iraq, with whom it fought one of the longest wars in the region, and Israel, whose existence in the Middle East Iran denies, and its nuclear program initially was developed to address its dual regional security concerns. The third conflict it got engaged in with the US made it more attracted to the nuclear program since this was an asymmetric conflict where Iran was a weak regional state trying to defend itself against a global opponent. Thus, the number of conflict engagements and conflict types determined Iran's nuclear choice. However, the pace of its nuclear weapons program was relatively slow till 2000 even though from 1990 to 2000 its nuclear program received renewed attention from the Islamic leadership. This was the period when the cold war ended, but Iran was still engaged in a conflict with the world's only superpower, the US, that identified Iran as a rogue state that was determined to jeopardize regional peace and stability in the otherwise orderly post-cold war world. The systemic change made matters more troublesome for Iran. With the US administration pursuing aggressive foreign policies toward Iran since 2000, the latter's security threat intensified. The Bush administration's declaration of Iran as one of the "Axis of Evil" states severely threatened and humiliated Iran; the threat exacerbated with the administration's war on Iraq in 2003 on the pretext that it was in possession of weapons of mass destruction. A society that was and still is split on many of the important domestic issues including democratization, modernization, and westernization, the Iranians remained united on the nuclear issue after the war on Iraq. The US decision to attack Iraq without the approval of the United Nations demonstrated the power of Washington in a unipolar world and proved that in the absence of a nuclear deterrent capability, Iran would soon be in the same position as Iraq and would be the US's next target in the Middle East for being one of the "Axis of Evil" states. Addressing its security concerns pertaining to this asymmetric conflict with the acquisition of a deterrent capability became pertinent for Iran. Consequently, Iran became relentless in its drive to acquire nuclear weapons and boldly announced its decision to enrich uranium so that the US would not be confused about its nuclear status. Improved and non-aggressive US policies toward Iran, which can be instrumental in terminating the prolonged Iran–US conflict, can convince Iran to renounce its nuclear weapons ambition.

The Iranian case is tested by using a theoretical framework on proliferation of protracted conflict states. Several causal factors are used to understand why Iran has been a determined proliferator. The project underscores the salience of protracted conflicts in proliferation decisions. Underpinning this idea is the assumption that non-proliferation may be achieved through the termination of intractable conflicts. Its aims are the following: 1) To understand that a state's decision to acquire nuclear weapons depends largely on its engagement in protracted conflicts; the number of conflicts it is engaged in and aggressive policies of the adversaries affect the pace of its nuclear drive. Resolution of protracted conflicts is pertinent for non-proliferation purposes. 2) To comprehend that although the number of conflicts makes a difference in terms of nuclear decisions, the presence of nuclear rivals intensifies the nuclear ambition, meaning non-nuclear status of the rival states can promote non-proliferation incentives in conflicting states inclined to proliferate. 3) To highlight that a long-running asymmetric conflict with a nuclear global power must be terminated because such a conflict invariably motivates the weaker party to the conflict to possess a nuclear deterrent capability to face off the superior rival even if the ramifications of such possession are politically and financially costly. 4) To explicate why standard non-proliferation strategies may be ineffective in attaining a non-proliferated world.

The rationale for this study is that although much scholarly attention has been paid on the proliferation drives of states in general and the Iranian nuclear motivation in particular, the efforts have generally revolved around the concept of security. It is pertinent to go beyond simple security logic and make efforts to understand why security is important to some states and not all, which kind of states are more insecure and why, what makes a protracted conflict state different in the realm of proliferation, how the number and type of conflicts a state is engaged in make a difference with regard to the intensity of proliferation, and what makes a weaker side in an asymmetric conflict with a global power almost a definite proliferator. Therefore, this study makes a significant contribution to both proliferation and conflict literature by examining the consequences of protracted conflicts in the domain of proliferation decisions of states and understanding the Iranian nuclear ambition from a theoretical perspective. The study also has significant theoretical implications. Major theories of International Relations that emphasize on power politics and military strength such as Realism and its strands are unable to explain Iran's propensity to acquire nuclear weapons simply by focusing on the structure of the international system, which is anarchic, or by investigating its security motivations. These theories fail to explain why states in intractable conflicts are more proliferation prone than others or why the need for deterrent capabilities differs even among protracted conflict states. It is important to underscore that the value and usefulness of deterrence depend on the number and type of conflicts a state is involved in, which the major theories ignore. They also do not investigate when and under what conditions some protracted conflict states become definite proliferators. This study fills the gap that the Realists create in their theories and builds on the central idea of Constructivism that "anarchy is what states make of it."[1] The meaning of anarchy is different for different states depending on the "structure of identity and interest."[2] Anarchy does not cause apprehension for all states or automatically generate proliferation. Anarchy becomes salient when states are engaged in intractable conflicts and that triggers proliferation decisions of different degrees depending on the types and numbers of conflicts that states are involved in.

One aspect requires noting before proceeding further. The study does not assume that Iran has nuclear weapons at the present time, but argues that this is a country that is expected to have a strong propensity to acquire nuclear weapons for being engaged in several seemingly un-resolvable protracted conflicts, most importantly, an asymmetric one with the hegemonic power of the world. Consequently, unless the conflicts are resolved, the danger of Iran's possible nuclear weapons acquisition will remain.

The book encompasses three parts – the first two consisting of a chapter each and the third composed of four chapters – and a concluding chapter with policy implications of the work. Following is a layout of the study:

Part I: Causes of proliferation

Factors utilized to comprehend Iran's nuclear weapons aspiration

The chapter primarily discusses previous scholarship on the subject. It entails the factors utilized by scholars to understand Iran's nuclear drive. By a detailed discussion of the factors provided by scholars and presentation of the significance of their works, it demonstrates the inadequacies of these works in understanding fully the Iranian nuclear ambition. The limitations lie in the fact that none of these studies have tried to analyze why security remains the central motivation for Iran in its quest for nuclear weapons acquisition. Although scholars have argued that security is the central drive for Iran's nuclear weapons program, they have not probed why security was the most important factor in this calculation or the connection between protracted conflict, security, and nuclear proliferation. The concept of intractable conflict was ignored by all of them in their studies. How asymmetric protracted conflicts make the weaker parties to the conflict proliferation prone, received no attention by scholars. The aspect of engagement in multiple conflicts was also ignored by almost all of them. The rationale and significance of the present study are highlighted by the presentation of the limitations of the previous studies.

Part II: Theory

Proliferation proclivities of protracted conflict states

This is the theoretical chapter of the book and the core of the study. It provides the primary hypotheses or unproved propositions of the study. It demonstrates the basic association between protracted conflict as an independent variable, security, prestige, and bargaining leverage as intervening variables, and proliferation as the dependent variable. It argues that proliferation is a function of a state's drive for security, prestige, and bargaining leverage, which in turn are products of a state being engaged in protracted conflicts. It then focuses specifically on protracted conflicts to understand which ones among them would be determined proliferators. It discusses the causal connections between the dependent variable, a determined

Introduction 5

proliferator, and the independent ones, the role of intractable territorial conflicts, the significance of engagement in multiple protracted conflicts, the offing where conflict rivals are allies, the presence of asymmetry in protracted conflicts, a situation where the weaker power faces a global opponent, the presence of nuclear rivals in conflicts, and the engagement in dyadic and proximate conflicts. It creates a theoretical framework of analysis and argues that these factors are instrumental in determining which states will be proliferation prone and why and which ones will want a fast-paced nuclear program and under what circumstances. The theory is expected to be applicable across protracted conflict cases, even though this study tests it against one case, Iran.

Part III: Case study: Iran

Iran's nuclear ambition and twin protracted conflicts between 1947 and 1979

The chapter focuses on Iran's nuclear ambition from 1947 to 1979. It demonstrates the fact that Iran wanted to acquire nuclear weapons for security considerations in general and in particular due to being engaged in twin protracted conflicts with Israel since 1947 and Iraq since the 1950s. Iran launched its nuclear program under the Shah regime. It was his personal interest in seeing Iran develop its nuclear capability and, ultimately, his cordial relationship with the US had paved the way to activate the program. Israel was an opaque proliferator since the 1960s and Iraq was suspected of having a clandestine nuclear weapons program in the 1970s. Iran's proliferation activity during this period was a function of its twin protracted conflicts where its rivals were also would-be proliferators. However, the chapter highlights the fact that Iraq was Iran's principal rival during this period although Israel's proliferation was a cause of concern. Thus, the chapter draws the connection between protracted conflicts and proliferation propensity of Iran and the existence of nuclear rivals and the inclination to proliferate.

Iran's nuclear program and triple protracted conflicts from 1979 onwards

This chapter demonstrates the significance of the Islamic Revolution in Iran in 1979 and the beginning of a new protracted conflict with the US, making it a state engaged in triple protracted conflicts simultaneously. The emergence of a new protracted conflict with a superpower having global reach and nuclear capabilities had tremendous significance for the proliferation incentive of Iran. However, the 1980–88 Iran–Iraq War kept Iran occupied in the war more than its proliferation activities. Although the Islamic clerics slowed down the nuclear program during the initial period of their rule and severe damage to the nuclear site was also caused by repeated bombings by Iraq, with time and when the war almost ended, that situation changed. Iran's nuclear weapons efforts gained momentum from the late 1980s when the leadership team changed and included Supreme Leader Ali Khameini and President Ali Akbar Hashemi Rafsanjani, who made serious efforts to strengthen Iran's strategic capabilities to address future security challenges

6 *Introduction*

effectively. The chapter, thus, presents the connection between multiple protracted conflicts and the intensity of Iran's proliferation interest.

The ramifications of the asymmetric Iran–US protracted conflict from 1990 to 2000 in Iran's nuclear domain

The chapter presents the consequences of the asymmetric Iran–US protracted conflict in the domain of proliferation. It shows how Iran became anxious to develop its nuclear program within the context of its protracted conflict with the US where it is a weaker regional power having no ability to fight the powerful hegemonic power. The Gulf War of 1990 and the US's lead in it, along with the almost-permanent security presence of the US in the Persian Gulf region in its aftermath, made Iran realize the value of possessing a deterrent capability to face an enemy like the US in the post-cold war unipolar world. The rogue rhetoric is also discussed in this chapter to understand its impact on Iran's proliferation activity during the time. Among other efforts, Iran's connections with North Korea during this period to develop nuclear and missile programs highlight its urgency to acquire deterrent capabilities to face off its most powerful extra-regional enemy – the US. The chapter essentially covers the association between asymmetric protracted conflict and the weaker regional power's strong inclination to acquire a nuclear deterrent capability.

Iran's fast-paced proliferation activity and hostile US policy since 2000

This chapter portrays reasons why Iran became relentless since 2000 in acquiring nuclear weapons and in the absence of one of the major regional rivals – Iraq – since 2003 with whom it fought one of the longest and bloodiest wars in the region. It focuses on the aggressive US policies pertaining to Iran since the beginning of the Bush administration and incorporates issues such as the US trying to create a linkage between Iran and Al Qaeda after the 9/11 attacks in 2001, the Axis of Evil speech by President Bush in 2002, The National Security Strategy of the US, and the subsequent war on Iraq in 2003 on the pretext that it had weapons of mass destruction and proliferating democracy in the Middle East was important to have regional peace and stability – all of which had tremendous impact on Iran's decision to make serious efforts to complete its enrichment program as soon as possible. The chapter connects the aggressive US foreign policies pertaining to Iran since 2000 with Iran's unrelenting efforts to develop the nuclear weapons program during this period.

Conclusion

This section is primarily intended to provide a summary of the study this book presents. It highlights the objectives of the study, provides a brief summary of the theoretical framework, and demonstrates whether or not the theory has been successfully applied against the case study, Iran. In other words, it shows whether or not the case study falsifies the theory or confirms the propositions and hypotheses of the theoretical framework. Finally, it provides theoretical and policy implications of the study, meaning what this study has to offer in terms of theories and policies. Based on the implications, it also offers some policy recommendations pertaining to US foreign policies and highlights the urgency to terminate the intractable conflicts to solve the seemingly un-resolvable Iranian proliferation problem.

Part I
Causes of proliferation

1 Factors utilized to comprehend Iran's nuclear weapons aspiration

Like any other research topic, Iran's drive for nuclear weapons was probed by scholars and policy-makers for decades and many causal factors or variables were analyzed to address the research puzzle. The factors were extracted from the three levels of analysis – systemic, domestic, and individual. While all of them seemed to have some significance in comprehending Iran's nuclear drive, the security motivation was highlighted as the most important variable in this regard.[1] Although scholars generally agree that security threats may have driven Iran towards a non-conventional weapons program, they failed to explore specifically why security threats are so important to Iran and not to other states such as Syria or Egypt or, to put it more bluntly, what makes Iran different from other states in the realm of proliferation. This chapter will critically analyze some of the factors that scholars have examined to obtain a sense of why Iran may need a bomb so desperately. The purpose is to highlight the need for a better understanding of Tehran's quest for nuclear weapons by analyzing the security aspect in a more detailed manner.

At the individual level, focus was on Mohammad Reza Pahlavi, the Shah of Iran, in the domain of proliferation. His role was mostly studied because Iran initiated its nuclear program during his rule. The Shah purchased a 5 Mega Watt research reactor from the US in the 1960s; by 1972 he announced Iran's intention to develop a massive nuclear energy program and to that end he established the Atomic Energy Organization of Iran (AEOI) in 1974, which was under his direct control. Given this, when in the late 1970s Iran showed signs of clandestinely developing a nuclear program,[2] proliferation scholars pointed fingers at the Shah with the argument that he wanted Iran to be advanced in nuclear technology and that desire was primarily instrumental in making Iran a proliferator. History provides examples of countries that have large-scale nuclear programs yet never had the intentions to acquire nuclear weapons – such as Canada and Japan. Therefore, it is pertinent to make a clear distinction between technology-driven and intention-driven nuclear weapons programs. Technological advancement in the nuclear realm may create a strong platform to opt for the weapons path, but specific decisions have to be made to build the bomb. This begs the central question: Did the Shah seek to acquire nuclear weapons? The Shah stated in 1975 that if other countries in the region acquired nuclear weapons at some point, Iran would be compelled to follow suit.[3] This proposition indicates two salient points: that the Shah had no intention of developing nuclear weapons when he started the research program or developed a large-scale nuclear infrastructure, but also that he was fully aware of the option to take the weapons path easily if technological advancement was achieved by Tehran. Which of these two points should be considered to assess the Shah's contribution to Iran's nuclear weapons aspiration? The first one seems more compelling. It was the Shah that signed the Nuclear Non-Proliferation Treaty (NPT) in 1968, the year it was actually opened for signature, and ratified in 1970, the year it came into force. If he had the inclination to develop nuclear weapons, like other regional leaders such as India's Jawaharlal Nehru, he could have stayed away from joining the NPT, which prohibits states from acquiring nuclear weapons once they sign and ratify it. He also proposed for a Nuclear Weapons-Free Zone (NWFZ) in the Middle East in 1974. Additionally, it was the Shah who declared the prospect of Iranian nuclear weapons "ridiculous" given the size of the superpowers' arsenals.[4] While it is hard to assess what the Shah had wanted during the initial stage of the development of the program, it is not difficult to argue that even if the Shah had such intentions from the start, other leaders had to follow in his footsteps for the nuclear infrastructure to develop and mature. The fact remains that when the Shah was overthrown with the Islamic Revolution of 1979, Ayatollah Khomeini had little desire to develop a program that was built by the West. He also found it against the interest of Iran's religious orientation – Islam. In the early post-revolutionary period, all kinds of non-conventional weapons were proclaimed contrary to Islam. Consequently, nuclear programs identified with the Shah were initially abandoned, particularly after nearly 3,700 of 4,500 AEOI scientists left Iran.[5] This automatically helps to understand that new leaders do not necessarily continue to pursue the policies undertaken by their predecessors and when they do pursue similar policies then it means that serious determining factors shape policies which cannot be overlooked even if the policies go against the personal inclinations of leaders.

During Ali Akbar Hashemi Rafsanjani's presidency, from 1989 to 1997, Iran once again made serious efforts to acquire nuclear weapons. Thus, it was believed that it was his personal inclination to see Iran go nuclear. By the time the eight-year-old Iran–Iraq War was coming to a close in 1987, Iran's President Rafsanjani ordered a nuclear weapons and delivery systems feasibility study.[6] It was also during his presidency that Pakistan's controversial nuclear scientist A. Q. Khan visited Bushehr nuclear facility, which was damaged heavily by Iraq during its war with Iran.[7] These facts associate Rafsanjani with the Iranian nuclear weapons aspiration. Rafsanjani's remarks about chemical weapons as "poor man's deterrents"[8] added more suspicion to his already tainted nuclear weapons-prone personality. When Iraq used chemical weapons in the Gulf War, which had tremendous negative impact on the morale of the Iranian military and civilian, Rafsanjani stated,

> ... the moral teachings of the world are not very effective when war reaches a serious stage and the world does not respect its own resolutions and closes its eyes to the violations and all the aggressions which are committed in the battle field.[9]

But was Rafsanjani able to march Iran towards a nuclear path or the war with Iraq and its negative consequences were instrumental in driving Tehran to consider proliferation seriously? Should one not seek to understand the context within which such a statement was made? These are important questions to ask because the answers are likely to offer plausible solutions to this crucial problem. If Rafsanjani's attitude had important bearing on the nuclear decision, why did it come so late into the game? He was the founding member of the Islamic Republic Party which was formed right after the Islamic Revolution in 1979 and had strong relations with Khomeini who was the Supreme Leader of the country for the next 10 years. He could have influenced Khomeini to reverse his decision in putting a lid on the nuclear program when that decision was made. Within the context of the Iran–Iraq War, that lid was gradually removed even during Khomeini's period, which indicates the necessity of moving beyond individual-level variables and focusing more on structural variables such as the security environment to understand the change in the dynamics of the program.

Iran's moderate leader, Mohammad Khatami, was the President of Iran from 1997 to 2005. He came to power on the platform of liberalization and reform policy. His theory of Dialogue among Civilizations, a response to Samuel P. Huntington's Clash among Civilizations, received attention not only from many countries of the world, but also from the United Nations, which named 2001 as the year of "Dialogue among Civilizations" – the purpose of which was to understand diversity comprehensively and to improve dialogues between the diverse groups of the world to prevent conflicts. After eight years of Islamic fundamentalist rule, he was a breath of fresh air for the Iranians who believed in open society and democracy. In 2005, Khatami urged all religious leaders to abolish chemical and atomic weapons,[10] but did he discontinue the program during his presidency? Unfortunately, he did not. On the contrary, Iran's clandestine nuclear program developed with some degree of direction, momentum, and speed during the presidency of Khatami. It was in February 2003 that the International Atomic Energy Agency (IAEA) Director Mohammad El Baradei confirmed the presence of a large-scale gas-centrifuge enrichment facility, Natanz, and a heavy water production site, Arak. Some contend that while Iran has purportedly made efforts to enrich uranium with lasers since 1991, it has also established a pilot enrichment plant in 2000 and conducted research on a rare element – named polonium – suitable for nuclear weapons.[11] In June 2003, an IAEA report stated that Iran did not fulfill some of the obligations and within a month IAEA visits discovered traces of highly enriched uranium in Natanz.[12] Although supportive of the EU3 (European Union 3) plan, Khatami declared that Iran would resume enrichment if necessary and that the nuclear program would continue even if it meant an end to UN oversight, asserting that Iran abhorred nuclear weapons.[13] That was not all. Throughout the first half of 2005, when he was still the president of the country, Tehran refused to provide information on P-2 or the source of nuclear contamination and disallowed IAEA access to suspected facilities at Kalaye, Parchin, and Lavizan II, threatened to unfreeze the enrichment program and withdraw from the NTP if the IAEA referred Iran to the United Nations Security Council (UNSC).[14] While Khatami was by far the most moderate leader Iran has had in its life, he did not stop the development of Iran's nuclear program during his rule. On the contrary, arguing that Iran had the right to peaceful nuclear energy he stated:

> If there is concern over nuclear bomb, why we, who have not yet achieved the peaceful nuclear technology, i.e. production of uranium with 3.5 percent enrichment – that serves as fuel for nuclear plants – are not trusted and put under pressure, while the powers that have hundreds of nuclear warheads in the region and are capable of producing tens of nuclear bombs a year, are not only put under pressure but are also supported? What is observed in the world is this double-standard logic; and we should in fact move into the world wherein we will be able to meet our needs by relying on our own power and on God.[15]

This statement points to the fact that nuclear logics must be comprehended comprehensively instead of narrowly focusing on a leader's role or attitude. While the role of the leadership can in no way be undermined, the strategic offing the country is in is the most crucial variable that determines whether or not to opt for non-conventional weapons, especially nuclear weapons.

Since 2005, Iran's President Mahmoud Ahmadinejad has been associated with the country's desire to acquire nuclear weapons. Like many others,[16] the book by the Emirates Center which describes a denial and deception strategy of the radical Islamic state, Iran, also focuses on the radical views of Iran's controversial leader Ahmadinejad and his inclination to make Iran a nuclear state.[17] In September 2005, Iran was declared to be "unequivocally in violation of its obligations in a Board of Governors resolution which cites article 12 of the IAEA statues, making it compulsory for a report to be submitted to the Security Council."[18] Before that year, even the IAEA seemed reluctant to recognize Iran to be in violation of agreements. Mahmoud Ahmadinejad's arrival in power, his inflammatory speeches, his determination to plough on at all costs and the feebleness of the international response to these developments all reinforce the skepticism and even the fear of some future catastrophe," states Therese Delpech.[19] Additionally, "The day Ahmadinejad took office in August 2005, Iran rejected yet another EU3 proposal; that week he restarted uranium conversion in Isfahan, unleashing a dramatic deterioration in negotiations with the EU3 and IAEA."[20] In April 2006, Ahmadinejad announced that Iran "has joined the club of nuclear countries" by successfully enriching uranium for the first time.[21] Because Iran defied the August 2006 UNSC Resolution, in December 2006 the UNSC agreed unanimously to ban international trade in nuclear and missile technologies with Iran and to freeze foreign assets of 12 individuals and 10 Iranian organizations. Ahmadinejad responded that the "UN resolution against Iran's atomic work has no validity for Iranians," describing the resolution as "a rusty instrument" that has "no effect." He further argued that "even if they issue 10 more such resolutions it will not affect Iran's economy and politics."[22] His aggressive statements obviously sent alarming signals to the international community.

Of all the leaders in Iran, Ahmadinejad's personal inclination to not step back from the program seems to be most important to study for the simple fact that by the time he became the President of the country, he inherited quite a developed nuclear program with enrichment facilities well in place and functioning to take Iran one step forward in making the ultimate weapon. The point is that perhaps when he came to power it was a matter of taking the decision that would be required to reach and cross the threshold and not a matter of technology so much. It is often stated that "the gradual advancement of a state's technical nuclear capacities inexorably leads to the eventual production of nuclear weapons."[23] So under the circumstances it was possible for him to have the greatest influence on the program compared to the others discussed in the preceding paragraphs. What the international community has acquired so far from the academic community is that Ahmadinejad spoke strongly about Iranians having the right to build the nuclear program or that Tehran would do anything or go to any length to ensure that the Iranians are not deprived of that right. The history of India and Pakistan, the two important proliferators, encompasses enough statements like this by leaders who were staunch supporters of the nuclear programs – Zulfiqar Ali Bhutto in Pakistan or A.B. Vajpayee in India. What proliferation scholars do not offer are two things: a systematic study of the cognitive variables of the leaders that trigger proliferation and how such leaders shape such an important policy. No study so far has offered this. Additionally, studies have not differentiated between determining and influencing factors. It is not only pertinent to distinguish them, but extremely important to show which one has triggered proliferation and whether or not one would work effectively in the absence of the other. For example, the security environment may be an influencing factor and the individual leader a determining factor in making a nuclear choice. A leader's personal inclination to go nuclear is not enough to make a country a nuclear state. Additionally, one of the most salient criticisms of this motivation is that it cannot be generalized across leaders. Each individual is different and his or her life, psychological makeup, cognitive perceptions are all unique and as such it is hard to use this factor from a theoretical standpoint.

Proliferation scholars inclined to develop individual level theories of proliferation contend that "to go nuclear is an ideal-typical 'big decision.'"[24] Security, prestige, or domestic political motivations is insufficient for such a serious policy choice. "Various voices in society may sound strong pro-or anti-bomb notes; but the responsibility for choosing wisely is much heavier for the top leader into whose hands the ultimate choice actually falls," argues Jacques Hymans.[25] Nuclear decisions are functions of the decision-maker's "national identity conception (NIC)," which is the leader's understanding of the nation's identity – his/her sense of what the nation stands for and how high it stands in relation to other states in the international system.[26] Oppositional nationalist leaders generally consider that their nation is at odds with and naturally equal to a particular external other and when they face the external other, they are predisposed to experiencing fear and pride. The decision to acquire nuclear weapons is not a means to the end of getting them, it is also an end in itself – a matter of self expression.[27] It is argued that bomb decisions are "the results of NIC-driven emotions that shape their information sets, their action tendencies, and indeed their very willingness to act at all on the nuclear issue."[28] Thus, oppositional nationalists desire the bomb, others do not. While all of this is correct, especially that decisions pertaining to serious issues such as the development of nuclear weapons are primarily made by the heads of states, it is unlikely for all leaders to be oppositional nationalists who would experience fear and pride when facing the external other and act defensively. It is evident that Iran pursued its nuclear program when both hawkish and dovish leaders – Rafsanjani and Khatami respectively – were in power. If Rafsanjani was an oppositional nationalist, was Khatami of the same kind too? Does it then mean that all leaders' understanding of the nation's identity has been the same or is it that only the one that initiates the program is an oppositional nationalist and the rest of the leaders simply follow the lead of the nationalist even though quite naturally their moral, psychological, perceptual, and cognitive perspectives differ? If this is correct, then changes in political administrations do not count with respect to policy changes.

A program needs time to take off. There are phases in each program which include a beginning, development, maturation, and continuation. Iran's nuclear weapons program is no exception. One needs to be careful in analyzing an individual level factor because individual leaders come and go, but where policies remain intact, it indicates that a much more consolidated factor was responsible for the continuation of the program – which most, if not all, leaders adhere to. Continuity with respect to determination and commitment is essential for the acquisition of a nuclear program. Although the Shah may have started the program, others never stopped the program during their periods and that shows the continuation of whatever Iran was trying to acquire in the nuclear realm. Therefore, to give credit to one person for the initiation of the program or to criticize a hawkish leader for continuing the program would be a wrong assessment of the overall endeavor. Every leader continued the program and when Iran was relentless in its efforts to build the bomb it had little to do with the leadership and more to do with the regional and international security environment it was in at the time, which no leader – oppositional nationalist or not – could ignore.

In the domestic/institutional realm, factors mostly studied to understand proliferation incentives are public opinion/people's demands, domestic turmoil distraction, cost-effectiveness of nuclear weapons – meaning bombs are cheap – and scientific/technological momentum – that scientists and military want bombs. With regard to the first factor, public opinion, proliferation may very well be a function of public opinion, although no state in the word proliferated for public pressure. In the context of Iran, it is hard to believe that leaders paid any attention to what people thought about the nuclear program. A country that has kept the nation in the dark about its policies with respect to world politics, domestic politics, human rights, or civil liberty would be unlikely to consider public opinion in nuclear choice. Anna Cahn writes, "On a question of such national importance as the nuclear option, it is clear that there will be no participatory decision-making."[29] Ray Takeyh contends that although much of the political debate is generally conducted in public, "the nuclear discussions are largely held in secret."[30] According to Shahram Chubin, Iranian public opinion was neither a driver nor a constraint on the development of the program until 2002, after which it was projected as a national issue.[31] Also, why would the Iranian people be enthusiastic about going nuclear when the country waged a costly and protracted war with Iraq? In fact, most scholars argue that Iran's populace largely opposes the nuclear program.[32] Moreover, when leaders needed to justify the program, they used public opinion or sometimes molded their opinions by making the nuclear issue a national issue for Iran. Additionally, it is important to bear in mind that public opinion may be positive about the nuclear program – energy program – but not with respect to the weapons program. People are supportive of Iran's rights, "but not keen to pay economically or politically from any confrontation with the international community."[33] To top it off, the more educated and elite class is also skeptical about the government's intentions. Consequently, the regime has not made efforts to discuss the matter with the people, which is not unusual in the case of any proliferator. The regimes have used words such as "denial," "double standards," and "rights" to rally people around the nuclear issue. The usage of these terms to rally people around the nuclear issue is clearly evident in the following statement:

> If today we insist on having [the] fuel cycle, [it] is because we want to generate scientific creativity and innovation inside the country. . . . Big powers want to prevent the developing countries from gaining these abilities. Having a nuclear fuel cycle significantly helps a country to reach stable development.[34]

Takeyh argues that "a highly nationalistic populace is beginning to coalesce around Iran's sovereign rights and invoking the all too familiar slogans of autonomy and superpower double standards."[35] However, what the nuclear issue stands for has never been thoroughly discussed and such discourses have never been entertained by any of the Iranian leaderships. Thus, even if the polls show that 80 percent of the people support the program, it is unclear what that "support" means. Popular support for independent nuclear energy capabilities should not be confused with support for nuclear weapons.[36] Chubin contends, "The nuclear program, especially its secret components, has been the 'baby' of a small group of people, among whom Hashemi Rafsanjani is the most prominent."[37] A final point to note is that if people came to know about the program when it has already been developed, then how can they drive the state to proliferate? Their contribution to the program is minimal. The development of a secret program of this nature is unlikely to be a product of public opinion.

Iran could have desired to acquire nuclear weapons for domestic political considerations. It is a country that projects political unpredictability and instability. There are elite factions that contend for power and they use the nuclear program as a source of legitimacy and support.[38] There are the pragmatic conservatives/the accommodationists/the reformists and the ideological conservatives/confrontationalists/the conservatives. Their views differ with respect to how the nuclear issue must be handled – whether to negotiate with the West and normalize relations with the world by using the issue as a bargaining chip to secure Iran's legitimate interest or to use it as an equalizer to compete with the West.[39] The reformists prefer the first option while the conservatives choose to opt for the second option. The point is that both groups use the issue to assert their predominance in the political apparatus of the country. Chubin believes that the nuclear issue is primarily a political tussle for power and legitimacy, and only secondarily about ideology.[40] He asserts that Tehran's progressive nuclearization has had stable political rather than security imperatives.[41] During the 1980s debacle with Iraq, weapons of mass destruction programs became powerful mechanisms of domestic survival, compatible with economic, political, military and technological self-reliance, anti-imperialism, sovereignty, and defiance of international regimes and under presumed western domination.[42] Iran's nuclear program in the 1990s, Chubin argues, was "in search for a rationale" not rooted in security imperatives but nationalism, prestige, and domestic drivers.[43] Takeyh argues that "the ultimate fate of Iran's nuclear program may still rest on the outcome of the intense power struggle going on inside the country."[44] According to Leonard Spector, Khomeini's close advisor Ayatollah Mohammed Beheshti told Iranian scientist Fereydun Fesharaki that "it is your duty to build the atomic bomb for the Islamic Republican Party,"[45] which means politics was very much a part of the nuclear issue. Along the same lines, others have argued that the nuclear issue has been one of the bases of Ahmadinejad's appeal to populism, threatening at once the clerics and vested interests of the establishment, while freezing out the diplomats.[46] This line of argument was agreed upon by the father of Iran's nuclear program, Asgar-Khani, who stated that while Iran's nuclear weapons provide "minimum deterrent"; they are

> necessary not only as a substitute for fossil energy but also for Iran's social cohesion and prestige ... Internally Iran is in a state of disarray. I would now argue that, only by becoming a nuclear weapons state, can Iran consolidate its social coherence. Iran needs both soft and hard power to regain national identity and prestige.[47]

There are many aspects to consider. First, Ahmadinejad came to power only in 2005 when the program had already gotten a strong shape and was up and running. Also, it is unlikely for any political leader to gain legitimacy and support of the people with the acquisition of nuclear weapons. History does not provide any evidence where a failed government could rest domestic disturbance or win support by going nuclear. Even if they do, people have to be aware of the nuclear program. In the case of Iran the nuclear issue became a public and important political issue only in mid-2002 when revelations of Iran's undeclared nuclear activities put Iran on the defensive. Also, Iranian leaders are not particularly concerned about the people's support and their own legitimacy, given the nature of the domestic/political system. In late 2002 tensions between the reformists and conservatives triggered popular protests, which the conservatives considered to be against the Islamic regime's interests, which brought the society close to widespread domestic revolt.[48] Students demanded a referendum to address Iran's future political status and violent clashes with the conservative forces erupted. The nuclear issue was not used to rescue the conservatives from this trouble. Islam provided a flexible normative foundation that was marshaled to justify the development and usage of WMD at certain times, but found incompatible with such weapons at other times.[49] Therefore, the radical leaders could not always use the nuclear issue, even if they wanted to, to win support due to religious reasons. Additionally, acquisition of nuclear weapons is a long-term goal and domestic unrest is often a temporary problem, which can change for the better within a short period of time. These points undermine the power of this factor in shaping a nuclear decision.

On the economic motivation, scholars have argued that a country can go nuclear for economic needs, meaning nuclear weapons are cost-effective weapons and a financially weak state can acquire such non-conventional weapons with the hope of being able to cut conventional expenditure because one bomb is enough as a deterrent capability. However, estimates show that Iran's defense expenditure increased and it wanted to rebuild itself in conventional weaponry after 1989 and that policy continued in the 1990s as well.[50] Also, Iran has regional rivals and nuclear weapons are useless in small scale or low-intensity violence that regional powers face in a volatile region like the Middle East. A protracted war with Iraq has taught it lessons pertaining to the necessity to possess advanced conventional armaments to face off such an enemy. Thus, Patrick Cronin argues that "Iran appears to have decided that a nuclear program, backed by other military means, is the best means of demonstrating its rising prominence, despite the risks attendant to such an exhibition."[51]

As for the last factor, scientific momentum, it is often stated that the Shah assumed that military power was closely associated with access to modern technology and that less-advanced armaments were undesirable. He believed in scientific modern high-tech military achievements and the acquisition of nuclear power was associated with scientific success and military power. Additionally, "mastery of the nuclear fuel cycle provides a valuable rallying nationalist theme, given that it requires vast investments in nuclear-bound human resources and technology, in the midst of economic stagnation, high inflation, and unemployment."[52] After Shah, other Iranian leaders also associated nuclear power with scientific success. It is often argued that bureaucratic constituencies conspire to perpetuate nuclear programs and "reinforce the strategic logic" that initially provoke the search for nuclear deterrence. Iran's case is no exception, according to Takeyh. There is pressure from the scientific community on the country to go nuclear. Both the scientific community and the Revolutionary Guards derive prestige and profit from the continuation of the nuclear program and are "emerging as stalwarts of Iran's proliferation machinery. As such a bureaucratic constituency congeals it would be difficult to divest Iran of its nuclear installations."[53] One important point needs to be highlighted here. Iran's clandestine nuclear program would not render the scientists or the government to enjoy and share the scientific momentum with the world. How can scientific achievement or momentum be enjoyed if the program is shrouded in secrecy? The achievement can only be shared if the program is openly declared, which is not the case in Iran. Given this, it is quite clear that the state-level factors do not provide adequate explanations for Iran's nuclear aspirations.

At the systemic level, the prestige motivation in the regional or international realm, the interest to bargain better with powerful states, and the quest for security are generally used to explain proliferation aspirations of states. There is national consensus pertaining to the nuclear program in Iran in the sense that "it is a source of pride and Iranians resist dictation from outside as to what they can and cannot have."[54] Iran spans the Middle East and the Persian Gulf and stretches into the Central and South Asia and possesses substantial energy resources on which a lot of the world's economic prosperity depends. Traditionally, Iran has been a major power in the Middle East and much weight was given to its role in the region. Since the Shah's period, "Iranian leaders believed that Iran's size, historical importance, and self-professed cultural superiority merit a significant role for the country in the region."[55] With the Islamic Revolution in the country and the emergence of radical elements in the political system, much of that evaporated. Consequently, Iran does understand that it needs other tools to win back the prestige it lost regionally and internationally. An Iran emboldened by a nuclear capability will undoubtedly play a more influential and hegemonic role in the region.[56] Its nuclear umbrella will enable it to dictate the outcome of future conflicts in the region or even affect the Arab–Israeli peace process.[57] Regionally, Iran has strived for a major power status and it still believes that it is one. Internationally, too, Iran expects to receive proper respect as a major Middle Eastern country. It expects the powerful states, especially the US, to consult it with respect to any endeavor in the Middle East. The perceived prestige of having nuclear weapons, another "Islamic bomb," is no doubt one element to consider.[58] Some argue that Iran's revolutionary aspirations did not imply territorial ambitions and that its revisionism was related to status and not land.[59] According to Robert Hunter, "more important to Iran is the matter of power and presence in the Persian Gulf. With the defeat of Iraq – a country now many years away from being in a position to compete for power in the region – and with rising risks of turmoil in Saudi Arabia, Iran is in a better position to compete for pride of place in the Gulf. Arguably, Iranian nuclear weapons could be a card to play in a contest for influence. That assumes that such a competition might be limited to the region and that Iran or any other regional actor could aspire to the role of the most influential country in the Gulf. Such an assumption makes little sense given the almost certain deep engagement of the United States and its allies in the Middle East militarily, economically, and politically for the foreseeable future."[60] However, one must understand that Iran is likely to achieve all of the aforementioned under two circumstances: if Iran is truly a nuclear state – which it denies aspiring for – and if it does not have a radical political system. One of the first reasons to believe that prestige – regional or international – was perhaps not the primary reason for Iran to go nuclear is that Iran's nuclear program was and still is somewhat clandestine. Nuclear weapons could conceivably place Iran at par with a number of key states, provided that it disclosed its intentions and refrained from signing the nuclear arms control treaties, the NPT or the Comprehensive Test Ban Treaty (CTBT). In reality Iran has signed both. By signing them, especially NPT, Iran became a legitimate non-nuclear weapons state. It clearly signaled to the world its intention to remain a non-nuclear country even though its real intentions may have been otherwise. As Sverre Lodgaard states, "NPT membership and IAEA safeguards shed legitimacy on Iran as a non-nuclear-weapon state (NNWS), in lieu of which a secret program could materialize – much the way Iraq pursued nuclear weapons in the 1980s following the Israeli bombing of Osiraq in 1981."[61] Although the denial and deception strategy has been used in some form or the other by all nuclear states, the newly proliferating countries have increased motivation to conceal their nuclear programs "because they are developing nuclear weapons in the context of strong non-proliferation regimes."[62] Whatever the reason for clandestine development of nuclear programs, such countries are unable to elevate their status by hiding their programs. In addition to joining the NPT, Iran has also been a strong advocate of the global nuclear disarmament drive, through which Iran also indicated its interest in maintaining a non-nuclear status. Some argue that Iran has two policies pertaining to nuclear weapons: "a declared policy advocating global abolition of such weapons and a secret policy to build and sustain" nuclear capabilities.[63] That may be the case, but the point is that this dual policy is of no use in providing Iran with regional or international prestige. Prestige is a function of crossing the nuclear threshold and acknowledgment of the possession of nuclear capabilities. Instead of elevating its status, clandestine development of such weapons has made Iran a rogue state or a state that violates international laws. Tehran's leaders understand that well not because of the title the country has gotten for the maintenance of such policies, but also for the sanctions that were imposed on it. Additionally, Iran's radical political system is not something that can bring it prestige or status. It has been called a rogue state because of its non-democratic political system, among others. Without changing that, it is unlikely for Iran to elevate its status simply by acquiring nuclear weapons. Therefore, even if this motivation has some value to it, given Iran's insistence for maintaining a non-nuclear status, this is unlikely to have primarily shaped nuclear decisions of Iran.

The other argument often used by proliferation scholars is that states sometimes go nuclear to bargain better with the West. The US may take a nuclear Iran more seriously than a non-nuclear Iran. With nuclear weapons in possession, Iran could possibly get a firm commitment from the US to forgo regime change in Tehran – which has been a recurrent theme in US foreign policy – provide security guarantees, end sanctions – which were imposed systematically since 1979 – and enable Iran's integration into the world economy.[64] There are those among the Iranian nationalists who see the US policy of containment as posing a direct threat to Iran's cultural, social, and political well-being and they support the government and associated revolutionary causes in part because of this resentment.[65] Takeyh argues that

> Iran's planners may be opting for a variation of the North Korean strategy, namely threatening to cross the nuclear threshold as a means of fostering better relations with the United States, including a resumption of economic ties. The economic dimension is particularly important as, in the last decade, Tehran has grudgingly come to realize that Iran's tense relations with the United States preclude its effective integration into the global economy and access to needed technology.[66]

Thus, the central argument here is that unless the US is threatened by something as big as nuclear weapons, Iran is unlikely to obtain economic concessions from the

US and sanctions will not be lifted either. Consequently, Iran's economy will suffer, making it difficult for the country to survive internally. After all, domestic stability is essentially dependent on economic stability and regime survival to a large extent depends on economic stability and domestic peace. Again, this argument may not be fully applicable in the case of Iran for its nuclear secrecy. The two former opaque countries, India and Pakistan, could not arrange any concessions from the US for more than a decade after their nuclear weapons capabilities became known to the world. Instead, the West imposed sanctions against Pakistan. After the Indian nuclear tests of 1998, the US tried to provide Pakistan with incentives, such as the delivery of the F-16s, to keep Islamabad away from testing its own nuclear weapons. Similarly, in the case of North Korea the five parties, including the US, decided to provide North Korea with incentives in exchange for the North's renunciation of the nuclear weapons program. This is not the case in Iran. As long as there is reason to question the actual possession of nuclear weapons, bargaining possibilities are slim. It is obvious that Iranian leaders are also aware of this line of reasoning. Some argue that

> the fact that Iran's nuclear program was not conceived as a bargaining tool does not mean that it could not ever become one. If the Europeans had not believed it possible, they would not make two attempts, on 21 October 2003 and 15 November 2004, to seek a negotiated solution with Tehran, proposing on each occasion the suspension of nuclear fuel cycle activities, with a view to discontinuing them. However they were always conscious that this was a risky gamble with a slim chance of success, and that Washington rather than London, Paris or Berlin held the trump cards, both economic and strategic.[67]

If this line of argument has any power, this too does not mean that the program has been a function of Iran's interest to bargain better with the West. With the maturation of the program this interest could be served along with other more vital interests, such as protecting security.

The only system-level incentive that is likely to have propelled Iran to acquire a secret nuclear weapons program is the security threat that emanates from the regional powers such as Iraq and Israel. Given this, Iran had to ask how the country could make conflict too costly for its opponent. Acquisition of nuclear weapons was the easy answer to the question. The possibility of Israel's possession of nuclear weapons added to the discomfort and Israel became the other motivation for Iran's need to develop nuclear weapons. By adopting a secret nuclear policy Tehran hopes to deter future unconventional and conventional attacks against Iranian troops and rear areas by developing the means to threaten retaliation in kind.[68] It is believed that Iran's quest for nuclear weapons has been a function of its security needs. Iran, like any other aspiring nuclear state, has been eager to avoid future wars with Iraq and Israel in the region. In 1994, Anthony Cordesman wrote that it was not possible to dismiss another round of fighting between Iraq and Iran.[69] Gregory Giles contends that "Iran's wartime experience and current threat perceptions together underscore why the Islamic Republic has concluded that nuclear, biological, and chemical weaponry is essential to its national security."[70] He further argues that "Iran has tried to deter possible Israeli conventional strikes by implicitly warning of its ability to retaliate with unconventional means."[71] In November 1991, Iran's Deputy President Ayatollah Mohajerani stated that if the Zionist regime has the right to possess nuclear weapons, then all Muslim countries have the same right and that Muslims should develop expertise in the nuclear realm to face the Israeli nuclear challenge.[72] This motivation seems to be the only one that may have driven Iran to take the nuclear path because even clandestine nuclear programs are taken seriously by the opponents and tacit nuclear deterrence works in between the rivals. India and Pakistan have been opaque proliferators for more than a decade before they tested their nuclear weapons and deterrence worked in the conflict relations. Israel has been an opaque proliferator for many decades and its regional security is primarily derived from that standing. Thus, states often make use of their clandestine nuclear programs to attain security goals. Given this, this incentive merits detailed explanation and analysis.

The salient books[73] that compete with this study are all descriptive works and mostly historical analysis of Iran's nuclear program. While facts are important for an understanding of the case study, which is what these books provide us with and which are the strengths of these books as research studies, theoretical explanations of the facts are essential, which they do not provide. For example, Chubin narrates the history of the Iranian nuclear program and argues that the central problem is not nuclear technology, but the fact that Iran is a revolutionary state and its interests conflict with the regional states and the West. Similarly, Venter portrays an alarming picture of Iran's nuclear and missile program. He primarily focused on Iran in the aftermath of the 1979 revolution and how the Mullahs have been able to silently march towards acquiring nuclear weapons. He looks at how Iran was able to make use of the nuclear black market in the development of the nuclear program and highlights Iran's reputation as a terrorist state. All these are simple facts surrounding Iran's nuclear program. However, his study is a little different in the sense that he looks at the South African clandestine nuclear weapons program, which he thinks is a model for Iran's secret program. Ray Takeyh in his book, *Hidden Iran: Paradox and Power in the Islamic Republic*, places the issue of Tehran's nuclear ambition within the broader context of Iran's relations with the West, particularly with the US, the "Great Satan." Takeyh argues that the hostile foreign policies of the Bush administration do not help the Iranian reformers who would like to change the course of their country's nuclear policies. In saying so, he contends that the US needs to have a better understanding of the domestic politics of Iran and must think about "selective partnership" with Iran.[74] While Takeyh's work is significant because he discusses the relationship of Iran with the West and his suggestion about partnership is also commendable, he fails to extract the variables that are connected to Iran's proliferation drive. The association of intractable conflicts with nuclear ambition is missing in his analysis. Why the US has not been able to trust Iran or give it the benefit of the doubt is also a function of their long-running conflict.

While scholars have argued that security is the central drive for Iran's nuclear weapons program, they have not probed why security was the most important factor in this calculation or the connection between conflict, security, and nuclear proliferation. The involvement of a state in protracted conflicts has been overlooked by analysts. The aspect of engagement in multiple conflicts was also ignored by almost all of them. Additionally, having global powers as long-running rivals of regional powers and how that impacts nuclear decisions has not been considered by them either. A theoretical work provides a causal connection between the variables under consideration, enabling one to understand why a decision was or is made. Alexander George and Andrew Bennett suggest that "case studies remain much stronger at assessing whether and how a variable mattered to the outcome than at assessing how much it mattered."[75] However, in a descriptive work the entire focus is on what decision was made and laying out the facts of the decisions. The basic strength of the book compared to others lies in the fact that it provides a theoretical analysis of the Iranian nuclear drive. Additionally, the concept and ramifications of protracted conflicts, and their numbers and types in understanding proliferation propensities of states are alien to these and other scholars who have written on Iran's nuclear ambition. None have grappled with the research problem this book investigates. The next chapter provides a theoretical framework to understand the connection between protracted conflict, security impetus, and proliferation propensities of states. It lays out the conditions that must be present for a state to be a determined proliferator. In other words, it portrays under what conditions is a state likely to be a determined proliferator. The theory is tested against the Iranian case in the four chapters that follow.

Part II
Theory

2 Proliferation proclivities of protracted conflict states

This chapter discusses when and under what conditions a state is likely to become the most determined proliferator. It builds a relationship between intractable conflicts and proliferation imperatives of states. It demonstrates that while the anarchic system influences proliferation propensities of states, not all states in general and conflicting states in particular are proliferation-prone. The influence of anarchy is dominant in proliferation decisions when states are engaged in certain types of conflicts. The chapter highlights that variables such as conflict types – protracted/non-protracted, territorial/non-territorial, dyadic/non-dyadic, proximate/non-proximate, and asymmetric/symmetric – number of conflict engagements, the regional or global status of the rival state, the nuclear and non-nuclear status of the opponent, and the relationship between different rival states shape or determine proliferation decisions. Thus, proliferation is not necessarily a direct function of being engaged in conflicts; there is more to it. This means that although conflict engagement is a necessary condition of proliferation, it is not sufficient to generate proliferation proclivity on its own. Additionally, among the proliferation-prone states, some are most determined to proliferate, meaning reversing the aspirations of such states is difficult, if not impossible. The reasons are primarily the aggregate effects of the variables/causal factors discussed earlier on proliferation. Given this, non-nuclear status of a state is essentially a product of non-existence of certain types of long-running conflicts. The principal objective of this chapter is to underscore the value of conflict resolution, especially where the above conditions are present, for attaining non-proliferation objectives. While it is true that nuclear proliferation is not unidirectional, for a state to give up its nuclear weapons aspiration, right conditions and incentives must be present in the offing. In order to know what conditions must be present, the conditions and factors that trigger proliferation incentives need to be presented and analyzed first.

States coexist in the anarchic international system, ensure their survival, and perceive that military capabilities can keep them secure from external attack. Power is a means to an end – the end being security. Nuclear weapons are especially valuable in this context. Structural Realist Kenneth Waltz states:

> Nuclear weapons deter nuclear weapons . . . The temptation of one country to employ increasingly larger amount of force is lessened if its opponent

has the ability to raise the ante. Force can be used with less hesitation by those states able to parry, to thrust, and to threaten at varied levels of military endeavor.[1]

For Waltz and other realists, war is always a possibility and states must be prepared at all times to face it. To most realists only military force is the final mediator of disputes between states. Nuclear weapons have made warfare less likely among the states that possess them. The big powers do not fight wars anymore because of their acquisition of nuclear weapons and small or weaker states still continue to fight wars due to the non-acquisition of these devastative weapons. Waltz states:

> Over the centuries great powers have fought more wars than minor states, and the frequency of war has correlated more closely with a structural characteristic – their international standing – than with unit-level attributes. Yet, because of a change in military technology, a change at the unit-level, waging war has increasingly become the privilege of poor and weak states. Nuclear weapons have banished war from the center of international politics.[2]

This, to Waltz, is because the mere probability of the usage of nuclear weapons requires extreme caution all around, so the likelihood of war decreases as more countries acquire nuclear weapons. The longest peace that prevailed between the two superpowers during the cold war years became a major research puzzle for the scholars in the post-cold war era. It has been argued by some scholars that the absence of wars generated the long peace between the two superpowers.[3] From this perspective, peace equals absence of war and absence of war is primarily a function of nuclear weapons acquisition. This also means that proliferation should be a natural form of state behavior between all pairs of states. However, in reality, the variations in proliferation are large, which commands inquiry.

While all states may have an inclination to proliferate because they worry about their security interests in an anarchical international system where there is no higher authority to protect the vital interests of states and nuclear weapons act as best deterrents against possible attacks, protracted conflict states have a natural tendency to be proliferation-prone because war remains a possibility in their conflict relations and, consequently, war-avoidance mechanisms and strategies must be developed. Therefore, even though all states generally worry about wars occurring between adversaries, the probability of wars varies from one type of state to the other. Before analyzing the connection between protracted conflicts and proliferation tendencies, it is important to define a Protracted Conflict (PC). A general definition of PC given by Edward Azar is: Protracted conflicts are

> hostile interactions which extend over long periods of time with sporadic outbreaks of open warfare fluctuating in frequency and intensity. They are conflict situations in which stakes are very high ... While they may exhibit some

breakpoints during which there is a cessation of overt violence, they may linger on in time and have no distinguishable point of termination.[4]

I define "protracted conflict" as a high conflict situation between two or more states that endures for decades without termination points, in which a number of crises are embedded, and where war remains a higher-than-normal probability due largely to the territorial nature of some of these conflicts.[5] As the definitions suggest, PCs generate crises and wars, or they are common conflict behaviors or manifestations. Michael Brecher and Jonathan Wilkenfeld state:

> Despite wide variation in their duration, geographic location, number of eruptions, and variety of issues, crises occurring within protracted conflicts exhibit characteristics that clearly differentiate them from crises occurring outside of such a conflict. Key among these differentiating factors is the question of violence.[6]

Studies reveal that actors in PCs are more likely to experience violent triggers and to employ more severe violence in crisis management.[7] All PC states are concerned about the extreme danger that such crises pose by virtue of their propensity to escalate to violence.

At this juncture it is important to differentiate war from violence. It is also important to conceptualize crisis and the relationship between crisis, conflict, and war. This is because war and crises are integral parts of a protracted conflict, as stated in the definitions. Also, crisis management mechanisms, and their salience and functions in conflicts are important to discuss. Scholars contend that crisis involves a threat to basic values, time pressure for response, and heightened probability of war.[8] The International Crisis Behavior (ICB) Project defines an international crisis as: 1) a change in type and/or an increase in intensity of disruptive interactions between two or more states, with a heightened probability of military hostilities; that, in turn, 2) destabilizes their relationship and challenges the structure of an international system.[9] Others have defined it differently, but included the "war probability" aspect. On war probability in a crisis situation Glenn Snyder and Paul Diesing write:

> The centerpiece of [the] definition is "the perception of a dangerously high probability of war" by the governments involved. Just how high the perceived probability must be to qualify as a crisis is impossible to specify ... [It] must at least be high enough to evoke feelings of fear and tension to an uncomfortable degree.[10]

Brecher and Wilkenfeld consider "heightened probability of war" as a necessary condition of crisis. They state that

> this probability can range from virtually nil to near certainty. For a crisis to erupt, however, perception of war likelihood need not be high. Rather, it must

be qualitatively higher than the norm in the specific adversarial relationship. This applies both to states for which the "normal" expectation of war is "high" and to those for which it is "low".[11]

In any case, they include war as an integral part of a crisis, which, in a nuclear situation, is inapplicable. War, which is an acute form of violence, becomes the pivotal concern of each party. War is defined as a militarized conflict involving at least one member of the interstate system on each side, resulting in a total of 1,000 or more battle deaths.[12] War avoidance mechanisms and strategies must be developed. States make efforts to prevent inter-state wars through, among other strategies, deterrence, arms control, domestic political and economic reforms, interdependent trade, preventive diplomacy, mediation, and arbitration. Although most of these options are employed by states to avoid wars, PC states that have developed hatred towards their adversaries, been engaged in several crises, or fought wars are unlikely to make use of any of these strategies with the exception of deterrence. For example, none of these strategies were utilized by PC dyads such as India–Pakistan, India–China, North Korea–South Korea, or Iran–Iraq, among others. The hostility surrounding the conflict prevents the adversaries from focusing on bilateral interdependent trade or from using preventive diplomacy to facilitate agreements to resolve disputes that trigger wars.[13] Consequently, domestic political reforms or economic restructuring may not be attractive options for such states to employ for war avoidance and they are unlikely to embrace the theory of democratic and trading states not fighting wars. Deterrence is the most attractive strategy for such states that are both weary[14] and fearful of war probability in the conflict setting. Deterrent capability refers to the capability that dissuades a state's adversary from initiating an attack. Nuclear weapons are assumed to deter wars in both a general and an immediate sense. A general deterrent capability is possessed by states to regulate their adversarial relationships when neither of the opponents is seriously considering an attack. Possession of such a capability is generally expected to make resorting to force unattractive to the adversary. An immediate deterrent capability is one where a state could use it as a threat to retaliate when one side is considering an attack.[15] States engaged in PCs are more likely to entertain the usage of the strategy of deterrence to prevent wars. However, among nuclear and conventional deterrence, nuclear deterrence is the preferred policy. Given this, PC states' needs to acquire deterrent capabilities are different from non-protracted conflict states'.

It needs to be noted that all PC states do not experience the same probability of wars. Variation in the occurrence of war among PC states is a product of the conflict types. Conflicts can be territorial or not and the probability of war varies depending on whether or not a conflict is territorial. States in territorial conflicts have a greater propensity to be war-prone because territory is an element of national power and as such is generally non-negotiable. Also, a zero-sum mentality prevails between rivals where territories are at stake.[16] To Hans J. Morgenthau[17] all state interests are defined in terms of power, and international politics is depicted as a "struggle for power," an eternal search for safety and superiority, where resources, population, and especially territory provide the means for success. Consequently, states are less inclined to part with territories that are in their possession and they wage wars to protect such assets. While wars may be fought over other issues, not all issues are resolved by wars. Conflict and war studies reveal that conflicts that end in wars are mostly over territorial issues. Kalevi J. Holsti argues that the percentage of wars involving territory during 1648–1991 has been very high.[18] Where war remains a higher-than-normal probability, PC states are likely to look for ways to avoid wars in the conflict setting. Nuclear weapons, being the best war avoidance weapons because of their devastating nature, very naturally factor into the calculation. Non-territorial conflicts are mostly over ideological, commercial, or religious issues; co-optive behavioral power can be used rather than coercive military power to settle such disputes. Wars are still likely in such conflicts, but are certainly not as probable as in the cases of territorial conflicts. History provides examples of territorial conflict states fighting wars frequently, such as India and Pakistan that fought wars in 1947, 1965, and 1971 or the Arabs and the Israelis that fought wars in 1947, 1956, 1967, and 1973. These two conflicts have also witnessed several interstate crises during the period of the conflicts. Although such conflicts have other issues involved in the conflict relations, as long as one issue remains territorial, it triggers wars easily. Additionally, such conflict relations witness more crises which are easily escalated to war levels unless non-conventional capabilities exist. India, Pakistan, Iran, Iraq, North Korea, South Korea, Israel, and the Arab states have all been involved in territorial PCs and have either proliferated or shown interest to acquire non-conventional weapons or wanted nuclear shield where acquisition – open or clandestine – became difficult.

The East–West PC was primarily over ideological issues and perhaps the Soviet Union gave up on the conflict after maintaining more than 40 years of rivalry essentially because it was an ideological conflict. However, one must not equate great power conflict with regional conflict. Such conflicts – whether territorial or not – can always be war-prone. Direct or proxy wars can be fought by great powers. The cold war period demonstrates the large number of proxy wars the superpowers have been engaged in to protect or defend their satellite states and to stop the adversaries from making any gains in their spheres of influence. The period also shows how easily the superpowers could have been driven into a nuclear confrontation with the eruption of a nuclear crisis in 1962 – the Cuban Missile Crisis. Since great power politics is much different from regional power rivalry, the two superpowers of the cold war years acquired nuclear weapons and throughout the period of rivalry maintained the strategy of mutual assured destruction (MAD) to deter wars in the conflict relations. Similarly, conflicts between great power and regional power may have more probability of wars since one state has much more power to wage a war on the weaker state. Such conflicts – whether territorial or not – are thus more war-prone, unless non-conventional weapons, especially nuclear weapons, exist in the hands of the weaker power. To the weaker power, the presence of a great power rival is threatening.

The great power has the natural power to bully the weaker state or to impose its terms on the regional power. The system type and the power of the global power are both important in this context. The international system can be unipolar as the present international system where the hegemonic power is able to dominate and dictate policies of all other powers in its vicinity and is able to defeat any other power or combination of powers that may fight it.[19] It can be bipolar like the cold war period where the two superpowers' relations have been central to international politics and where each of them dominated a coalition of allied states and competed with its rival superpower for influence over non-aligned countries.[20] It can also be multipolar like the European politics in pre-World War years where several major powers of comparable strength cooperated and competed with one another in shifting patterns.[21] While scholars disagree about whether or not today's world is truly unipolar or hegemonic, it is important to comprehend the difference between polarity and power configuration/structure. The world may consist of various major powers and structurally the system may be called multipower, but it can still be a unipolar international system if there is just one pole operating in the system. As Damon Coletta states, "A pole differs not just in magnitude but in kind from other bodies in the system because its special combination of powers makes other units bend toward its position rather than the other way around."[22] A unipolar world is one where there is just one polar configuration. All states are somewhat allied to the global power. Where the system is unipolar and the rival is the hegemonic power, the weaker regional state is invariably and seriously threatened. The situation becomes a structurally-determined rivalry. Given this, the global power is seen by the regional state as more of a threat if the international system has one superpower only. This essentially means that in a one-polar international system, this feeling of threat for the weaker party is exacerbated or pronounced. This is primarily because there is no other power that is equal to the global power that could defend or protect the weaker power in times of military confrontations with the former power. Where the world is unipolar, the situation is always grave for such small states. Iraq, a regional power, and the US, a global power, may not have had any territorial conflict, but their conflict was war-prone, at least for Iraq, since one of the parties to the conflict was a superpower. Similarly, the Iran–US conflict has one party that happens to be a global power and has the ability to inflict serious damage on the opponent and the other is simply a regional power. Wars can easily be waged by the stronger power to dictate its terms on the adversary that is weak on every level. The war on Iraq in 2003 to oust Saddam Hussein from power based on the pretext that Iraq was developing WMD, even though there was no indication of Iraq doing so at least at that juncture of the relationship, is a striking example of this. In the context of the Iran–US conflict, the security predicaments are obviously different for Iran compared to the US. Iran constantly feels threatened by the power structure of the US and the fact that its hegemonic ambitions can be forcefully imposed on Tehran. Such ambition may have much to do with interests such as instilling liberalism in the economy and polity and changing Iran's status in the region. Thus, where states are threatened by a superpower, they feel the most vulnerable amongst all kinds of PC states. The relationship between them is highly politicized and deeply adversarial because a regional state that is supposed to be bandwagoning with the global power is instead competing against it. The global power singles out such states as the most salient threat. It identifies such states as "rogues" or "states of concern" and develops security strategies to address such threats not because these states will take over the powerful states, but because these states are causes of global security troubles such as proliferation problems or terrorism. The global power also believes that such states jeopardize regional and global stability. Given this, it develops new technologies and armaments to deal with such problem cases. To address such regional problems, newer strategies and techniques are required – sometimes new armaments are also built. This state forms coalitions, where possible, or acts unilaterally, where necessary, to deal with such states so as to minimize potential threats from such arrogant states. While a hegemonic power is able to use coercive military or economic power, soft power – cultural attraction, ideology, and international institutions – or even co-optive behavioral power – getting others to want what one wants[23] – in most cases, military or economic coercion is chosen as the best mechanism to deal with such problem cases, especially in a unilateral international system where other powers are less likely to create troubles when the sole superpower takes actions against the trouble-maker. The international environment is important to consider in this context. No one has the power or the motivation to unnerve the decisions taken by the sole global power. All also feel that the regional power is somewhat arrogant in trying to compete with a global power and disrupt global and regional stability. Additionally, they also feel that it is difficult to engage such an arrogant country diplomatically.

Misunderstanding or miscalculating the intentions and the capability of the weaker party is prominent in this situation. The global power tends to do that most of the time. This is not unusual given the fact that weak states have not only fought and sometimes won wars with the big powers of the world, but have initiated wars where conflicts were asymmetric. It is argued that "the weaker challenger can initiate war against the relatively strong adversary if its key decision-makers believe that they can achieve their political and military objectives through the employment of a limited aims/fait accompli strategy."[24] Additionally, "short-term offensive capability and windows of opportunity may be exploited if the weaker state comes under the control of militaristic decision-making groups that lack political legitimacy."[25] Argentina's war with Britain over the Falklands islands in 1982 is a case in point. Consequently, the stronger power exaggerates the aggressive intentions of the regional rival. It also believes that such an arrogant state is likely to use non-conventional weapons against the world's sole superpower. Unless that were the case, such states would prefer to cooperate with the global power or not disturb peace of the international system by remaining arrogant. The weaker party also has the propensity to misunderstand the intention of the global power in such an international system. It believes that the global power will invariably impose its terms on the weaker regional state. There is thus extreme trust deficit in the relationship. The weaker state is prone not to trust the global power's less-hostile attitude or policies, where such policies are pursued. It perceives that in such an environment, it must rely totally on itself to defend against such a strong opponent. No power will come to rescue it in case of need. No power also has the power, even if intentions to defend it are there, to protect its interest. The absence of other powers to protect it combined with the power of the global power to impose its terms on the weaker state with the usage of coercive mechanisms trigger acute insecurity for the weak state. Thus, the environment is more confrontational; the weaker state perceives extreme insecurity and is in dire need of some quick addressing mechanism to compensate for the insecurity faced by it. Waltz believes that nuclear weapons eliminate the likelihood of miscalculation of the degree to which a war will be costly. Consequently, to Waltz, "the probability of major war among states having nuclear weapons approaches zero."[26] Given this, under such circumstances, the weaker parties to conflicts are proliferation-prone even if territorial issues are not at stake or the conflict is not over territorial issues.

The central point then is that in a conflict where war probability is high, proliferation tendency is high. Although war probability is higher where conflicts are over territories, compared to non-territorial conflict cases, conflicts between superpowers or between global powers and regional powers are always war-prone. Thus, such conflict rivals desire nuclear weapons for war-avoidance. Three salient points that have been raised by now then are: First, PC states are likely to proliferate among the universe of states; Second, territorial PC states are more proliferation-prone due to high war probability; Third, non-territorial PC adversaries may also be war-prone and in turn proliferation-prone if such conflicts are between superpowers or among global and regional powers.

This proliferation tendency exacerbates where a state's conflict rival has nuclear weapons because first, there is a natural tendency to close the gap and reach parity with the rival state at the strategic level and, second, unless the state has similar weapons, the conflict turns into an asymmetric one where wars can be easily waged on it due to the absence of nuclear weapons and it is unable to use the same war strategy against its rival state due to the possession of such weapons by that state. Regional states are particularly interested in closing the gap and reaching parity with the rival states at the strategic level. India and Pakistan have focused on this kind of nuclear arms race most of their life or at least since the introduction of nuclear weapons to the conflict and so did other regional powers such as Iran and Iraq or North Korea and South Korea, among others. This interest is a function of security imperative as well as interest in maintaining symmetry of weaponry in conflict relations, which essentially is demonstrative of the image/prestige preservation. Under these circumstances, nuclear weapons acquisition becomes an end in itself. Arms race is an integral aspect of conflict relations. Each state wants to match the capability of its adversary. No rival state wants to be disadvantaged by maintaining an asymmetric conflict and remain the weaker power. This rule applies for all cases of PCs because, as stated earlier, conflicting states are uneasy about strategic asymmetry. Once a conflict starts, a zero-sum mentality prevails between states and they begin to focus on the idea of relative gains in the relationship. Power "is not a characteristic of the nation itself, but a characteristic of its relationships with other nations," states A. F. K. Organski.[27] Although Realists in general and Neo-realists in particular argue that all states are concerned about relative gains and cooperative endeavors are not encouraged by states primarily because of the relative gains concept, in reality, not all states are worried about relative gains. Only PC states are mostly worried about relative gains. Each state wants to be more powerful than the other. They try to maintain an action–reaction policy as far as military capabilities are concerned. As stated earlier, arms race becomes an essential and chronic characteristic of the conflict. Therefore, as soon as one state acquires a nuclear capability, the other follows suit. Additionally, this becomes a matter of status degradation and fractured prestige for states if they are unable to match the power of the opponent. The idea that "parity preserves peace" is also acknowledged by both parties. Where this is the situation between somewhat equal regional rivals, then in conflicts between global and regional powers where the former possesses nuclear weapons, the latter is naturally more inclined to have a similar capability. This is mostly because of the desire to match the capability of the adversary – in this case a global power. As stated before, every PC rival tries to match the capability of its adversary and a regional power is no different than a global power. There is a natural tendency to match it for security reasons. Here, matching the capability of one's rival is a function of rivalry. However, one point needs to be noted carefully: if a global rival has nuclear weapons, the regional rival has more of a tendency to acquire a similar capability because on other levels it is unable to be at par with the global power. It is impossible for a regional power to try to match the global power on any level. After all a global power becomes one due to its global reach and capabilities. For example, in the contemporary world, the US is "the sole state with preeminence in every domain of power, economic, military, diplomatic, ideological, technological, and cultural – with the reach and capabilities to promote its interests in virtually every part of the world."[28] No other country in the world or a number of countries combined has the power to bring it down. Such a state dominates all other states in the international system.[29] If this power has a regional rival, the regional rival is automatically threatened by having a global power as its rival. If major powers are in no position to compete with this global power, it is impossible for a regional and weak developing country to match the capability of the global power. Success in war depends largely on the weaponry available to the opposing sides.[30] Since success in war with a global power is unlikely for the weaker side, it tries to deter wars. Additionally, because the enduring rivalry demands ensuring security of the weak state, the latter tries to address the strategic disparity with the acquisition of nuclear weapons. Under the circumstances it seeks to acquire the ultimate war-deterring capability – nuclear weapons. The purpose may not necessarily be only to dissuade the global power from taking a military action against the weaker state, but also to persuade the adversary to take this actor seriously, acknowledge its rightful status in the region, and not to impose its terms on the state. What a weak state cannot do without the possession of nuclear weapons, it can do once it develops them. These are particularly important when its rival is a global power. The acquisition of nuclear weapons provides a state of this nature with a lot of advantages compared to other states that have somewhat equal rivals. With nuclear weapons the game is quite simple – one weapon is enough of a deterrent for a weaker state, which is not the case with conventional weapons. The weaker power will never be in a position to match the conventional capability of the global power. On the economic and strategic level, it is not a match. Thus, it strives more to maintain a capability that has the ultimate capacity to deter its global adversary. States prefer general deterrence because it plays the predominant role of maintaining conditional peace between adversaries where the conflict relationship is less heated and less acute.[31] As a result, all states, whether regional or global, that has regional or global rivals with nuclear capabilities will try to acquire similar capabilities to close the gap between them at the strategic level and to maintain some degree of prestige in the rivalry relationship. The weaker regional power in conflict with a global power has the most incentive to match such capability for prestige and bargaining reasons in addition to security imperatives.

If the conflict is already asymmetric where one power is weaker than the other, the weaker power will have a natural propensity to proliferate to address its weakness. This is applicable against all cases of asymmetric PCs. Pakistan is a case in point. It strived to acquire nuclear weapons, some say, even before India ever contemplated acquiring primarily because it was the weaker party to the conflict. Asymmetric conflicts between regional and global powers are the worst kind of conflicts as far as proliferation impetus is concerned. Where a regional power is involved in a PC with a global power, the weaker power is even more inclined to acquire nuclear weapons to restrain the stronger power from waging wars or imposing its terms on the weaker state. The strong is hard to deter when power is unbalanced, a generally accepted notion in international politics. As mentioned earlier, the stronger power has the power to inflict enough damage on the opponent with its capabilities. The weaker power is in no position to compete with the stronger power, which the weaker power is fully aware of. To compensate for its weakness on other levels, it undertakes security policies that drive it to acquire nuclear weapons. States generally formulate their security policies on the basis of worst-case scenarios and are always "wary of the time required for them to catch up with the technological and military capabilities of other states. The result is a constant effort by countries to increase their capability to defend themselves and deter aggression."[32] Weaker regional states always have the apprehension that the global power will attack them at any time and they understand fully well that even with time they can never catch up with the military capabilities of the global power. Generally, a "hegemon does not have to do much to generate fear among the other states in the system," John Mearsheimer states that "its formidable capabilities" alone can scare others and push other major powers to balance against their "dangerous opponent."[33] But how is a weak regional state supposed to balance the power of a global rival? This could apply against great power dyad, but not against an asymmetric global–regional power rivalry. Under the circumstances the fear that the global power instills in a regional rival pushes the latter to develop non-conventional capabilities that may simply help to defend it from potentially aggressive moves of the global adversary. Nuclear weapons acquisition becomes important within this context. Interestingly, for such states nuclear weapons are more fungible compared to the global or strong major powers. Fungibility refers to "the ease with which capabilities in one issue-area can be used in other issue-areas."[34] Nuclear weapons provide security, prestige, and bargaining chip simultaneously for weaker states in the conflict where other means of competing with the adversary are unavailable, unaffordable, and useless. For example, Iran cannot match the power of the US on any level and consequently it strives to acquire nuclear weapons first to secure itself from the US's military attacks and then to swagger its capability to prove that it is also no less important a state in the international system and finally to be able to bargain better with its global adversary. Therefore, for such states, although security and survival are the most important reasons for proliferation, they are also inclined to obtain prestige through the possession of nuclear capability and bargain better in an asymmetric conflict. Concepts such as status inconsistency, power, and prestige become blurred with security motivation.

The situation becomes worse and is ignited for the weaker regional state where the global power pursues aggressive foreign policies against its weaker rival. Generally speaking, a global power often pursues aggressive foreign policies in these situations. It has the power to conquer and no reason to demonstrate its benign intentions to the weaker states in the international system. Stephen Van Evera states,

> When conquest is easy, states have less faith in agreements because others break them more often. They also bargain harder and concede more grudgingly, causing more deadlocks; they find that compliance with agreements is harder to verify; and they insist on better verification and compliance. As a result, states negotiate less often and settle fewer disputes; hence more issues remain unsettled, and misperceptions survive that dialogue might dispel.[35]

The usage of force by the US against Iraq after the Gulf War is a good example of a policy of the global power based on the notion of coercion. Instead of moderating Iraq through the usage of carrots, such as economic interactions, the US firmly used a stick.[36] Even if the global power does not pursue aggressive policies, the weaker power most often misperceives the intentions of the stronger power because of its superiority in terms of capabilities. Rivals assume the worst about the hegemon's intentions which reinforces the fearful state's motivation to deter it and "maybe even weaken it if the opportunity presents itself."[37] Assuming the worst about the intentions of an adversary means exaggerating the hostility of the opponent, which drives decision-makers into making wrong decisions based on poor judgments in the realm of security. Jack Levy contends that

> exaggeration of the hostility of the adversary's intentions is the most common form of misperception. It derives from system-induced worst-case analysis, the tendency to define intentions in terms of available capabilities, diabolical images of the adversary, and psychological constraints on information processing.[38]

The weaker party to a conflict operates on the basis of a preconceived evil image and notion of its stronger adversary. Janice Gross Stein argues that images of the enemy are embedded in the minds of the decision-makers in deep-rooted conflicts and changing the existing enemy images may be very difficult because they are "deeply rooted and resistant to change, even when adversary attempts to signal a change in intent to another."[39] This leads to two salient points: first that the rival is likely to develop an evil image of the enemy state where conflicts are intractable, which automatically leads it to misperceive the intentions of the enemy, and second, this image is unlikely to change even if the enemy makes good gestures pertaining to the conflict relations. These two points boil down to one conclusion: misperception of the enemy's intentions is a constant factor in such a conflict. However, misperception becomes worse when aggressive policies are contemplated or pursued by the global power – meaning usage of coercive economic or military power. Consequently, a strong response is preferred by the weak state. Levy argues that "response to perceived hostility is to increase military capabilities in order to deter aggression and to prepare for war in case deterrence fails."[40] Misperception in essence promotes arms racing. It is impossible for a regional power to increase its conventional military capabilities to deter aggression of a global power. Given this, non-conventional weapons are desired. One ultimate weapon can secure the weaker state in an asymmetric conflict. Nuclear weapons acquisition, thus, becomes a function partly for such misperceptions, which is common in enduring hostility. In order to acquire such a capability, the weak state indulges in secret endeavors and violates the norms of agreements in the realm of proliferation. It worries about negotiation in good faith and considers survival mechanism as the best possible solution under the circumstances. Van Evera states that "the secure state," in which case offense dominates such as a global power, "can afford the luxury of negotiating in good faith, but the insecure must worry more about short-term survival. Their worry drives them to deceit and sudden betrayals of all kinds."[41] However, as the weaker power decides not to bandwagon with the stronger one or to give in to the pressures of the global power, it very naturally conveys a threatening message to the opponent by demonstrating its eagerness to acquire the most devastative weapons the world has seen. It portrays itself as a risk-acceptant state willing to dissatisfy a global power. Here, too, although it is to secure itself from a military attack, there is more to it. It is also to give the signal to the opponent not to mess with the internal political dynamics of the state and to stop pursuing such foreign policies. Thus, sometimes such states do not mention the word deterrence in a manner one would expect for security reasons. The point is that where a small regional country does not abide by the norms of the international system and maintains an enduring rivalry with a global power, it is naturally misunderstood by its rival state. The rival, even if a global power, misperceives its intentions and capabilities and does not give the country the benefit of the doubt. It believes that this country is adamant to disrupt peace and security of the world. Its decision-makers' statements are not believed and given respect; neither is its governing institution respected. Given these, misperceptions of intentions and capabilities work both ways in an asymmetric conflict, leading to additional difficulty in an already problematic enduring rivalry.

Additionally, this incentive to proliferate very naturally increases when states are engaged in more than one or multiple PCs because as the number of rivals increases, the likelihood of wars also increases. If war probability is less in one conflict that does not necessarily mean that war is less likely in another conflict it is engaged in. The more conflicts it has, the more likely it will want to acquire nuclear weapons because once possessed, such weapons can protect the state against all sorts of enemies – regional or global, small or big, proximate or non-proximate. Also, if states are involved in dyadic conflicts the chances are more that nuclear weapons will be desired because wars are more likely in dyadic conflicts and there is no one to depend on for security purposes in dyadic conflicts unlike non-dyadic conflicts where responsibilities can be shared even informally. Perhaps all Arab states were not so inclined to acquire nuclear weapons to deter the Israeli nuclear threat because Iraq was developing nuclear weapons clandestinely and Iran too, although a Gulf state but part of the conflict due to its connections with Syria, was developing a nuclear program since the 1970s. Other Arab states such as Syria had other non-conventional weapons such as chemical weapons to deter Israeli aggressive actions, and finally all were together in this conflict – even though there was always covert and even overt Arab disunity, which even Israel was aware of. Response by the coalition states to the adversary's possession of nuclear capability was thus often muted. In a coalition responsibilities are unclear and the key interests of each member state are not easily understood. If some states in the coalition have the deterring capability, most other states consider that their rival can be effectively checked by that state and consequently their desire to proliferate may be less intense.[42] The point is, buck-passing was possible in the Arab–Israeli conflict, which was not possible in the Iran–Iraq conflict. Thus, both Iran and Iraq were inclined to acquire nuclear weapons for their involvement in the Iran–Iraq dyadic conflict. Additionally, proximate rivals are the most dangerous ones to compete with and war is always a possibility due to the fact that borders can flare up at any time which might be potentially disturbing for escalation possibilities. Such states have to remain prepared for the unexpected crisis situations and the acquisition of nuclear weapons is the best means to secure a state under the circumstances. India and Pakistan as well as Iran and Iraq are examples of proximate states engaged in dyadic conflicts that acquired or showed aspirations to acquire nuclear weapons. If a state is engaged in multiple conflicts, it prefers to proliferate simply because one deterrent capability enables it to defend itself from all sorts of enemies. A regional state is incapable of defending itself effectively solely by depending on conventional weapons. The point of nuclear weapons being cost-effective comes in at this juncture. The argument is that the acquisition of nuclear weapons may actually help a country in reducing its defense expenditures. When the cost of conventional forces is too high and the state is no longer capable of maintaining such high defense expenditures, "acquiring nuclear weapons would permit the nation to maintain (or increase) its military capability with less of an economic burden."[43] Countries such as France and Britain have cut down on conventional weapons expenditure due to the acquisition of nuclear weapons. It was argued by the Indians and Pakistanis as well that they will follow in the footsteps of those two nuclear powers. However, that is not always possible for states that have to protect themselves from proximate rivals. Borders have to be well protected and conventional forces and capabilities are as important as non-conventional ones. Also, proximate rivals need to be careful about radiation effects of the usage of nuclear weapons. While scholars sometimes have argued that nuclear weapons are cost-effective and countries may have gone nuclear for this incentive, nuclear weapons are mostly cost-effective for states that are engaged in multiple conflicts. It is impossible for such states to defend themselves with conventional means. In fact, they can cut down on such forces if the ultimate weapons are possessed. George Quester argued more than three decades ago that Iran may be able to reduce its defense expenditure by going nuclear.[44] A nuclear Iran may have to spend much less on conventional weapons to defend itself against attacks from its regional neighbors and global rival. However, it must be noted that even such states do not develop such weapons for cost-effectiveness. While security remains the main driving force for the nuclear decision, the economic factor is also factored into the calculation, just as prestige, swaggering, and bargaining politics are.

The aforementioned situation becomes even more troublesome if a state's conflict rivals are allies of one another. If one state has multiple rivals and the rivals – all or even one – of them are allies, the situation becomes more threatening for the state because it can be attacked from different fronts by enemies who are allies. There is of course difference between allies that are "value or norm-driven," such as democracies being generally allies and not fighting each other, or "interest-driven allies"[45] such as the US and Israel with respect to the Middle East. The first is where there is a feeling or sense of community due to shared political ideology and principles. The second is more complicated. Here allies become allies because of some common purposes, such as security threat. Also, when enemies are friends of each other, there is a natural situation of power disparity. Where two or more enemy states are allies the state in question is bound to consider the conflicts as asymmetric and feel extremely vulnerable. If a global power has a regional ally and both are adversaries of another regional state, then the latter feels doubly threatened. The regional ally has to spend less on defense for the support it obtains from its global ally compared to the one that does not have any such ally. In conventional realm, it is impossible to deter such adversaries or match their capabilities. Resorting to nuclear weapons capability may become the best option for such a country that cannot easily calculate the capabilities of its adversary because there is more than one state involved in the adversarial coalition. The psychological or emotional vulnerability is also taken care of with the possession of nuclear capability. If one of its enemies that are allies of each other is a global power, asymmetry is more pronounced. If one enemy is a global power and the other regional, it is very disturbing for the state because the global power has easy access to the region through the regional power. Where the global power has easy access to the region through a regional power that is a proximate rival of a state, its security dynamics change easily. The state becomes extremely concerned about its security and survival under the circumstances. Proximate rivals are the worst rivals. As stated before, borders have a tendency of flaring up and crises escalation is a common situation between bordering rivals. India and Pakistan are good examples of border disturbances leading to disputes and crises. Here the problem is not only being involved in a rivalry with a global power, but also the fact that the rival has easy access to the region or has bases in countries of the region that are close by. Iran falls into this category of states. It has the US as its global rival that has Israel as its primary ally in the Middle East, which is also an enemy of Iran, and has Iraq, another enemy state with common borders where US troops are stationed. This is a precarious condition for Iran. To address these simultaneous security problems, it requires mechanisms that cannot be undermined by regional and global powers. It desires to have capabilities that will dissuade adversaries from taking any action against it and that will give it respect and negotiating power. If regional powers were its only concerns, perhaps it would not be so relentless in developing its nuclear program. The feeling of isolation and insecurity dictates its security, defense, and foreign policies. Miscalculations of intentions of adversaries are evident. Adversaries are seen as very aggressive. Aggressive intentions of the adversary are overinflated. Trust deficit is a common characteristic of such conflicting states. Trusting adversaries who seem to be planning to trap the country from all ends is difficult, if not impossible. Where trust is not achievable and where pressure to trust remains, deception path is undertaken. While some degree of deception is evidenced between most conflict states, a state having multiple conflict adversaries and global adversary is the most likely candidate for walking through a deception path. Unless they deceive the international community, such states cannot secure themselves. Under the shelter of the civilian nuclear program, they make efforts to develop nuclear weapons capability. The relationship between civilian and military technology is complex. The simple linear relationship between military technology and civilian nuclear development becomes complex due to the conversion of weapons. "The development of atomic energy for peaceful purposes and the development of atomic energy for bombs are in much of their course interchangeable and interdependent. From this it follows that although nations may agree not to use in bombs the atomic energy developed within their borders the only assurance that a conversion to destructive purposes would not be made would be the pledged word and the good faith of the nation itself."[46] Given this, if nations want to deceive others they can quite easily do so if the intention to deceive is there. Time is of essence for such states. They cannot rely on other states to protect them. Deceiving becomes the practise under the circumstances because security is at stake. Security guarantees are not trusted and negotiations are either rejected or not taken seriously. All these are functions of lack of trust, which is a product of the enemies being allies. This is the worst kind of situation in the proliferation world. Such states are the most determined to proliferate and stopping them from doing so requires multiple conflict resolutions simultaneously.

If a state is engaged in territorial PCs and has a global power rival, faces nuclear adversaries, is involved in asymmetric and multiple conflicts – including dyadic ones – its conflict rivals are allies and some are proximate states, it is likely to be the most determined proliferator of the world. Thus, deterrent weapons are extremely valuable to such states. Nuclear weapons, being the best deterrent, are naturally attractive to such a state. To recap, the central propositions are:

1 Among states in the international system, PC states are likely to acquire nuclear weapons.
2 Territorial PC states are mostly proliferation-prone because of higher war probability in the conflict setting.
3 PC states facing dyadic conflicts have more desire to proliferate.
4 PC states having proximate rivals have a great propensity to proliferate.
5 Regional states engaged in PCs – whether over territorial issues or not – with global powers are extremely prone to proliferation.
6 A PC state facing a nuclear adversary, regional, global, or both, is almost inevitably proliferation prone.
7 A PC state engaged in an asymmetric conflict where it is a weaker regional power against another strong regional power or a global power is strongly inclined to proliferate.
8 A PC state engaged in multiple PCs, where some are dyadic, is propelled to proliferate.
9 A PC state whose enemies are allies of each other considers nuclear weapons acquisition essential.
10 A PC state faced with all of the aforementioned points are likely to be the most determined proliferator.

Figure 2.1 demonstrates a general connection between protracted conflicts and proliferation propensities of states.

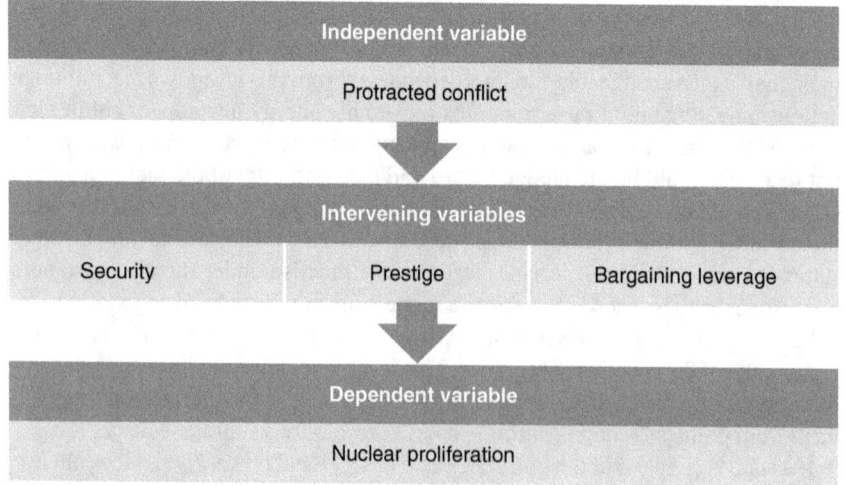

Figure 2.1 Nuclear proliferation: variable connection.

Protracted conflicts and nuclear weapons 43

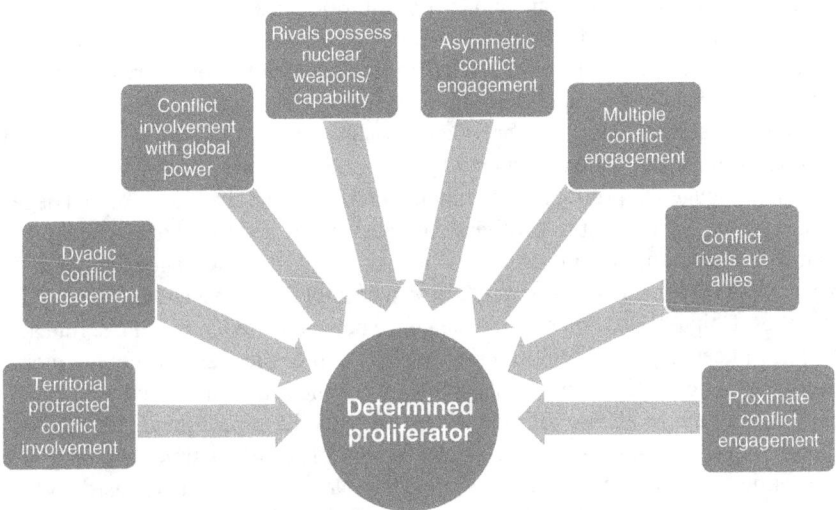

Figure 2.2 Protracted conflicts and a determined proliferator.

Figure 2.2 shows the variables that make a state the most determined proliferator among the protracted conflict states.

A study of the proliferation cases reveals that all proliferators in the world have been involved in some form of PC. The five nuclear states – US, the former Soviet Union, Britain, France, and China – have all been engaged in PCs when they became nuclear states, and so were the three regional proliferators, India, Pakistan, and Israel. Other regional states that have made efforts to proliferate such as Taiwan, South Korea, and Libya have all been in PCs during the time they showed their desire to proliferate. The three "Axis of Evil" states, North Korea, Iran, and Iraq, have all been involved in PCs. Even the only country in the world that renounced its nuclear weapons program, South Africa, was also in a protracted conflict when it acquired nuclear weapons. Thus, to date, all proliferators have been PC states. All regional proliferators have also been involved in territorial PCs such as India, Pakistan, Israel, Iran, Iraq, and North Korea. Countries like Iran, Iraq (before 2003), and North Korea have additional incentive to proliferate for having a global power as a rival even though with the global power they do not have territorial issues. The argument that where rivals are nuclear states proliferation propensities are higher also holds in the cases of all proliferators. The former Soviet Union's unrelenting drive to acquire nuclear weapons at the earliest possible time once the US detonated its weapons in Hiroshima and Nagasaki is a known fact. In the South Asian region, Pakistan's persistent drive to have the bombs at any cost was evidenced after India detonated its peaceful nuclear device in 1974 and it is argued that the latter developed its nuclear weapons program to primarily address its security concerns pertaining to its extra-regional nuclear rival, China. In the

Middle East, Iraq's desire to be a nuclear state emanated from Israel's nuclear weapons development program and Iran's ambition started because of its bilateral rival Iraq's efforts to acquire nuclear weapons. In the Asia Pacific region, North Korea felt threatened by the US's nuclear umbrella in South Korea, creating strategic imbalance in the Korean Peninsula. The proposition that PC states in asymmetric conflicts facing global rivals are even more likely to proliferate can also be used against cases. North Korea, Iran, and Iraq (before 2003) are striking examples of PC states engaged in protracted asymmetric conflicts with the US – a global hegemonic power – that want to proliferate by any means and using any technique – denial or deception. The proposition which stipulates that states engaged in multiple PCs are very proliferation-prone can also be applied against the universe of the PC cases. China, India, and North Korea have been involved in twin PCs. Iran and Iraq have been engaged in more than two PCs. All of these states showed more-than-normal desire to acquire nuclear weapons. When states are faced with multiple PCs and the rivals are allies, they are very likely to proliferate also applies against cases. Iran is one such case that faces multiple conflicts simultaneously and its enemies, such as Israel and the US, are allies. North Korea is also a case in point. It is interesting to study these cases to understand the value of these propositions and test them against cases. Where all of the propositions we have discussed can be applied against a case, that state is likely to be the most determined proliferator. Iran seems to be such a case.

The next four chapters test the theoretical framework of the study against the Iranian case. The purpose is to evaluate the empirical power or the applicability of the theory. Iran was chosen for the study because it is a highly controversial case in the realm of proliferation that needs comprehensive investigation. Additionally, it is also engaged in PCs. While Tehran alarms the international community with its nuclear program that enables it to make nuclear weapons, it is important to understand why it may require such weapons, whether or not it is likely to relinquish its nuclear weapons program, and what needs to be done to attain that goal.

Part III
Case study: Iran

3 Iran's nuclear ambition and twin protracted conflicts between 1947 and 1979

The previous chapter presented a theory of proliferation among protracted conflict states and this chapter and the ones that follow test that theoretical framework against the Iranian case. The chapter deals with Iran's nuclear aspirations and standing first and then analyzes its twin protracted conflicts from 1947 to 1979. The purpose is not simply to probe the two conflicts during the specified period, but to demonstrate that its nuclear program had developed and received a certain degree of momentum for its twin intractable conflicts at the time. Iran is engaged in both conflicts till now. The two conflicts and their ramifications in the nuclear realm are consequently discussed from the beginning till the present time. During the specified period, Iran was engaged in a protracted, territorial, and dyadic conflict with Iraq, a proximate rival that was also suspected of clandestinely developing nuclear weapons capabilities, and a non-dyadic protracted conflict with Israel that had nuclear weapons capability since the 1960s. The only positive aspect for Iran during this period was that none of its enemies were allies of each other. Thus, although the desire to acquire nuclear weapons seems to be present, the effort in that realm was still modest.

Iran's nuclear program

Iran launched its nuclear program under the Shah regime. The Shah of Iran, Mohammad Reza Pahlavi, became an important ally of the US after the US–UK sponsored coup against Prime Minister Mohammad Mossadeq in August 1953. While it was the Shah's personal interest in seeing Iran develop its nuclear capability, his cordial relationship with the US had paved the way to develop the program. As part of the Atoms for Peace program, the US offered nuclear research facilities and training to its cold war allies, Iran being one of them, and in exchange Washington wanted commitments from them not to develop nuclear weapons. The Shah came under this commitment and in 1957, Iran and the US signed a nuclear cooperation agreement, "which eventually led to the supply of a basic five-megawatt (MW) light-water research reactor and related laboratories, commissioned at the Tehran Nuclear Research Center (TNRC) in 1967."[1] The following year Iran signed the NPT, which it ratified in 1970. By 1974, Iran came under full-scope safeguards agreement with the IAEA according to which it complied to accepting IAEA inspections on all sources of fissionable materials in all peaceful nuclear activities within the country.[2] The AEOI was also established in 1974 and there were plans to generate 23,000 MW of nuclear energy within the next 20 years and to acquire full-nuclear fuel cycle including facilities to enrich uranium, fabricate fuel, and reprocess spent fuel to obtain plutonium for civil fuel purposes.[3] As part of this plan Iran made agreements with Germany, France, and the US and it obtained 22 reactors for generating 23,000 MW of electrical power. The Western allies had helped Iran in developing a comprehensive nuclear program under the umbrella of cold war alliance politics and with the understanding that Iran will never have the ambition to acquire nuclear weapons.

The Shah was in power until 1979, but from 1975 onwards the US became suspicious of Iran's massive nuclear program which, according to the US, could have dual purpose. By that time, Tehran had acquired nuclear fuel cycle capabilities with both civilian and military applications. While for the past two decades the international community has been discussing Iran's intention to reprocess uranium, this is not the first time Iran has been inclined to reprocess uranium. In fact, since the beginning of the nuclear program Iran has given this aspect serious consideration. As early as 1975, Iran had problems with the US with regard to where the plutonium would be reprocessed. Iran insisted on having reprocessing facilities located in Tehran, while the US had apprehensions about that.[4] In 1976, Iran expressed serious interest in acquiring uranium enrichment technology. During that period Iran's budget for the Atomic Energy Organization was increased from $30.8 million in fiscal year 1975 to more than one billion dollars for the fiscal year 1976.[5] Also in the year 1976, South Africa came to an understanding with Iran according to which South Africa would supply $700 million worth of yellowcake to Iran and in return Iran would finance an enrichment plant in South Africa.[6] In a discussion of Iranian investment schemes in nuclear technology during the 1970s, it was noted that in 1976 Iran decided to purchase "an experimental laser system" capable of enriching uranium. Tehran bought four gas lasers from Lischem, a US company, and decided to invest and conduct more research in this area. US Department of Energy's (DOE) nuclear export division's head James Kratz commented on the sale and reported that they didn't think it was a viable process for uranium.[7] It is also interesting to note that Iran's intention not to accept safeguards pertaining to its nuclear program was even evident at the initial stage of its development. Thus, that is not a new policy of Tehran either. In fact, talks between Iran and the US on nuclear cooperation were suspended for a while after disagreement on nuclear safeguards in 1976.[8] By the late 1970s, but still during the Shah's rule, the US received intelligence information indicating that the Shah had set up a clandestine nuclear weapons development program.[9] Additionally, according to Akbar Etemad, Director of the AEOI until October 1978, researchers at the TNRC had been involved in laboratory experiments with applications for reprocessing spent fuel.[10] Leonard Spector stated that the nuclear program that Iranian Revolutionary leaders inherited was "by far the most ambitious in the Middle East."[11] Given these, it is quite evident that its nuclear program had dual purpose from the start and that was primarily a function of the threat emanating from Iraq. Thus, although the general belief is that the Iran–US relationship was cordial prior to the demise of the Shah era, in reality during the last few years of the Shah's rule the relationship with the US was not so smooth. From 1975 to 1979, the Ford and Carter administrations had taken stern actions against Iran in the nuclear realm. In 1975 the US decided to use a veto power over Iran's desire to reprocess US-supplied nuclear power fuel and in 1977 Jimmy Carter refused to offer reprocessing and enrichment assistance to Iran and wanted it to accept comprehensive IAEA safeguards as a condition for any Iranian nuclear exports.[12] The US also made efforts to persuade France and Germany not to assist Iran in its reprocessing and enrichment activities – just what the Clinton and Bush administrations have done in more recent years – which, of course, were not effective. Back then, the US's apprehension was for two reasons: India tested its peaceful nuclear device in 1974 which alarmed the international community and Iran's nuclear program was comprehensive enough that it could be used to build nuclear weapons at some point in time, should the political will be there to pursue that path. The US also believed that Iran would not restrain from developing nuclear weapons if other states proliferated in the region. The US National Security Council Memo stated that year, "despite Iran's present benign attitude towards the NPT and non-proliferation, some are concerned over its possible longer-term nuclear weapon ambitions should others proliferate."[13] Given this, it is important to understand the motivations behind Iran's nuclear aspirations at the initial stage of the nuclear program and how that contributed to today's more complicated nuclear ambition. However, before going into that, comprehending Iran's current nuclear program's standing is pertinent since the contemporary program is a product of the program that was initiated during the Shah period and the motivations, back then and today, are connected. In other words, the central motivations for a dual purpose technology have been constant from the very beginning till today, even though today's incentives may be more pronounced and known.

The Shah's contribution to Iran's nuclear program cannot be denied, but his aim was simply to see Iran as an economic power in the region. He believed in the possession of conventional deterrent weapons and thought that nuclear weapons were less credible deterrents compared to the conventional ones. Some believe that during this period there was no political decision taken by the Iranian leadership to acquire nuclear weapons, but there was appreciation at different quarters of the Iranian administration that the option to acquire such weapons remains open if Iran decides to do so later.[14] However, others contend that it was during the Shah period that Iran began a nuclear weapon research program centered at the Amirabad Research Center, where studies of weapons design and plutonium recovery from spent reactor fuel were conducted.[15] Scholars also believe that Iran sought laser enrichment technology and had probably set up a secret nuclear weapons group since the reign of the Shah.[16] There is controversy and debate as to what the Shah was really up to with regard to the nuclear program. However, one point was recognized by both groups: that the weapons aspect was important for the Iranian leadership. Iran was obliged to never acquire nuclear weapons under its NPT commitment and consequently it could never come out in the open and discuss proliferation potential or possibilities if there was any weapons component to its nuclear program. In fact, Tehran continued this secrecy till almost 2003, when it made a detailed declaration to respond to a Resolution of the IAEA Board of Governors that set a deadline for the disclosure of its program.[17] This is not unique to the Iranian case. Iraq and North Korea have also pursued the same path, although the two outcomes were completely different. North Korea tested its nuclear weapons and used it as leverage over the US to bargain better and Iraq could not even develop a nuclear weapons program. All proliferators have been engaged in some form of secrecy during the infancy of their nuclear weapons program and the reasons are obvious. No country is supposed to proliferate. Interestingly, even Pakistan and India, countries that did not sign the NPT, did not disclose or discuss nuclear matters publicly. The only difference between them and Iran, however, is that the latter is obliged to allow full inspection due to its commitment to NPT and IAEA, which the former states are not.

After Shah's rule, Iran's nuclear program continued under the leaderships of Ayatollah Khomeini, Ali Khameini, Ali Akbar Hashemi Rafsanjani, Mohammad Khatami, and Mahmoud Ahmadinejad, as discussed in Chapter 1. The Revolutionary regime of Ayatollah Khomeini inherited two partially completed German-supplied power reactors at Bushehr, the construction of which the leader froze and later it was severely damaged by Iraqi bombings during the 1980–88 Iran–Iraq War, one of which was later constructed with the help of Russian aid after the 1995 agreement between Iran and Russia.[18] Thus, after the Islamic Revolution, the pace of its nuclear program slowed down a lot. From 1979 to 1989, under Ayatollah Khomeini, the nuclear program did not make much progress because he viewed "nuclear technology with theological suspicion."[19] However, after fighting a protracted war with Iraq, Iran's nuclear weapons efforts gained momentum from the late 1980s when the leadership team changed and included Supreme Leader Khameini and President Rafsanjani, who made serious efforts to strengthen Iran's strategic capabilities to address future security challenges such as the Iran–Iraq War effectively.

From 1980 to 1990, even though Iran had more than two conflicts to deal with, Iran's primary security threat which initially triggered it to focus on the nuclear weapons program was Iraq. With Iraq, the conflict was between bordering countries and Iran's experience was bitter. Tehran did not want a repetition of the protracted war with Iraq. Its other security concern was obviously Israel, a country that Iran would like to see wiped out from the map of the Middle East and that which possessed nuclear weapons.[20] Otherwise why would Iran decide to initiate a secret uranium centrifuge enrichment program in 1985 in the midst of an exhausting war with Iraq[21] and also when, according to the Islamic clerics, nuclear weapons have been a western innovation and un-Islamic? In the missile realm, Iran was not advanced. Iran's delivery systems suffered increasing attrition as the Iran–Iraq war progressed and the disparity in longer-range strike capabilities led Iran to seek ballistic missile capabilities in order to strike Baghdad and other major Iraqi population centers. By the mid-1980s it attained assistance from China in that realm, and by 1985 and 1986 it acquired Soviet Scud-B missiles with a range of 280–300 km from Libya and

Syria. By 1988 it obtained a larger number of the same missile from North Korea which gave it the ability to strike Iraq and respond to Iraqi strategic missile attacks.[22] With the conclusion of the war, Iran began a more dedicated and comprehensive missile program with assistance from North Korea, China, and Russia. It possessed Shehab 1 (Scud-B) with a range of 300 km, Shehab 2 (Scud-C) which has a range of 500 km, and Shehab 3 (No-Dong) with a range of 1300–1500 km.[23]

Interestingly, while on the one hand the Gulf War of 1990–91 diminished Iran's threat emanating from Iraq due to the constraints on Iraq's conventional and non-conventional weapons programs, on the other hand it brought to the forefront an even more potential threat – the US. With the waging of the Second Gulf War with Iraq, the US "expanded its permanent security presence in the Persian Gulf"[24] region, which was a serious security threat for Iran. In this security environment after the 1990–91 Gulf War, seeing no alternative, Iran reached an agreement with North Korea around 1993 to obtain the facilities and expertise required to build intermediate-range Shehab 3 missiles[25] and, in 1998, Iran successfully test-fired Shehab 3, which would allow it to hit all of Iraq and strike the key ally of the US – Israel.[26] The purpose, it is believed, was to strengthen Iran's leverage vis-à-vis the US.[27] When Mohammad Khatami, a moderate leader, came to power in 1997, it was expected that the nuclear program in Iran would receive less attention because of his interest in engaging Iran more in the international stage and in particular with the US. However, Iran worked on its nuclear program more seriously during this regime and its drive became unrelenting in the post-2002 period due to very prominent hostile foreign policies of the US directed against Iran, discussed in Chapters 5 and 6. The 2003 war in Iraq rang a new threatening security alarm for the Iranians. Although there was a moment of relief for Iran as Iraq's dictatorial regime fell, the American military presence in Iraq for an indefinite period threatened Tehran like never before. Instead of feeling more secure in the absence of a protracted conflict rival – Iraq – the presence of the hegemonic power along its border made matters worse for Iran. The threat was exacerbated because the US and Israel were allies.

In the present world where nuclear proliferation remains a major threat to global peace, Iran is a key state in the Middle East that is suspected of having a nuclear weapons program. While Iran claims that its nuclear program is exclusively for peaceful purposes, the US and some of its allies are increasingly of the opinion that Iran's program is structured for a dual purpose. Even the European intelligence and the IAEA agree that Iran is intent on developing the bombs. As stated earlier, Iran has been a signatory to the NPT since 1968 which allows it to enrich uranium for civilian fuel programs only. However, from 2000 to 2002, for 18 months Iran concealed its enrichment activities from the IAEA inspectors, making the international community more suspicious of its real intentions pertaining to the enrichment programs. In April 2006, Iran's controversial President Mahmoud Ahmadinejad announced that Iran joined "the club of nuclear countries" by mastering the entire nuclear fuel cycle and being able to enrich uranium for power stations.[28] The concern of the US and its European allies is that if Iran can master enrichment to fuel grade, it can master enrichment to weapons grade because the processes of mastering these are the same. Although Iran officially does not acknowledge that its nuclear program is for weapons purpose, evidence suggests that the program is not for peaceful purposes. Its program certainly is for military purposes, argues Meir Javedanfar,[29] who provides several reasons for his assessment. He argues that

> in 2002, it [Iran] hit the nuclear program and IAEA visits to Tehran were rejected. How to mold uranium into warheads was a design Iran purchased from somewhere else – perhaps from A.Q Khan. P2 centrifuges are not needed for civilian purposes. It is unclear what Iran did with its plutonium. Polonium 210 is basically the trigger for nuclear reaction – which Iran possesses.[30]

For all these reasons even if Ahmadinejad did not speak about Iran's aspirations pertaining to nuclear weapons, the world would have reasons to worry about Iran's nuclear intentions. Estimates on how long it would take for Iran to make a nuclear bomb range from a couple of years to a decade. In 2006, the Institute of Strategic Studies reported that Iran would be able to produce enough nuclear materials in three years. According to the International Institute for Strategic Studies' *Military Balance 2009*, Iran has in fact acquired enough enriched uranium to produce one bomb by late 2009.[31] Additionally, the report doubts US intelligence estimates that Iran halted its work on nuclear weapons six years ago in 2003. It also states that Tehran continued to develop its long-range ballistic missiles able to reach targets in Israel and more.[32] This means that Iran continued to deceive the international community in general and IAEA in particular with regard to its nuclear program.

Just as there is disagreement between the US and its allies on the time that will be required for Iran to produce nuclear weapons, there has also been disagreement between them with regard to what measures – diplomacy, sanctions, or military action – should be taken to prevent the country from acquiring the devastating weapons. In 2006, Seymour Hersh wrote that although publicly the Bush administration was focusing on diplomacy to resolve the issue, covertly it was planning a military attack on the country not only to crush its nuclear weapons program, but also to change the regime in power.[33] However, some believed that neither sanctions nor bombing Iran would resolve the present Iranian nuclear crisis.[34] Essentially, the US and its allies need to come up with a solution that may comprehensively solve the root causes of Iran's drive to acquire nuclear weapons. Given this, it is pertinent to have a lucid understanding of what caused Iran to proliferate and why it cannot relinquish its nuclear program even though the consequences of its determination to maintain the present nuclear status could be extremely grave.

Facing a dyadic conflict with proximate and nuclear weapons-ambitious Iraq

Iran developed a dyadic conflict with Iraq in 1959, which still continues. Although the conflict has multiple roots, including control and influence in the Islamic world, there are two significant territorial disputes in the conflict. The first is over the Shatt-al-Arab waterway in the Gulf and key strategic points along their land border and the second is about their respective parts of Kurdistan. Until today, both of these issues remain unresolved and the conflict still protracts. Shatt-al-Arab, according to an International agreement of 1937 – the previous Ottoman Turkey/Iran agreement – was fully an Iraqi territory except for a length of three miles where the frontier was to run along the line of the maximum depth of the river. The Shah of Iran was not particularly happy with this accord and had shown dissatisfaction over the agreement. That became more prominent when he expressed deep dissatisfaction with the agreement after the overthrow of the Hashemite Kingdom in Iraq in 1958. In 1959, the Shah stated in a press conference that the status quo of the Shatt-al-Arab was "intolerable" which triggered the first crisis between Iran and Iraq and marked the beginning of the half-a-century-old conflict. Iraq continued to claim the waterway and emphasized on the agreement of 1937 as a valid basis for its claim. Border clashes ensued and Iran placed its military forces on alert and moved to the Iraqi border. The same issue gave rise to another crisis in 1969 and finally the 1980–88 war was waged over this same dispute. In 1975, the Algiers accord was reached between the two countries according to which Shatt-al-Arab was to be the common border between Iran and Iraq. Saddam Hussein expressed his dissatisfaction with the accord and waited for an opportunity to punish Iran. There were severe border and air clashes between Iran and Iraq a few years after that. Finally, Saddam made a strategic choice to exploit Iranian domestic turmoil after the Islamic Revolution and initiated a war on Iran – when the country focused on an inward-looking policy – which continued for the next eight years. Thus, the immediate causes of the war include disputed borders and right to the Shatt-al-Arab waterway, which is primarily a connecting point of the Arab and Persian states. For oil exports from the Iraqi and Iranian ports, this is pivotal. Both believed that it was worth fighting a war over this strategically important waterway. Consequently they continued a protracted war till Iran was war-weary and incapable of putting up with a fight against Saddam's stronger conventional forces. As stated before, the war was waged on Iran for which it was not prepared and was initiated at a time of political instability in the country. Iran learned lessons from the war and strongly focused on its defense policy in the aftermath. The war proved that Iran needed to defend itself better and the idea pertaining to the utility of non-conventional weapons came to the forefront.

Iran and Iraq fought one of the deadliest and longest wars in the century – the Iran–Iraq War of 1980–1988 – which was not only costly for the Iranians, but also inconclusive and most Iranians believe it was a defeat for them because of Iran's acceptance of the cease-fire while being weak. They have had seven foreign policy crises and four international crises since then. While at war with Iran, Iraq obtained financial backing from Saudi Arabia and its smaller allies in the newly formed Gulf Cooperation Council, and received massive shipment of weapons from the Soviet Union, China, France, Germany, the UK and the US.[35] Iraq also acquired chemical and biological weapons manufacturing capacity from many western nations and used chemical weapons on thousands of Iranian forces and civilians in the mid-1980s. Iraq was not punished for using these weapons in the war. On the usage of chemical weapons Hashemi Rafsanjani stated: "With regard to chemical, bacteriological, and radiological weapons training, it was made very clear that these

Case study: Iran

weapons are very decisive."[36] The UN Security Council did not name Iraq as the aggressor state due to the aforementioned states' influence on UN decision-making, even though it was clear that Iraq's invasion of Iran triggered the war. Iran, a victim of Iraq's invasion, literally fought the war alone without support from the international community. The war proved many things to the Iranians: that a surprise war with Iraq was always a high probability; that Iran cannot rely on the international community or even the supranational institution, the United Nations, to protect its interests in case of a war; that non-conventional weapons may be used to kill tens of thousands of people in a war and the violator of the norm pertaining to the usage of non-conventional weapons will not be punished; that the taboo pertaining to the usage of the chemical weapons has been lifted; that other non-conventional weapons – the absolute weapons – must be developed to deter the potential adversary from waging wars against Iran.

There is obviously no doubt that Iran embarked on a comprehensive nuclear program during the Shah period, as stated earlier. During that period, Iran's primary threat emanated from Iraq and it intended to address that with the acquisition of nuclear weapons. In 1975, the Shah stated that Iran had "no intention of acquiring nuclear weapons but if small states began building them, then Iran might have to reconsider its policy."[37] Iran was suspicious of Saddam's nuclear program and had to be prepared for the worst case scenario. Unfortunately, Iraq was involved in twin protracted conflicts of its own – one with Iran and the other with Israel. The Arab–Israeli conflict started in 1947 and Iraq was a direct actor in that conflict on the Arab side. As a member of the Arab coalition against Israel, Saddam reportedly described Iraq's nuclear program as the first attempt at Arab nuclear arming against Israel.[38] Saddam's desire to acquire nuclear weapons for his twin conflicts was there, but which one of these conflicts was most important to him was difficult to gauge. While the conflict with Iran was more pressing because it was dyadic and Iraq was weaker in terms of power resources – land and population – but Iran still did not have nuclear weapons capability, even though its comprehensive nuclear program alarmed Saddam's Iraq. On the other hand, Israel was a small state in the Arab–Israeli conflict, but had nuclear weapons capability ready for assembly on short notice since the 1960s and by the 1970s the conflict witnessed four wars between the adversaries. Thus, deterring Israel became extremely important for Iraq, which other Arab states did not have the ability to do with nuclear capability. Although it is difficult to assess which protracted conflict adversary motivated Iraq to acquire nuclear weapons capability, it is safe to say that Iraqi nuclear weapons acquisition addressed its dual security needs simultaneously without having to pay equal attention to each one of them separately. Unfortunately, the problem with such a situation is that even if the weapons are not primarily meant for one adversary, that adversary still feels threatened under the circumstances and arms race in the realm of that conflict ensues. Iran was not certain about Saddam's intentions as far as nuclear weapons development was concerned and that increased its threat, which required addressing mechanism. Consequently, Tehran had to reconsider its nuclear policy since smaller states in the region, especially rivals, were making efforts to acquire them.

The war with Iraq led Iran to embark on its nuclear program somewhat aggressively. The memories and bitter experiences of the war triggered an added incentive to build a program that would enable Iran to acquire nuclear weapons. After almost two decades Iranian officials still echo the pain Iran experienced at the war and expresses Tehran's dissatisfaction with the UN in helping Iran when it was in dire need of assistance from the international community. Iran's Foreign Minister Manuchehr Mottaki stated in relation to sanctions imposed on the country due to Iran's nuclear program at the UN Security Council on March 23, 2007:

> This is not the first time the Security Council is asking Iran to abandon its rights. When Saddam Hussein invaded Iran 27 years ago, this Council waited seven days so that Iraq could occupy 30,000 sq kilometers of Iranian territory. Then it unanimously adopted resolution asking the two sides to stop hostilities, without asking the aggressor to withdraw. That is, the Council – then too – effectively asked Iran to suspend the implementation of parts of its rights; at that time it was its right to 30,000 kilometers of its territory. As expected, the aggressor dutifully complied. But imagine what would have happened if Iran had complied. We would still be begging the Council's then sweetheart, President Saddam Hussein, to return our territory. We did not accept to suspend our right to our territory. We resisted eight years of carnage and use of chemical weapons coupled with pressure from this Council, and sanctions from its permanent members.[39]

The Iran–Iraq conflict has been a dyadic one and there was no power that Iran could depend on to defend it in case of a future Iraqi attack. The war itself was proof of that. Tehran could not win the war with Baghdad with conventional weapons and that "reinforced its determination to develop a nuclear arsenal in the 1980s."[40] As stated before, in the conflict Iraq was the weaker side in relative strength, at least in terms of land space and population – Iran was four times larger in land than Iraq and had three times the population – which made Iran a confident actor in the relationship. Given this, Saddam's Iraq had more of a reason to develop nuclear weapons to deter an attack from Iran that was also planning to proliferate its Islamic ideology and install Islamic regimes throughout the Middle East beginning with Iraq. Iraq pursued its proliferating ambition primarily for that. However, Iraq initiated a war on Iran at a time of tremendous political instability in Iran. The war actually validated the argument that weaker states are likely to initiate a war in an asymmetric conflict where the window of opportunity is present and in the absence of nuclear weapons. Due to experiencing an unexpected war and as a result of Iran's inability to capture Iraq with conventional means and mechanisms, Tehran "became even more convinced that the bomb was the way."[41] In fact, the war changed the mind-set of the Iranian leaders. Conventional or traditional strategies were no longer considered to be useful means in addressing future threats from countries like Iraq. Non-traditional strategies and means were given serious consideration during the time. The war, in essence, became the most important influence on Iranian foreign policy throughout most of the 1980s, a decade in which, energized by that war and its regional fallout, terms such as "terrorism," "suicide bombing," and "Islamic revolution" worked their way into the lexicon of international relations across the globe.[42]

Iran tried using several of these non-traditional mechanisms and strategies to fight its rivals in the region and around the world. However, its effort to build a nuclear program with a weapons component in it continued all the while. Although it is the general belief that Iran gave up on its nuclear program after the Islamic Revolution and that the Revolutionary leaders were against building such weapons, it is interesting to note that for security considerations and as a consequence of the surprise attack from Iraq, Iran's clerics reconsidered their thoughts on the development of the nuclear program. In the mid-1980s when chemical weapons were used by Saddam's forces against the Iranian forces and civilians, the new thinking was given further consideration. Iran's efforts pertaining to building the program were evident even as the war went on. During the war, Iran made efforts to restart its nuclear program,[43] which led to many cooperation deals with several major nations capable of providing materials for the development of a comprehensive nuclear program for Iran. In 1985, China provided Iranian nuclear experts training and Iran received a research reactor and calutron from China which started functioning in 1987.[44] In February 1986, Pakistan's leading nuclear scientist Abdul Qadir Khan secretly visited Bushehr and later that year Iran and Pakistan signed a secret nuclear cooperation agreement.[45] Iraq attacked Bushehr in mid-1986. In 1987, Iran reached a cooperative agreement with North Korea on nuclear weapons development which included assistance in the realm of uranium mining and exploration.[46] In the same year, construction started on a nuclear research and production center for weapons-grade fissile material at Moallem Kalayeh – the facility which is believed to contain uranium labs and laser enrichment equipment and have been run by the Islamic Revolutionary Guard Corps.[47] In mid-1987, *The Star* of Johannesburg reported that Iran was secretly buying uranium from a British-run mine in South African-occupied Namibia and that Tehran has been buying uranium from the mine at Rossig for the past eight years.[48] Around the same time, South African media reported that Iran was in fact developing nuclear weapons with the help of South Africa and Argentina.[49] Iraq attacked the Bushehr nuclear plant again in 1987. Iran rebuilt the Bushehr reactor with the help of German assistance.[50] When the war was almost terminating, the President of Iran, Ali Khameini, in his address to the Atomic Energy Organization stated:

> Regarding atomic energy, we need it now . . . Our nation has always been threatened from outside. The least we can do to face this danger is to let our enemies know that we can defend ourselves. Therefore, every step you take is in defense of your country and your revolution. With this in mind, you should work hard and at great speed.[51]

In 1987, an exiled nuclear physicist revealed that Abdul Qadir Khan revisited Bushehr and Iran held a secret meeting in Tehran's Amir Kabir nuclear research center with key Iranian nuclear decision-makers, where it decided that new funds would be allocated to develop an atomic bomb.[52] While in July 1988 Iraq once again attacked Iran's Bushehr nuclear power plant, in October 1988, at an annual conference held to bring back Iranian nuclear scientists living in exile, Rafsanjani appealed to the participants to return to Iran and openly called for the development of nuclear weapons.[53] In 1988–89, the Iranian leaders also reportedly obtained large quantities of yellow-cake from South Africa for enrichment in Iran or even Pakistan. Iran approached Pakistan seriously to help it in enrichment of uranium.[54] During the same period Iran made nuclear deals with China and later with Pakistan.[55] The timing reveals the cause for its nuclear aspirations. This was also the time when Iran made nuclear deals with China and later with Pakistan that would support its nuclear weapons program. These demonstrate that Iran's major threat during the period emanated primarily from its proximate rival, Iraq, an aggressive state throughout the life of the protracted conflict.

One important aspect that needs to be highlighted here is that Iran perceived serious security threats from Iraq when its nuclear weapons program was revealed to the world due to the Osiraq bombing of 1981. It was not only the revelation of what Iraq had, but Saddam's intentions to acquire them at any cost that made Iran more nervous. After the destruction of Osiraq, Saddam stated:

> I believe that anyone or any state in the world which really wants peace and security and which really respects peoples and does not want them to be subjugated to foreign forces should help the Arabs in one way or another to acquire atomic bombs to confront the actual Israeli atomic bombs, not to champion the Arabs and not to fuel war, but to safeguard and achieve peace. Irrespective of the Arabs' intentions and capabilities and even if the Arabs do not want them and are unable to use them, I believe that any state in the world that is internationally and positively responsible to humanity and peace must tell the Arabs: here, take these weapons in order to face the Zionist threat with atom bombs and prevent the Zionist entity from using atomic bombs in wars.[56]

This statement proves that Saddam believed in the need for an Arab deterrent capability against Israel and Iraq's drive for nuclear weapons in the 1980s has mostly been due to the desire to have mutual deterrence in the Middle East.[57] The ramifications of such statements for Iran have been grave. As discussed before, although initially the Islamic clerics have been suspicious of Iran's nuclear program which was developed with American and western help, they continued the program with new momentum and fervor during their rule due to the insecurity the regime perceived from Iraq. That fervor became more pronounced in the 1990s.

Iran launched a rapidly expanding nuclear weapons program in response to Iraq's nuclear weapons program that was rediscovered as the 1990–91 Gulf War came to a close, which will be discussed in the next chapter in order to understand the impact of all three protracted conflicts on the nuclear decision of Iran. Its

58 *Case study: Iran*

long-running conflict with Iraq, the long Iran–Iraq War, and Iraq's nuclear weapons ambition were all instrumental in inspiring Iran to develop a security program that would defend it from future aggressive moves of Saddam Hussein. After the 1990–91 revelations, Saideh Lotfian stated, "The fact that Iraq is temporarily restrained by the UN-imposed sanctions is not reassuring in the long-run and the Iranian government cannot afford to ignore security threats from its western neighbor."[58] He added that the existence of Iraq with a known chemical and biological weapons (CBW) capability provides an incentive for Iran to develop a deterrent in kind, and "given the possibility of war with an Iraq that retains a residual CBW capability, Iran has good reasons to bolster its deterrent by any means that do not undermine the legitimacy of the government."[59] These and other important statements simply demonstrate how Iraq was seriously factored into Iran's security calculation in general and nuclear weapons program in particular.

Addressing non-dyadic regional conflict with nuclear-capable Israel

Iran's other regional conflict is with Israel, a small state in the Middle East surrounded by rival Arab states. While the conflict, known as the Arab–Israeli conflict, started with the independence of Israel in 1947, Iran, a non-Arab state, did not become part of the conflict until the early 1980s. Iran did not have any direct dispute with Israel. In fact, both have been hostile towards Iraq for a very long time. In general, it became involved in the conflict because of its connections with the Muslim countries that fought against the Jewish state of Israel, but more specifically following the revolution in Lebanon in 1982 when the Syrian President Hafez al Assad allowed Iran to play a more central role in the conflict by seeking its help in creating a guerrilla force, the *Hezbollah*, and by seeking financial and military help from oil-rich Iran. Therefore, due to Iran's connections with Syria, it became actively engaged in the Arab–Israeli conflict. It is noteworthy then that although Israel was another protracted conflict rival of Iran in the Middle East and it simultaneously had two security threats in the region, the threat from Israel for Iran came much later. In the 1970s, when its nuclear program started to develop with full force, Iran was primarily embroiled in addressing Iraqi threat even though threat from Israel was also there. As Ray Takeyh puts it, "Iran's nuclear calculations are not derived from an irrational ideology, but rather from a judicious attempt to craft a viable deterrent capability against an evolving range of threats."[60] In the hierarchy of threats for Iran, Israel came after Iraq because the Arab–Israeli conflict was in a multi-power region where other actors were also involved and Iran was not directly a party to it till the early 1980s. However, Israeli threat was also factored into the nuclear calculation because Israel had nuclear capability by then and also for its anti-Islamic ideology.

The Arab–Israeli conflict, which began in 1947, had its roots in the Arab rejection of the Jewish state of Israel and the latter's demand for statehood. From 1947 to 1993, the conflict generated 25 international crises and the first crisis had six direct participants including Iraq, Egypt, Jordon, Syria, Lebanon, and Israel. Iran,[61] as stated earlier, was not a party to the conflict, but over time it became actively involved in repudiating the state of Israel. The parties fought wars in 1948, 1956, 1967, and 1973. Israel has been an opaque nuclear state since the late 1960s. It has maintained secrecy about its nuclear weapons program for decades. Although it maintained an opaque status for many decades, in 1973 it was very clear that Israel had nuclear weapons. Robert Harkavy states that Israel "leaked the material in the *Time* article indicating that it had been prepared to use nuclear weapons after only the first week or so of the 1973 war."[62] It did not sign the NPT even though it signed the CTBT in 1996.[63] It has clearly refrained from renouncing its nuclear weapons option. Israeli leadership has consistently argued that nuclear weapons are important for the country's security because it is surrounded by rival states. It is also a country that has been conventionally weak in quantitative terms as compared to its Arab neighbors. Estimates of Israel's nuclear capabilities are difficult to confirm. Some of these estimates are based on the Israeli technician Mordechai Vanunu's testimony according to which Israel had about 200 nuclear devices in 1986. Seymor Hersch reported that its capabilities were far more advanced than what Vanunu had revealed and that the country possesses low-yield enhanced radiation-type warheads and thermonuclear weapons as well.[64] More recently, George Perkovich and James M. Acton stated, "The country is believed to possess sophisticated nuclear warheads with a range of yields, and it has aircraft, land-based missiles and, most importantly, submarines with which it could deliver nuclear weapons to any of its likely adversaries."[65] Iranians, for their part, see Israel as an implacable enemy and believe its nuclear capability is a threat to Iran's security.[66]

Iran argues that Israel should not be allowed to exist as a state and that it should not have a place in the map of the Middle East. On Israel, "there is almost universal agreement that the Jewish state is an active regional rival bent on checking Iran's political and military power and undoing Iran's achievements."[67] While Iran has highly complex relations with the states in the Middle East, it has maintained close relations with Syria, especially after the Camp David Accords of 1977 which took the Arab states by surprise and created a split between Egypt on the one hand and the Arab states on the other because of the hand of friendship Egypt stretched towards Israel. Egyptian–Israeli friendship threatened Syrian security and it sought to address that by seeking Iranian friendship and assistance. According to Iran, if the Zionist state has the right to acquire nuclear weapons, then all Muslim countries have the same right and they should develop expertise in the nuclear field to face off the Israeli nuclear challenge.

Since the creation of the state of Israel, the US and Israel have been allies. That created further complexity in the conflict relations between Iran and Israel, which will be discussed in greater detail in the next chapter. While the US has always viewed the survival of Israel in the Middle East as a matter of its national security,[68] Iran says that "the basic problem in the Islamic world is the existence of the Zionist regime, and the Islamic world and the region must mobilize to remove this problem."[69] Also, Israel has been the only real democracy in the Middle East, which is appreciated by the US and which Washington wants others in the Middle Eastern region to adopt in their political institution. This is something Iran has always feared and perceived to be a threat to its security and survival, especially after the Islamic revolution.

Interestingly, the US also does not have problems with Israel maintaining an opaque nuclear status and not signing the NPT. The Iranians wanted to make the Middle East a nuclear weapons free zone in the 1970s, but Israel's opacity has made it impossible for that dream to be fulfilled. Other Middle Eastern countries such as Egypt have been equally dissatisfied with Israel's stand on the nuclear issue. Although this should have been an internal problem of the region, the US's support for Israel on the nuclear matter adds fuel to the fire for countries such as Iran.

As stated before, Iran's creation of Hezbollah has made the relationship between Iran and Israel bitter. According to Israel, it is "entangled with Iran in a life-or-death struggle because of Iran's involvement with terrorism."[70] Hezbollah, according to Israel and the US, is a terrorist organization, sponsored financially and militarily by radical Iran which uses Lebanon as a platform to attack Israel. *Hamas* also received support from Iran even though the ideologies of Hamas and Iran differ. Their common interest has always been to destroy Israel. It has also funded other regional organizations such as the Palestinian group Islamic Jihad.[71] While Israel is suspicious of Iran's intentions and worried about its continuous terrorist activities against Israel, Iran worries that Israel's nuclear weapons are for using against the Islamic world. What would Israel need nuclear weapons for? More importantly, why would it acquire tactical nuclear weapons? Israel is the only country in the Middle East that has nuclear weapons capability[72] and that which is allowed to possess them by the international community. This is also a country that is allied with the western world in general and the US in particular and possesses not only strategic weapons, but tactical weapons to use in the battlefield. Israel has the kind of "relatively low-yield tactical nuclear weapons that can be selectively fired to eliminate specific targets. Low-yield 'tactical nukes' could be used to hit the type of hardened underground centrifuge firm which Iran has built at Natanz to enrich uranium."[73] These low-yield nuclear weapons can be launched from air and sea. Israel began developing Jericho missiles for the larger nuclear warheads in the 1960s and is very advanced in missile development programs. Israel emphasizes on the Samson Option that the country would be using extreme measures if its survival were at stake. For example,

> in a crisis with Iran, the Samson Option has been used to mean that Israel would attack Iran in a preemptive war and would be willing to use nuclear weapons. Israel would be willing to attack Iran even if the result of an Israeli preemptive strike ended up being retaliation by Iran that ended up with Israel's destruction. The Israelis judge that destruction in a military conflict with an aggressor like Iran would still be better than doing nothing and waiting to be destroyed.[74]

Such strategies threaten Iran. Israel's intention is not to allow any country in the Middle East to acquire nuclear weapons. Iran's possession of nuclear weapons is perceived as a threat to Israel's survival. It says that it will not introduce nuclear weapons in the region, but will not be the second either. That policy has been maintained since the 1960s. After so many years, Israel still pursues the same policy that it "cannot accept a nuclear Iran nor can America."[75] Perkovich and Acton argue that "even if all other nuclear-armed states agreed to eliminate their nuclear arsenals, Israel would not join them unless political, security, verification and transparency conditions specific to the Middle East were to its satisfaction."[76] All these are not only threatening and unacceptable to the Iranians today, but were threatening and unacceptable to them for several decades. Ray Takeyh states that "the Islamic Republic perceives a nuclear-armed Israel as an existential threat not just to itself but to the entire Islamic world."[77] Thus, Israel is considered a military as well as an ideological threat and Iranian leaders agree on the strategic value of a strong nuclear program.

Iran has more reasons to worry about Israel than Israel has about Iran, according to the Iranians. It is true that Israel learned lessons from the holocaust, but that made the post-holocaust Israeli leadership aggressive. Michael Evans and Jerome Corsi state, "Passivity in the face of aggression has always been judged to be a mistake the European Jews made against Hitler."[78] Israel's strategies pertaining to conflicts and confrontations had changed and the country has had less patience for negotiations. In extreme situations it is expected to attack Iran, preemptively or preventively. Iran has always believed that the holocaust was primarily used by the Israelis to be militarily stronger in the Middle East and to wage wars against the Muslim world. Iran argued that nuclear weapons would place it on a par with Israel. "An equalizer" is often seen by Tehran "as a necessary insurance policy."[79] Although Iran has not been able to attain a nuclear weapon yet, and continues to deny that it wants anything more than a peaceful nuclear program, scholars believe that to the Iranians "deterrence could be achieved through the manipulation of uncertainty."[80] It is difficult for the country to come out in the open and declare its desire to acquire such weapons to an international community that strives to attain a non-proliferated world. It is further difficult for Iran to declare its nuclear status because of its adherence to the NPT. Consequently, a "denial and deception strategy" is undertaken by Iran, like other proliferators such as Iraq in the pre-2003 period. Iran has been using low-intensity violence in the form of terrorism in the Middle East, especially with Israel, since the 1980s. It is likely that the strategy will soon change when Iran is fully capable of acquiring nuclear weapons or is nuclear-capable. A degree of confidence will ensue as a result of that and some degree of stability is expected in the Iran–Israel conflict theatre.

Iran had twin concerns until 1979 and that made it quite a serious proliferator. All efforts during the 1980s prove that Iran was intending to undertake the nuclear weapons path. That is not surprising given its twin conflicts with Iraq and Israel simultaneously and the newly initiated conflict with the US. Although the conflict with America started in 1979, which will be the focus of the next chapter, the first few years of any conflict is considered as a setting stage and during that time it is hard to tell what the intensity of the conflict will be and whether or not the conflict will be intractable. Therefore, for the next few years, Iran's focus was still on Iraq

62 *Case study: Iran*

and Israel as far as the nuclear weapons program was concerned. Well into the 1980s, Iran understood the depth of this new conflict and that is when its policies pertaining to nuclear weapons acquisition changed even more. The next chapter explicates Iran's strong need for nuclear weapons based on its triple protracted conflicts since the Islamic Revolution of 1979.

4 Iran's nuclear program and triple protracted conflicts from 1979 onwards

The previous chapter enumerated Iran's twin protracted conflicts and how they determined Iran's decision to build a comprehensive nuclear program with dual purpose. This chapter goes beyond that and examines Tehran's third protracted conflict with the world's superpower, the United States, and demonstrates its proliferation propensity as a function of all three conflicts from 1979 onwards. The argument is that although Iraq and Israel have been Iran's security concerns for a long time and addressing them with non-conventional weapons was important for Tehran, its third conflict with the US was even more salient because this was a conflict between a regional and a global power where asymmetry on every level was evident. The problem was more pronounced because one of Iran's protracted conflict rivals, Israel, has been an ally of the US and Iraq obtained military assistance from the US during its protracted war with Iran, which allowed it to defeat Tehran in the war.

The evolution of the Iranian nuclear weapons program reveals that security threats from Iraq, Israel, and the US – its three protracted conflict rivals – have primarily compelled Tehran to be attracted towards building a nuclear weapons program. While Iran's intractable conflicts with Iraq and Israel in the Middle East lasted for more than half a century, its long-running conflict with the US is also 30-years-old. It is one thing to have a regional rival and be engaged in a more or less symmetric conflict, it is entirely another thing to have a superpower or a hegemonic power as a rival state of a regional power and be engaged in an asymmetric conflict. Although the world focus was always on two of the most prominent conflicts in the Middle East – the Iran–Iraq PC and the Arab–Israeli PC which made Iran a party to the conflict on the Arab side, the other two conflicts between a regional power and a global power – the Iraq–US and Iran–US – were largely ignored by the international community as well as the academics dealing with international politics of the Middle Eastern region. With the war on Iraq in 2003 and the subsequent fall of the Saddam regime, civil war erupted in post-Saddam Iraq, along with extreme hostility towards the American military in the country. Given this, it is easy to see to what extent insecurity and hatred still shroud the US–Iraqi relationship. It will be interesting to see whether or not the PC between Iraq and the US ultimately terminates once the Iraqis enjoy a stable domestic and democratic political life in the post-Saddam era. It is intriguing that in three of the four protracted conflicts in this

64 Case study: Iran

region, Iran has been a party and, consequently, war on Iran was always a possibility for which the country needed to be militarily prepared. Given this, possessing a nuclear deterrent capability became almost a necessity for Iran to prevent wars[1] that could be initiated by any one of its three rivals, one of which remains a world power. More importantly, two out of the three rivals possessed nuclear weapons, the US being a declared nuclear state and Israel an opaque nuclear state, while the other rival, Iraq, was suspected of having the capability for more than two decades. Interestingly, although Iran's primary bilateral conflict was with Iraq and its need for the nuclear capability was primarily to prevent a war with Iraq, its hatred towards the Zionist regime in Israel gave it additional impetus to proliferate in the nuclear realm. However, with time, its reasons to move on with the nuclear program and relentlessly try to build a nuclear bomb had shifted from these two countries to the US. The US became its primary security concern after the end of the cold war and since 2000, with the introduction of more aggressive foreign policies of the US in and around the Middle East and in particular against Iran. Thus, although security motivation still remains the driving force behind Iran's acquisition of nuclear weapons, it is important to question: security against which country? Iran has three rivals, but if placed in a hierarchical order, the US is placed at the top and Iraq at the bottom. Israel was and still is in the middle. This is not because Israel is less of a threat to the Iranians, but because the Arab–Israeli conflict is a multi-power conflict and there are other states on the Arab side to check Israel from making a military move. Iran–Iraq and Iran–US are both dyadic intractable conflicts, requiring more attention and preparedness for military attacks. Iran's nuclear capability, which allows it to deter the US from attacking it, invariably helps in maintaining its regional security. This is somewhat similar to what Indians had to say about having a nuclear capability to deter Chinese threats which would automatically keep India secure from Pakistan's aggressive military moves against India.

Iran's intractable and asymmetric conflict with America

From 1979 to 1990, three major developments in Iran made the headlines: the Islamic Revolution led by Ayatollah Khomeini in 1979 with which the Islamic clergy seized control of all political, judicial, educational, and media institutions and systematically suppressed any opposition,[2] the 1980–88 war with Iraq which devastated the Iranian economy thoroughly, and the death of Khomeini in 1989. However, this was also the period that witnessed the beginning and the development of a long-term rivalry or a protracted conflict between Iran and the US. In January 1979, Iran witnessed civil unrest and the Shah was forced into exile. The following month Ayatollah Khomeini returned to Iran after about 15 years in exile and was given a heartfelt welcome in the country. The military under the Shah's rule had to announce its neutrality and, following that, the monarchy collapsed. By April of 1979, Khomeini controlled power in Iran and proclaimed the Islamic Republic of Iran.[3]

> The euphoria in Iran on the arrival of Imam Khomeini unnerved the United States, because till then America had a near monopoly on Iranian oil, which

was suddenly lost. Khomeini was heading a people's revolution, and the born-again Iranian nation was full of confidence and pride. The Islamic revolutionary government had come to stay, and this rankled Washington and Tel Aviv.[4]

Prior to 1979, Iran and the US enjoyed a special bilateral relationship due to which Tehran's security was strengthened with military procurement, but its economy began to increasingly suffer. That and the Shah's suppression of secular dissidents contributed to the revolution which ultimately overthrew the Shah of Iran. In October 1979, the US allowed the Shah to enter the US and get treatment for cancer. The revolutionary government repeatedly raised objections to the US over this matter, but Washington ultimately ignored the objections.[5] As a consequence of that, on November 4, 1979, the radical students attacked and seized the US Embassy in Tehran and took 63 embassy personnel hostages. Khomeini complimented the students and referred to the US as the "Great Satan."[6] While there is still controversy about whether or not the attack was directed by the Islamic leader or simply an endeavor of the militant students, the fact remains that "the seizure of the hostages became the axis around which all US–Iranian relations subsequently revolved."[7] A revolutionary Iran was not deterred by threats from America and was "cognizant of US conspiracies to reinstall the Shah."[8] Khomeini's hostility to anything American was "bitter, stubborn, zealous – and total."[9] He has proved to the US that

> the challenges to the West are certain to get more and more complex, and that the US will ignore this fact at its peril. He has made it plain that every effort must be made to avoid the rise of other Khomeinis. Even if he should hold power only briefly, the Ayatollah is a figure of historic importance. Not only was 1979 his year; the forces of disintegration that he let loose in one country could threaten many others in the years ahead.[10]

With Khomeini's encouragement Muslims have staged anti-American protests and riots in countries such as Libya, India, and Bangladesh. During the same period, in Islamabad, a mob burned the US embassy.[11] These not only threatened the US, but made it act negatively against Iran. America realized that there could be many Khomeinis in the world and Iranian kind of Islamic ideology must be contained. This was also a revolution that had dramatic impact on the western economies and the world economy moved from oil surpluses to recurrent shortages. The West in general and the US in particular realized how close it came to be dependant on oil imports from Iran, a highly unstable and fragile country.[12] While nothing much could be done overnight in order to reduce that dependence, the threat that Iran posed on the security and economic levels was evident, which America needed to address. Thus, it is argued that "since the 1979 hostage crisis, the US government has viewed Iran as a threat to American interests in the region, branded it a state-sponsor of terrorism, and targeted it with a panoply of economic sanctions."[13] Where this was the case, Iran had ample reason to worry about the intentions of the world's superpower vis-à-vis Tehran. Iran not only felt threatened as a result of this, but was also humiliated and insulted. Iran believes that it is pivotal in the Middle East region. It is rich in terms of culture and heritage and should be given the rightful status in the region. Instead of that, Iran suffered humiliation in the aftermath of the revolution, which triggered a long-term worry.

The Iran–US PC started with the Islamic Revolution in Iran in 1979. The otherwise friendly Iran–US relations of the 1960s and 1970s changed to one of hostility overnight. The Carter administration froze Iranian assets in the US, severed diplomatic relations with Iran and proposed at the United Nations to impose sanctions against Tehran.[14] Ultimately, the crisis came to an end with the signing of the Algiers Accords on January 19, 1981 according to which the US agreed not to interfere in the internal affairs of Iran, to unfreeze Tehran's assets, and lift trade sanctions in exchange for the hostages. They also agreed that both governments would cease litigation surrounding the hostage crisis.[15] While the Iran–US crisis that started in 1979, which triggered a conflict between the states, ended with this accord in 1981, the conflict continued and became protracted. The conflict witnessed several crises, which have or have not always ended, but the hostility that started in 1979 still continues. On the impact of the revolution for both Iran and the US, Ali M. Ansari states:

> For the adherents to Iran's revolutionary ideology, the Islamic Revolution indicates a definitive break with the past, defined by the termination of relations with the United States. This termination is defined by the seizure of the US embassy in November 1979 ... For the Americans, on the other hand, the embassy seizure was the defining moment and the cause of the collapse in relations. Such was the sense of humiliation of the 444-day hostage crisis ... in the popular conception the hostage crisis marked a definitive break with the past, much as it did for the Iranian revolutionaries.[16]

Interestingly, for the revolutionaries, the hostage issue marked the termination of Iran–US relations, but for the US "it marked the beginning of an obsession with Iran."[17] For security and conflict studies, this was the beginning of an intractable conflict which has lasted for 30 years and continues to be protracted.

The Iran–US conflict was premised on ideological/religious/political differences and the incompatibility over these issues continues even at the present time. There is extreme hostility, leading to tremendous hatred on both sides, in the relationship, which needs to be addressed and the intractable conflict terminated before any progress can be made in Iran's nuclear realm. Many Iranians believe that the nuclear program and the development of Iran's intermediate-range missiles are all a function of its insecurity emanating from the US and ultimately the intention is to bargain better with the US on equal terms to end so many "years of hostility."[18] It was also argued in 2006 that "nearly 27 years of heavy sanctions imposed directly by the United States have not prevented Iran from proceeding with its nuclear program."[19] Even though there is reason to underscore this perspective given the permanent existence of Iran–US hostility, surprisingly, the US government has never tried to effectively probe what drives the Iranian leaders to acquire nuclear weapons and what the US could do to resolve the problem.[20] Although there was no direct war between the contending states in the life of the conflict, many crises erupted in the conflict setting and all impacted negatively on the overall relationship. For example, the capture of US military and diplomatic personnel from the American Embassy in Teheran cannot be forgotten by the US. Although there was a seemingly short-lived thaw during Bill Clinton's Presidency, that situation quickly changed with George Bush's power-taking in 2001, which will be discussed in the next chapter. Interestingly, like any other protracted conflict states, Iran and the US "have made significant overtures to each other at least nine times since the end of the hostage crisis in 1981."[21] Some of these were the US–Israeli initiative of 1985 – the Iran contra affair – official attempts at dialogue during George H. W. Bush and Bill Clinton's administrations, collaboration between the two countries after the 9/11 attacks, high-level communication on the nuclear issue, and unofficial Track II meetings between former Iranian and US officials.[22] All these efforts, however, have failed to bring about any resolution to the issues that create incompatibility of interests between the two states and the future of any such endeavors does not look promising either.

What is really intriguing is that even though today one hears about America's determination to install democracy in the Middle East, it was something America had masterminded since the Islamic Revolution of 1979. The US administration believed that regime change in Iran would reduce the threats posed by the country. This is not unusual given the freedom and liberty the people of the US enjoy and the level of human rights violation the Iranians had to put up with during the entire period of Khomeini and to some degree have to endure even today. Democratic regimes do not only respect their own citizens, but also citizens of the world. The US not only believed in this theory with respect to Iran, but had in fact funded the anti-regime groups in Iran, "mainly the pro-monarchists, during the 1980s."[23] The goal was obvious – to bring about a change of regime in Iran that would be democratic, but more importantly, pro-US. Although all efforts failed, the idea of the US trying to change Iran's regime by using groups within Iran to work for the US's interest brought a new dynamic to the serious security problem Iran was already faced with pertaining to the conflict with the US. To Iran, such activities on the part of the US goes against the Algiers Accords which settled the Iranian hostage issue and which stipulated non-interference in the internal affairs of each state. That the US did not respect the rules of law was proven by this act. Additionally, the US has also been questioning Iran's human rights issue since then. Iran has demonstrated disturbing human rights abuse record, which the US has been particularly concerned about since the Khomeini period. However, to Iran, this is Tehran's internal issue, which only the Iranians should deal with.

Since then the US became obsessed with the new Iran that it had not seen before – an Iran that humiliated the US, betrayed it, and created the terror organization *Hezbollah* in 1982 after the Israeli invasion of Lebanon which would be Iran's proxy in the Middle East and a bone of contention between Israel and Iran. To the Iranians, when Israel invaded Lebanon, it prompted Iran to deploy its Islamic Revolutionary Guards to the Bikaa Valley in order to aid the Lebanese Muslims to fight against the Israeli forces and vehemently protest the US support for Israel's actions. Following this, operatives from American-backed Lebanese Christian forces kidnapped four Iranian diplomats which included the commander of the Revolutionary Guards in the Bikaa Valley and the Charge D'Affairs.[24] Consequently, retaliatory kidnappings by Iran followed in the next few years. Iran maintains a close relationship with Lebanese Hezbollah which is a *Shiite* militant group that was created in 1982 by Lebanon's Shiite clerics that were sympathetic towards Iran's Islamic Revolution, maintains military forces along the border over which the Lebanese government has no control, and committed "several acts of anti-US and anti-Israel terrorism in the 1980s and 1990s."[25] The US became more obsessed with Iran after 1983 following the suicide attacks on the US embassy and marine barracks in Beirut, which were the acts of Hezbollah, supported by Iran. As a result of that President Ronald Reagan declared Iran "a state sponsor of international terrorism."[26] Thus, even though much has been discussed and analyzed about Iran being one of the rogue states since the 1990s, not much has been stated about Iran's earlier titles given by the US, which also impacted Iran's nuclear decisions negatively in the pre-1990 period.

> In January 1984 following the 1983 bombing of the US marine barracks in Lebanon, Iran was added to the terrorism list. The list was established by Section 6(j) of the Export Administration Act of 1979, sanctioning countries determined to have provided repeated support for acts of international terrorism. The terrorism list designation bans direct US financial assistance (Foreign Assistance Act, FAA) and arms sales (Arms Export Control Act), and requires the United States to vote to oppose multilateral lending to the designated countries (Anti-Terrorism and Effective Death Penalty Act of 1996, PL 104–132). Waivers are provided under these laws, but successive foreign aid appropriations laws since the late 1980s ban direct assistance to Iran (loans, credits, insurance, Eximbank credits) without providing for a waiver. Section 307 of the FAA (added in 1985) names Iran as unable to benefit from US contributions to international organizations, and require proportionate cuts if these institutions work in Iran. No waiver is provided for.[27]

Thus, by the mid-1980s Iran's economy was in shambles, it was badly humiliated, and had to handle three enduring rivals, who were all somewhat connected, if not allies.

Iran's primary intention was to export the Islamic ideology, which the Revolutionary leaders believed in, to Lebanon and the rest of the Middle East. Interestingly, Iran also masterminded the hostage crisis in Lebanon in the 1980s. Eighteen Americans were captured during the crisis and all were not released until 1991.[28] By the mid-1980s Iran, in the midst of a war with Iraq, required arms which it requested to buy from the US in exchange for the release of the hostages. In 1989, Iran's President Ali Khameini stated on the context of the release of the hostages in Lebanon, "These are our conditions: stop being aggressive, stop your arrogant actions, discontinue the transgressions against the rights of the Iranian people and return what you owe us."²⁹ In January 1989, President George H. W. Bush created a platform for a rapprochement with Iran saying that "goodwill begets goodwill," meaning that better relations with Iran was possible if Iran released the hostages held in Lebanon by Hezbollah. While Iran supposedly did help in releasing those hostages which was completed in December 1991, no thaw followed in the Iran–US relationship.³⁰ This was partly because Iran continued to back the terrorists and used them as proxies and opposed US-sponsored Middle East Peace Process, which was a major US endeavor by then, and partly because Iran was targeted by the US as a state sponsoring terrorism and the US tilt towards Iraq in the war was unacceptable to the Iranians. Iran was supposedly involved in state-sponsored terrorism in different places, such as the airline hijackings. Alireza Jafarzadeh states,

> Three months after the September 1984 bombing in northern Beirut, Iranian terrorist proxies killed two more Americans during the hijacking of Kuwait Airways flight 221. The hijackers diverted the flight to Tehran on December 3, 1984, and demanded the release of the Kuwait 17; two passengers who worked for the United States Agency for International Development were shot and killed when demands were not met. Iran allowed the airliner to land and to remain at the airport as the terrorists killed the two passengers and continued to make their demands. Playing the crisis from both sides once again, the regime sent in a security force to storm the plane and arrest the hijackers, but rather than putting the terrorists on trial – as they promised the world they would do – they released them and allowed them to leave the country. Once again, Iran used the grisly tactics of terrorism by sponsoring these acts while seeking concessions from the West and trying to show a cooperative face.³¹

Iran has used such tactics not only during the 1980s, but also in the aftermath and continues to do so. The problem is that Iran and US views of what constitutes a terrorist group differ. To Iran, financially supporting Hamas or other radical Palestinian groups is not "irresponsible or out of bounds," partly because "the Gulf states and their citizens provide considerable support for these groups with little public US criticism."³² One of the primary reasons for using these proxies is to unnerve the rival states because Iran has no other way to pass on its message to its enduring rivals who are allies. Tehran also prefers to employ this issue as leverage against Washington.³³ For the two rivals of Iran, the primary ramification of the attacks was that Hezbollah became a major enemy of the US and Israel and, consequently, Iran became the primary target of these states due to its connections with this terror organization.

America's support for Iran's primary regional rival, Iraq

What made matters worse for Iran was that the US tilted remarkably towards Iraq in the 1980–88 Iran–Iraq War. These included diplomatic attempts to block conventional military sales to Iran and providing battlefield intelligence to its enemy, Iraq.³⁴ The US also proved that it was tilted towards Iraq in that war during the "1987–88 direct skirmishes with Iranian naval elements in the course of US efforts to protect international oil shipments in the Gulf from Iranian attacks."[35] Iran's major challenge came from Iraq when it invaded Iran in 1980. Iran was totally crippled with the war that killed more than one million people. Throughout the Iran–Iraq War, Washington supported Baghdad with economic and military assistance. In February 1982, Iraq was removed from the State Department's list of states that have "repeatedly supported acts of international terrorism."[36] One of the impacts of this was the increasing economic ties between the two countries, which helped Iraq fight a war with Iran more effectively. This had a tremendous negative impact on the Iran–US relations. As stated earlier, by 1984 Iran was included in the list of states sponsoring terrorism, which Iran perceived as a double standard in American foreign policy. Additionally, although the US condemned any state that tried to develop chemical and biological weapons, Washington did not even question Iraq for developing such non-conventional weapons and to the world's surprise it never condemned the usage of chemical weapons against Iran during the war.[37] Interestingly, after Saddam Hussein was captured, one of the first allegations used against him was the usage of chemical weapons against the Kurds yet the US did not take effective measures against Saddam when non-conventional weapons were used against Iran. To the minds of the Iranians this has always been there, which triggered Tehran to take the necessary steps to secure it against such elements in the future. As Shaul Bakhash states, "No one said anything about Iraq using chemical weapons. International community primarily supported Iraq. The trauma had a tremendous impact on strategic decisions in Iran."[38] How much it hurt the Iranians and impacted its future policies is evident in the speech of Iran's president after more than 20 years. In 2005, Iran's President pointed out the failings of the countries and pointed his fingers at the US for aiding Saddam with weapons. He stated,

> For eight years, Saddam's regime imposed a massive war of aggression against my people. It employed the most heinous weapons of mass destruction including chemical weapons against Iranians and Iraqis alike. Who, in fact, armed Saddam with those weapons? What was the reaction of those who claim to fight against WMDs regarding the use of chemical weapons then?[39]

As a result of this, the Iranians also lost faith in international norms, rules, procedures, or treaties. Nationalistic spirits came to the forefront and sovereign rights were focused upon. Ray Takeyh contends,

> The legacy of the war reinforces a nationalistic narrative that sees America's demands for relinquishing of Iran's fuel cycle, an implied right at least under the NPT, as historically unjust. This is a country that has been historically subject to foreign intervention and imposition of various capitulation treaties. Therefore, it is inordinately sensitive of its national prerogatives and perceived sovereign rights.[40]

Iran also began to realize that all its regional enemies are allied to the US, its rival, in one way or the other, even though Iraq and the US were not traditionally allies.

This also meant that all cards were in the hands of the US and when this country wanted, it could make its enemy an ally for its own national security or economic interests. That the Reagan administration approved the clandestine shipment of military equipments to Iran through Israel to free the hostages held in Lebanon itself proves how far the US can go for the sake of its interests. Although the Iranians were benefited by this, American unfair strategic game in the region was unacceptable to the Iranians. It was simply impossible to turn the game around if Iran remained on the same platform. The conflict was substantially asymmetric to begin with and where regional powers bandwagoned with the US, even if temporarily, the imbalance became much more threatening. Iran can be brought down to its knees if regional powers aid the US in doing so and in fact it perceives that the war with Iraq was lost primarily for the help Iraq received from the US. Consequently, an alternative to that situation was more aggressively sought. Superpower game, domination, and bullying had to be stopped and that would only be possible by developing a comprehensive nuclear program which would provide them with the capability to build nuclear weapons. Even at the present time Iranian leaders think that

> they are being challenged not because of their provocation or treaty violations, but because of superpower bullying. So in a rather peculiar manner, the nuclear program and Iran's national identity have become fused in the imagination of the hardliners. Thus, the notion of compromise and acquiescence has rather limited utility to Iran's aggrieved nationalists.[41]

Iranians argued that instead of the US being able to bully them, they could do so by using the nuclear card and contain America from getting involved not only in wars with Iran, but also in interfering in the internal affairs of Iran. As Enders Wimbush argues,

> The opportunities nuclear weapons will afford Iran far exceed the prospect of using them to win a military conflict. Nuclear weapons will empower strategies of coercion, intimidation and denial that go far beyond purely military considerations. Acquiring the bomb as an icon of state power will enhance the legitimacy of Iran's mullahs and make it harder for disgruntled Iranians to oust them. With nuclear weapons, Iran will have gained the ability to deter any direct American threats, as well as the leverage to keep the US at a distance and to discourage it from helping Iran's regional opponents.[42]

Thus, nuclear weapons seemed to solve a lot of problems simultaneously and seemed to be a fungible weapon to Tehran that faced a superpower rival.

America's regional ally is Iran's enemy

Since the formation of the State of Israel in 1947, the US and Israel have been allies. The US has always viewed the survival of Israel as a matter of American national

Case study: Iran

security and historically the only true democracy in the Middle East has been Israel.[43] The relationship was more than cordial during the aforementioned period. During President Reagan's presidency, the relationship was elevated from friendship to strategic partners. In 1979, after the Islamic Revolution, Reagan stated that

> the fall of Iran has increased Israel's value as perhaps the only remaining strategic asset in the region on which the United States can truly rely; other pro-Western states in the region, especially Saudi Arabia and the smaller Gulf kingdoms, are weak and vulnerable.[44]

This naturally made Iran much more nervous than it originally was about two of its rivals being allies. It must be noted that Iran and Israel had some degree of relationship in the 1970s – even though Israel was Iran's other protracted conflict rival through the latter's connections with the Arab states as part of the Arab–Israeli conflict – and that continued well into the 1980s. The relationship became bitter since the Israeli invasion of Lebanon and Iran's involvement in it through Hezbollah, as discussed before. Since then the two countries have been bitter enemies of each other. The situation was further aggravated with Washington's support for Israel in the region. Iran watched how Washington supported Israel in the region in the 1980s, even when Tel Aviv violated international security norms. It showed the world how strong the US–Israeli friendship was by remaining silent when Israel carried out an air strike on Iraqi nuclear reactor in 1981. While the hardliners in the Reagan administration wanted the US to impose economic and military sanctions against Israel for attacking, Reagan believed that a dovish approach should be pursued and, in fact, adopted a sympathetic or even empathetic stance toward the Israeli position.[45] This is interesting because Israel, a country that did not sign the NPT and which was involved in illicit proliferation activity, simply took out a nuclear reactor of another country and the world's greatest power, the US, watched it doing so. For Iran, it proved that the US was maintaining a double standard in its foreign policy. Iraq was not allowed to have the nuclear reactor, but Israel was allowed to have opaque nuclear weapons.[46] Interestingly, during the same period Washington led the global opposition to nuclear assistance for the Islamic Republic of Iran.[47] Moreover, later that year, Israel and the US signed a Memorandum of Understanding (MOU), which was a significant symbol of Reagan's commitment toward Israel.[48] Although Iran was more than happy to learn that Iraq's nuclear reactor was destroyed by Israel, it was less than enthusiastic to know that America did not take any measure against Israel for doing so. The bond of its two rivals was not only disturbing, but also fearful, which triggered its desire to emphasize more on its nuclear program. Scholars argued even much later that "Iran's policies toward Israel and the US are often an exception to its overall shift toward prudence. Restrictions on relations with both countries remain one of the strongest remnants of the revolutionary legacy."[49] Addressing security issues in relation to Israel and the US became much more salient to Iran since then. Thus, many argue that "Israel and its over-the-horizon ally, the United States, take up much of the national security debate in Iran."[50] What is interesting, however, is that some believe that even if the Arab–Israeli conflict is resolved, the problem with Israel will still continue for Iran simply because of Israel's connections with the US. The relationship with Israel may be simply muted, but Iran will be part of the diaspora that will not agree with any peace agreement. Shaul Bakhash argues that "there is genuine hostility with Israel. Part of the hostility is simply leverage against the US – if you can call me a terrorist, then I can hate Israel."[51] He further contends that "as long as Iran has something to fear from America, it will be in this [conflict with Israel]."[52] Given the security environment Iran faced, it was believed that "the strongest impulse to build nuclear weapons, in Iran, as everywhere else, comes from the fact that its key enemies are nuclear-armed and the resulting belief that a nuclear deterrent is therefore essential to Iran's national security, or at least the security of its regime. Iran's primary enemies – Israel and the US – have nuclear capability."[53] Nuclear adversaries and triple conflicts have strongly impacted Iran's strategic decisions during that period.

Developing the nuclear program

Generally, nuclear aspirants desire the ultimate weapon to address pivotal security threats. Scholars argue that

> because not all threatened countries covet nuclear forces, the emergence of a security threat, even a very intense threat, is not a surefire indicator that proliferation is likely to follow. The rise of an acute security threat is a necessary – though not a sufficient – condition for a country to start a nuclear weapon program . . . not every civilian or military member of a threatened country's leadership will agree on the character or intensity of the threat, or on the need to acquire nuclear forces to counter it.[54]

This is a noteworthy point because in reality all threatened countries are not proliferators and most states perceive threats in their environments in some form or another. However, when security threats come from different directions and a state is targeted by multiple conflict rivals, who also happen to be allies or at least obtain help from each other, the targeted country's leadership may have to be in agreement about offsetting these real security predicaments. Additionally, even if one of the threats may be ignored, all will not have the same intensity and may not be ignored. Asymmetric conflicts with global powers pose serious security threats for a regional power. There is huge gap between the two states in the conventional military realm, which the regional power can never close. The US, for example, does not need to depend on nuclear weapons to deter a regional rival; its conventional weapons are enough to do so. Some argue,

> Not only would the US be able to respond to a nuclear attack by conventional means but, more importantly, it might feel able to deter one without its own nuclear weapons because its conventional military (and possibly also its "cyber," or information warfare) capabilities mean that it could inflict intolerable damage on any government and on the terrorists whom it could locate.[55]

74 *Case study: Iran*

This demonstrates how powerful the US is compared to a regional state. Given this, such threats are sufficient conditions for proliferation. Although Iran's nuclear program started in the 1960s and its strategic decisions revolved around the two key regional rivals, Iraq primarily and also Israel, after 1979, a third rival joined the club of conflict rivals and this time the rival was a superpower with nuclear weapons. The strategic calculations that Iran was used to doing had changed dramatically. It is one thing to address regional security threats; it is entirely another to deal with global powers. The Iran–US rivalry is the most important one in the hierarchy of conflicts that Iran has been engaged in during that period. As Colin Dueck and Ray Takeyh argue, "Israel may be peripheral to Iran's nuclear calculations, the American shadow looms large."[56] They further contend that "the only way in which the long-term American challenge can be negated is through the possession of the 'strategic weapon.'"[57] The asymmetry of power between a regional state and superpower is the greatest concern for the regional state engaged in a conflict with a global power. Farideh Farhi highlights the conflict asymmetry and Iranian leaders' desire for nuclear weapons. She states, "You can't tell your people that you give in because your enemy is powerful."[58] The global power has the capacity to wage war or inflict damage on the regional power easily. The regional power will have no choice but to accept the terms of the superpower. Thus, the regional power perceives extreme fear, especially when hostility and incompatibility over issues ensues. It was reported in a conservative newspaper in Iran that "in the contemporary world, it is obvious that having access to advanced weapons shall cause deterrence and therefore security, and will neutralize the evil wishes of great powers to attack other nations and countries."[59] Some believe that "given the power asymmetry between the two states," and instead of allowing the US to wage war on Iran and bully it constantly, "a presumed nuclear capability seems to be the only viable deterrent posture against an adversary that has never accepted the legitimacy of the Iranian revolution and has long sought to isolate and contain the Islamic Republic."[60] Its triple conflicts triggered a new incentive to develop the nuclear program that was originally developed by the Shah. The eagerness to acquire nuclear capability was a function of the US joining the club of its conflict rivals. Handling three conflicts became not only difficult for Iran, but impossible, especially when Israel was an ally of the US, Iraq seemed to have built a new relationship with the US in the midst of the protracted war with Iran, and the US was a nuclear power. Deterring all three adversaries with nuclear weapons became important and being at par with the superpower at least on one level by projecting nuclear strength was also important. Nuclear weapons became attractive within this context. Thus, for Iran "this is a weapon of deterrence and power projection."[61]

While Israel is still a regional state that could have been deterred by other military means – including other non-conventional mechanisms – how is it possible for a regional state to deter a superpower without nuclear weapons, especially when the rival is a nuclear state? "A relatively small nuclear outcast will be able to deter a mature nuclear power. Iran will become a billboard advertising nuclear weapons as the logical asymmetric weapon of choice for nations that wish to confront the United States."[62] Additionally, the issue of prestige is factored into this strategic calculation. Iran has been historically, culturally, and strategically different from the Arab states in the Middle East and, consequently, the Iranians see themselves at the "center of gravity" for the region. Iran "wants some of the obvious things from the US: lift sanctions, stop trying to isolate and demonize Iran, recognize Iran's role in the Middle East, and acknowledge the Islamic Revolution."[63] For them, "the way to achieve a measure of parity with the United States and attain some sort of regional superpower status is you have to talk the talk the US is talking. Capabilities like nuclear weapons."[64] Consequently, even though the Supreme Leader did not give the development of nuclear program high priority, "even during this time of turmoil, Iran undertook a small-scale clandestine program with the help of centrifuge technology acquired from Pakistan."[65] Despite a number of setbacks, "research and planning for a nuclear arsenal continued."[66] What was more interesting is that Iran began "its nuclear quest in earnest during the 1980s, when the country was locked in mortal combat with Iraq – and Saddam Hussein had made no secret of his own nuclear ambitions."[67] In 1984, Tehran focused on building a new research laboratory at the Isfahan Nuclear Technology Center (INTC) and Chinese assistance in developing this research center included supplying a "training reactor" in 1985.[68] The Center's research experiments involved uranium conversion and fuel production.[69] It secretly imported the uranium in 1982 for research purposes.[70] Interestingly enough, all these were very conveniently hidden from the IAEA. According to the IAEA reports, "all of the materials important to uranium conversion had been produced in laboratory and bench scale experiments [in kilogram quantities] between 1981 and 1993 without having been reported to the Agency."[71] By 1985 Iran decided to start a full-fledged nuclear program with Chinese and North Korean assistance.[72] According to some sources, Iran and Pakistan came to an agreement in 1987 which provided Iran with a centrifuge to enrich uranium.[73] The transfer of nuclear technology began in 1989. Attention towards the fuel cycle was given more specifically in 1988–89.[74] Two reasons explain that: the Islamic leaders were generally against the western nuclear program and Iran was in a war with Iraq which drained all resources from the country. Thus, although the three conflicts had to be addressed simultaneously, it was unable to do much to develop the nuclear program in the midst of an ongoing war which crippled the economy of the country. However, this was also a period that was the defining one in terms of nuclear program development. This was the time when Iran realized that addressing all conflicts at the same time required it to acquire nuclear weapons. It was more important because Israel was an opaque state and the US, a nuclear rival of Iran, was Israel's ally. Saddam's ultimate intention to develop nuclear weapons was also revealed during the same period. No leadership – Revolutionary or Reformist – could ignore the security environment or conflict settings. Consequently, the triple protracted conflicts triggered a new drive towards proliferation. However, it must still be noted that during this period the nuclear program was not a crash program, but one that was "characterized by persistence and incrementalism."[75] This was primarily the period when Iran's program was at a resetting stage and when the rivalry with the US in particular was still to be institutionalized, although the two regional rivalries were already very well-founded by then. Ten years is not enough to test a relationship and when a major war is absent in the setting, it is a little difficult to understand where the relationship is heading towards. Thus, Leonard Spector states that in 1985 when the US was supporting Iraq, Iraq was still the number one enemy of Iran,[76] even though with the US Iran has its own share of conflict issues such as terrorism and US foreign policies. With Israel, there was great hostility, but it was not a threat of the same magnitude for Iran. There was no territorial ambition of Israel.[77] However, if the US did not support Israel so strongly and did not provide assistance to Saddam in the Iran–Iraq War, perhaps Iran's relationship with the US could change with the death of Khomeini in 1989. That could not and did not happen because in those 10 years the US had proved to be the greatest enemy of Iran – by calling it a terrorist state, supporting its regional rivals, trying to change its regime, and keeping it from making economic or security gains. Several unresolved crises during the period also made matters worse and the relationship embittered severely. Both started to mistrust each other and the trust deficit was institutionalized within this period. Consequently, settling the differences was out of the offing.

The following chapter gives a detailed account of Iran–US conflict since 1990 and the ramifications of it on proliferation decision in Iran. It demonstrates that the conflict that started in 1979 reached a more difficult period after a decade and Tehran continued its veiled nuclear program more vigorously due to this institutionalized conflict with the US.

5 The ramifications of the asymmetric Iran–US protracted conflict from 1990 to 2000 in Iran's nuclear domain

This chapter portrays Iran's nuclear ambition based on the asymmetric conflict with the US from 1990 to 2000, a period when the conflict was somewhat institutionalized. It argues that Iran made quite serious efforts to develop a comprehensive nuclear program during this period. The end of the cold war, US aggressive foreign policies pertaining to Iran, the rogue rhetoric, the continuous imposition of sanctions on Tehran, and overall asymmetry in the conflict setting have been the main contributors to Iran's focus on the nuclear program at the time.

After the end of the cold war, President George H. W. Bush proclaimed the potential for a

> new world order . . . freer from the threat of terror, stronger in the pursuit of justice and more secure in the quest for peace. An era in which the nations of the world, east and west, north and south, can prosper and live in harmony.[1]

According to him, this was the new world order that the community of states had longed to be in place for a very long time. While the cold war had just ended and the world seemed to have entered a different stage, unfortunately the US policy-makers faced a vexing problem in determining which countries were friends and which ones were enemies in the emerging international system. However, regional aggression took center stage in 1990 with Iraq's invasion of Kuwait. The potential of regional aggression and instability having a swell effect in the international system worked to transform and draw the attention of US foreign policy-makers.[2] It was believed that the otherwise peaceful international system would face instability due to some arrogant and aggressive regional states. These states would shake regional stability, which would ultimately impact global peace and stability. Combating these new problem states became important to the world's existing superpower, the US. Consequently, American foreign and security discourse since that period revolved around these potential problem states. According to Michael Klare, "From 1990 on, the general model of a rogue state ruled by an outlaw regime armed with chemical and nuclear weapons became the standard currency of national security discourse."[3] Paul Hoyt provides details on rogue characterization and asserts that there were four categories into which statements on rogue activities could be classified. These categories were the development of WMD, involvement in international terrorism, posing either a global or regional military security threat, and challenging international norms.[4] More recently, the policies of the pursuit of WMDs and support for terrorism were reaffirmed as important identifiers of rogue states.[5] Policies in pursuit of WMDs and support of terrorism represent very explicit and salient threats which Washington's policy-makers can point to when singling out rogue states.[6] To Miroslav Nincic, these indeterminate threats hovering by rogues fall into two kinds: first, massive internal repression and second, overt aggression against another state.[7] Thus, in addition to the pursuit of suspicious policies, the perceived nature of rogue states as non-democratic regimes appears to be of equal importance.[8] It is also important to note that these states function in ways that the US policy-makers deem outside the parameters of the international community. In essence, these states are anti-western in their orientation. Iraq, Iran, North Korea, Libya, and Syria very naturally achieved the status of rogues.[9] Combined, the first four states comprise 94 percent of all instances when a state was specifically referred to as being a rogue.[10] In light of these points, it was not difficult to see how Iran perfectly fit within the framework of the rogue states. It is a non-democratic country that harbors terrorism, makes efforts to acquire weapons of mass destruction including ballistic missiles, and, in doing so, challenges international norms, and also poses regional and global threats. Above all, it has been an anti-US state since 1979 and calls the US the "Great Satan." Thus, Iran was not only engaged in an intractable conflict with the world's only superpower that dominates and dictates other states in the international system, but was also identified as a rogue state by its global adversary – to make matters worse for Tehran in this asymmetric conflict setting. This humiliated and insulted the Persian Gulf state that strives to be a preponderant power in the region.

What is interesting is that the US policy-makers did not simply label some states as rogue states, they actually added this term to their vocabulary and used them frequently. Paul Hoyt reports that from 1993 to 2004, the policy-makers used the term in their foreign policy discourses at the highest levels. During the Bill Clinton years he accounted for 23 percent of all instances where the term was found in documented public statements. When combined with the statements of President Bush, presidential statements discussing rogues accounted for nearly a third of all the collected statements. From 1993 to 2004, US administrations mentioned this word to refer to Iraq 32 percent of the time and 29 percent of the time in the case of Iran, while North Korea was mentioned 20 percent of the time, and Libya 13 percent of the time.[11] What is more intriguing is that although the conventional wisdom is that George W. Bush was harsher with the rogues compared to Bill Clinton, during Clinton's years, especially during his second term, the administration used the term "rogue" much more in foreign policy discourses.[12] In examining the public statements of US foreign policy elites during the period 1993–2004, K. P. O'Reilly witnesses an increasing and continuing usage of the rogue label at the highest ranks of foreign policy decision making. The usage of the term abounds in the statements by key diplomatic actors, both Presidents and Secretaries of State alike.[13] Klare states,

> Given the history of US relations with these five states and the frequency with which they have been named as rogues and renegades by the media, it has not

been difficult for the Department of Defense to persuade US policy-makers of the need to be prepared to defend America's "vital interests" against their aggressive intentions.[14]

Iranian efforts to obtain nuclear, chemical, and ballistic missile technology were particularly troubling to the US within this rogue framework. The CIA Director Robert Gates told the Congress in May 1992 that "Iran has embarked on an across-the-board effort to develop its military and defense industries."[15] Although details of the situation in Iran were not provided by Gates at the time, in just about five months, the CIA reported that Iran had launched a clandestine effort to develop nuclear weapons, with the help of Chinese and western sources.[16] Iran has generally adhered to anti-western and anti-American positions, maintained a non-democratic political regime, and focused on a costly and ambitious military program to rebuild its military capability that was shattered in the 1980–88 war with Iraq, as stated earlier. In July 1998, it also test fired Shehab 3 medium range ballistic missile, with a range of 1350 km, which would allow it to hit Israel and Iraq easily, stated in the previous chapter. It was also developing Shehab 4 which would have a range of 1940 km and Shehab 5, an intercontinental ballistic missile. Although Washington was nervous with the news of these new nuclear and missile developments, Iran's efforts during the period were shaped by America's categorization of states as rogues and non-rogues and its discriminatory policies against these so-called rogue states. The discriminatory policies of the US have been apparent in many cases. Akbar Ganji elaborated on American discriminatory and contradictory policies. He stated,

> The US and Britain supported states that were corrupt in the Middle East prior to 2003. When Egyptian president Hosni Mubarak was forced to have free elections in Egypt, he said to the US that fundamentalists will emerge and win. That is when the democratization drive went on vacation.[17]

It is difficult for Iran to accept such discriminatory policies of the US, especially when it is called a rogue state for not only being a state engaged in terrorism and developing WMDs, but also for its non-democratic political regime. Since combating rogue states was a priority of the US, Tehran had more of an urgency to protect itself from evil and aggressive behaviors of the US in a unipolar new world. After all, the Gulf War did not only prove the "validity of the Rogue Doctrine," but also provided the US with the "preferred strategic template for all future wars,"[18] which threatened the so-called rogue states such as Iran that were engaged in an intractable conflict with the world's only surviving superpower, the US.

At the systemic level, Iraq's ambitious and aggressive behavior towards Kuwait alarmed the US and made it aware of the possibilities of other regional states' militaristic moves in the future. Thus, American focus was also fully on Iran. At the domestic level, the Pentagon may have inflated these threats coming from the rogue states for defense budgetary reasons. Unless there is serious threat, they cannot justify spending more on defense when Soviet threats disappeared from the world scene. At the individual level, both George W. H. Bush and Bill Clinton believed the three states – Iraq, North Korea, and Iran – to be rogues that posed serious threats to the Americans. To Iran, all these were unacceptable. Iran has never acted like Iraq. Although Iran did not join the coalition in the Gulf war, it did not support Saddam Hussein in attacking Kuwait. Additionally, Iran was a victim of a long war with Iraq; it did not initiate an attack on Baghdad. It also was not directly involved in a war with the US. Therefore, America should not judge the intentions of Iran based on the Iraqi behavior. Until the 1990s Iran did not have ballistic missiles. Thus, they did not have the capability to hit the US and there was no reason to worry about that. Rather, the focus that they had given on missile development became much more aggressive after the rogue rhetoric and the swaggering of the US power and position in the early 1990s. Thus, while the Americans thought rogues were threatening the US and planning to jeopardize the long-sought stability that the world was waiting for, to the rogues, in particular Iran, targeting them was unacceptable and threatening. Additionally, sanctions imposed by the US unilaterally was not only disturbing and unfair to the Iranians, but were also threatening as they indicated that the US was bent on disallowing Iran to protect itself militarily from regional adversaries. Iran had two regional rivals to be worried about and it was pertinent for it to stay militarily at par with its rivals. Military strength is dependent on economic viability and Washington seemed determined to crush Tehran economically and turn it into a vulnerable regional state. The threat emanating from the US exacerbated within this context. Consequently, the determination to acquire nuclear weapons to deter the only superpower from making gains vis-à-vis Iran became much stronger. This resolve was connected to the asymmetry Iran faces in the Iran–US conflict dynamics. O'Reilly eloquently states,

> Rogue states, while painted often as regional bullies capable of threatening their neighbors, pale in the light of comparison with the power capabilities of the US. It is precisely this wide gap in capabilities that is seen as driving these rogue states to develop and acquire WMDs.[19]

The US–Iran relationship is asymmetric on several levels including "unequal power base, leveraging tactics"[20] among others. Shaul Bakhash states in simple terms, "America is a superpower. There is huge difference between America and Iran."[21] While general asymmetry on all levels between the US and Iran in the overall protracted conflict perturbed the latter, American swaggering and boasting of power after the end of the cold war disturbed the overall conflict relations further. Americans boasted of American power and spoke about being a benevolent hegemon after the demise of the Soviet Union. Madeleine Albright stated in the 1997 G-7 Summit: "The US is the indispensable nation. We stand tall and hence see further than other nations."[22] These are statements that infuriated regional powers to whom American bullying was unacceptable and who were also afraid of American expansionist policies to promote its interests and policies. The Middle East was the hot bed for that recipe and Iraq and Iran were the principal targets in the region. The US also spoke of universal application of the American principles, practices, and institutions. That was not all. Washington pressured other countries to adopt American values and practices pertaining to human rights and democracy.[23] While all these may be acceptable to some states in the international system, it became increasingly difficult for countries such as Iran to tolerate such behaviors of the US. This is because of several reasons: first, Iran and the US were involved in an asymmetric conflict and Tehran was already in a vulnerable position within the conflict framework; US swaggering only made security threats more pronounced for Iran. Thus, Leonard Spector states that although radical ideology is there in Iran, its acquisition of nuclear weapons has been a function of its national security – an insurance against US attack – and also national and international prestige. Its weapons would be used to enhance its confidence in the world.[24] In a similar vein, others also argue that for Iran a nuclear weapon is a symbol of national pride and success.[25] Meir Javedanfar states that

> Iran wants to be a regional superpower. It is no match with America, but in the Middle East, the Iranians want to be at parity with the Americans. Nuclear weapons acquisition is the cheapest way to be at parity with the US.[26]

This is more salient within the context of its asymmetric conflict with the US. Second, Iran was one of the regional countries that did not adhere to westernization in this globalized world and did not accept that American values and principles are universally acceptable ones. They believed that what are human rights violations to the West in general and the US in particular are not human rights violations for the Iranians. Rights are culturally defined; Islamic culture prescribes certain rights to the Muslims that may seem alien to the people who follow Christianity. Thus, American or western ways of thinking and living are not acceptable to the Islamic Republic. Rather they want Americans to recognize and acknowledge the Islamic Revolution and its ways. Third, Tehran saw how easily America formed a coalition of states in fighting Saddam Hussein's army during the Gulf War and how the Iraqi forces had to retreat. In "Operation Desert Storm" brilliant military victory was achieved by the US and the coalition with little cost. While the overall success may have made the Iranian leadership happy because Saddam learned a lesson, it also made them worried about American predominance in the Middle Eastern region and support from the regional states. Iran has always wanted to be a regional superpower which means that "the US has to negotiate with Iran and ask for permissions if it wants to come to the Middle East."[27] Instead of that happening, the war proved that US foreign policy would not be limited to regions close to the US even at a time when it could rest after decades of cold war with the Soviet Union. One point needs to be noted here. When almost all regional states supported the US in its fight against Saddam's army in Kuwait, Iran did not show support or join the coalition.[28] Iran considered the war on Iraq a war by the West on Islam. This proves what kind of mindset the Iranians had pertaining to the US during the 1990s. Additionally, it proved that states would bandwagon with the only existing superpower in case of another regional war and Iran needed to be prepared for that. Finally, to top these off, Iran became fully aware of the fact that America was pursuing a policy of global unilateralism. It was promoting its own interests with little reference to those of others. As Samuel P. Huntington states, America itself had become a "Rogue Superpower"[29] by then. America's intention and agenda, coercive use of power – through the imposition of sanctions and waging military intervention – and actions were all very threatening to the leadership in Tehran. Michael Mazarr states,

> Taken at the level of strategy, the focus on asymmetric war in defense policy assumes a foreign policy that would have the United States leaping into one stability operation after another in service of a guiding ideology that assumes that Washington and its allies can and must create order in failed states. Such an ideology is highly questionable on empirical grounds, and as a foreign policy, it almost certainly will not sustain public support. The American people, especially in the wake of war in Afghanistan and Iraq, have no appetite for endless nation-building schemes. Yet, a defense strategy committed to preparing for asymmetric war presumes that the United States will commit itself to precisely such a campaign.[30]

Consequently, some argue that at the domestic political level, there was and still is "great solidarity that Iran should have an independent foreign policy."[31] Shaul Bakhash states that although the American administration wants the international community to believe that there are wide differences between the leaders in Iran, "the differences between the leadership are grossly exaggerated."[32] He uses the example of the nuclear issue and states that "within the leadership there is agreement on it" and "even public opinion agrees to move on with the program."[33] Some argue that the

> Iranians will stop at nothing to preserve their homeland – the taking of hostages, terrorism, and nuclear weapons are just instruments for them to scare America out of their backyard. America remains an enemy that has repeatedly expressed its desire to overthrow the Iranian government. Most Iranians believe the Khat-e-Imam took the American embassy to destroy its network of spies and put an end to American plans to launch a military coup in Iran.[34]

The US presence in the region after the Gulf War was also very disturbing to Iran. Tehran's desire to pursue a "nuclear weapons capability may also have been encouraged by revelations following the 1991 Gulf War that Iraq had been able to conceal a massive nuclear weapons program, and perhaps by the growing US security presence in the region."[35] Restraining America from proceeding towards Iran to promote western ideals and values in this new world became pertinent for Iran. The nuclear ambition got further attention by the policy-makers in Iran during this period. Although it is believed that George W. Bush's aggressive foreign policies embittered relations between US and Iran from 2001 onwards which had great impacts on Iran's proliferation decisions, Spector states that Iran's connection with A. Q. Khan started in 1995, during Bill Clinton's presidency, when Iran focused on its nuclear weapons program with a lot of vigor.[36] Iran's resolve to acquire nuclear weapons increased and it made clandestine efforts to attain that goal. Bakhash mentions an Iranian diplomat who said, "We were forced into the black market" because the US prevented Iran from getting any nuclear technology.[37] American foreign policies in the unilateral world along with the asymmetry in conflict relations were instrumental in encouraging Tehran to make determined efforts in the nuclear realm. The desire to enhance Iran's prestige in this conflict setting also "had a lot to do" with its need to go nuclear.[38]

The development of a nuclear program takes years and where states pursue clandestine processes to work on their nuclear programs they take even longer due to secret deals and frequent abandonment of the programs for suppliers' restrictions. What needs to be stressed here is that while capability development may take long, the intention is what needs to be gauged. The intention can, however, be assessed by the effort the country has invested into the nuclear program. Iran's drive to acquire nuclear weapons became much more pronounced during this period. Shame and humiliation due to being called a rogue state were partly responsible, but mostly it was the security threats that were generated by placing Tehran under the rogue category. Iran's engagement with the US in an asymmetric and long-running conflict was also instrumental in driving them towards new clandestine efforts to complete their nuclear program. How much the asymmetric conflict impacted Iran's decision to move on with its nuclear program seriously in the 1990s was evident in Iran's disinterest in extending the NPT unless the big five nuclear states, or the vertical proliferators, decided to dismantle their nuclear weapons. In April 1995, *Deutsche Presse-Agentur* reported that Iran decided not to sign an indefinite extension to the NPT unless the five nuclear powers also agreed to decrease and eventually eliminate their nuclear weapons. Ali Akbar Velayati, Iran's foreign minister, demanded that the nuclear states end production of weapons-grade nuclear material, and make accommodations to facilitate the transfer of nuclear energy technology to other states in need of other forms of energy production.[39] Although such was Iran's desire, Tehran still did not make relentless effort to acquire nuclear weapons during this period, as was the case after 2000.

There was one upside of the Gulf War, which helped Iran in incrementally moving on with the nuclear program during this period. The war proved that US may get involved in a limited probe, and may not conquer. During the Gulf War the main intentions of the US were the restoration of Kuwait's legitimate government and the unconditional and complete withdrawal of the Iraqi forces from Kuwait. The war aims of the US were limited. This gave Iran ample reason to believe that unless it proves to be more aggressive than Iraq, it is highly unlikely that the US would try to use force to change its military or political course. It is important to note that "Iran's military doctrine and capacity is defense of its own territorial integrity only. Iran has never attacked any of its neighbors in the region in the past 300 years, even when it was badly provoked in 1998 by the Taliban in Afghanistan."[40] Thus, unless Iran does anything different from its earlier strategies, it is unlikely for the US to start a fight with Iran at the dawn of this changed world order just because it has been declared a rogue state and for its terrorist support, which was part of Iran's policy since the 1980s. Consequently, although the threats were high, it still gave

Iran some hope to move along with its nuclear program within the timeframe that was expected and feasible. Consequently, during this period Iran was pursuing a broader effort to produce dual-use nuclear technologies, with both civilian and military applications, and was not simply focusing on a "dedicated nuclear weapons program."[41] This is not to suggest that Iran did not intend to acquire nuclear weapons capability, but simply to mean that even though the threat perception was high, it was not high enough which would trigger a crash nuclear program.

After the death of Khomeini in 1989 Iran's nuclear program got renewed attention from the new leadership team which included Ayatollah Sayyid Ali Khameini, who took over as Supreme Leader, and Ali Akbar Hashemi Rafsanjani, who was elected President in August of that year. From 1990 onwards "Iran embarked on a more ambitious nuclear program with both civilian and military applications."[42] Rafsanjani pursued the nuclear program more vigorously in the midst of the end of the cold war. He hired Iranian scientists from all over the world.[43] To that end, Tehran stepped up its efforts to buy nuclear technology abroad at the start of the UN offensive against Iraq. According to a US State Department official, Iran was researching uranium enrichment methods and probably had agents in Europe who were "scouring the market" for enrichment technology. The US believed that Iran may acquire or already had acquired an unsafeguarded enrichment facility for which it might get parts from Eastern Europe.[44] Pakistan's army chief General Mirza Aslam Beg proposed to create a strategic alliance with Iran, which included the sharing of nuclear weapons technology. By then Pakistan and Iran both received large amounts of nuclear-related assistance from China, which raised the possibility of a three-way nuclear trade in the future.[45] From 1990 to 1992 China provided Iran with an assortment of small research reactors and laboratory-scale laser enrichment equipment for laser research at the Tehran Nuclear Research Center.[46] By May of 1991, *Nucleonics Week* reported that Iran had a nuclear cooperation agreement with Pakistan and clandestine nuclear agreements with South Africa and China. European officials expressed concerns that Iran may well seek Pakistan's assistance in enriching uranium obtained under a secret nuclear cooperation agreement from South Africa in 1988–89.[47] Around the same time, US officials also believed that China and Pakistan were assisting Iran in the development of a nuclear bomb.[48] In fact, the *Boston Globe* revealed that on his recent trip to the US, Mohammed Mohaddessin, foreign policy spokesman for the Mojahedin Iranian opposition group, stated that Iran was seeking nuclear weapons. He asserted, "What the regime is doing is concentrating on research in order to develop nuclear weapons themselves. They are looking for technical assistance, for materials."[49] He claimed that Iran by then had created a special unit of the Republican Guards to secretly develop nuclear weapons without the knowledge of the IAEA. According to him Iran had sent a number of nuclear experts and researchers to China for training purposes and to obtain the expertise.[50] Although neither Iran nor China came out in the open to say they made nuclear deals, when France did not agree to supply highly enriched uranium to Iran, Rafsanjani said that Iran could get it from other countries, such as China and North Korea.[51] Iran's dual nuclear program was very much there since the early 1990s. According to the Iranian physicist

Alireza Assar, in the early 1990s Iran had two parallel nuclear programs – the civil program which was run by the AEOI, and was organized around the Bushehr nuclear power reactor, and the military program which was controlled by the Ministry of Defense and Iranian Revolutionary Guard Corps. The plan of this latter program was to develop a vast uranium enrichment program. That is what was revealed in 2002.[52] In August 1992, Russia and Iran signed "an umbrella agreement for bilateral nuclear cooperation" which was followed in January 1995 by "a specific agreement to complete one unit of the Bushehr Nuclear power plant with Russian nuclear technology."[53] Russia also offered Iran a large research reactor, fuel fabrication facilities and a centrifuge enrichment plant, which meant that "Moscow was offering Tehran a full civilian fuel cycle and off-the-shelf nuclear break-out capability."[54] In fact, by 1992, Iran's nuclear program had an annual research budget of $800 million, and had major facilities at Tehran University, Moallem Kalayeh, and Isfahan.[55] Iran also declared the Isfahan site to the IAEA for the first time.[56] CIA Director Robert Gates testified the same year that Iran was seeking nuclear weapons and could procure one by 2000 if the West did not intervene.[57] Because of US complaint to Russia about the fuel cycle assistance the latter agreed to cancel its assistance to Iran. Thus, by September 1994, according to a senior Iranian official, seeing no alternative, Iran considered withdrawing from the NPT since western nations continued to deny it nuclear technology, even though it had complied with the NPT's requirements. The official statement confirmed "rumors" circulating in the western intelligence community that Iran might decide to leave the NPT. In January 1995, *The Guardian* reported that Iran was trying to obtain support to prevent the extension of the NPT, and the US was increasing its efforts to deny nuclear technology to Iran. Iran was unhappy because its efforts to acquire nuclear technology for peaceful use were being thwarted by nuclear suppliers following the US lead.[58]

At the third session of the Preparatory Committee for the 1995 NPT Review and Extension Conference in Geneva, the Iranian delegation claimed that Iran was not being granted access to technology designed for peaceful use of nuclear energy as stipulated by Article IV of the Treaty. Iranian delegates to the IAEA General Conference in Vienna said that Iran would postpone its decision on withdrawal from the NPT until closure of the final Preparatory Committee meeting for the 1995 NPT Review and Extension Conference. A US official noted that Iran had nothing to gain from leaving the NPT and would be "better off" gauging the extent of the support of the Non-Aligned Movement (NAM) at the January 1995 PrepCom meeting. A Japanese official remarked that because North Korea had succeeded in withdrawing from the NPT and was "rewarded with power reactors," Iran might attempt a similar course. Officials also observed that although the Iranian delegation to the General Conference seemed sympathetic to the NPT and uneasy with the hard-line stance ordered by Tehran, "quitting the NPT is a card" Iran could play at any time. Pakistani sources confirmed Iranian claims that the US pressured Pakistan into denying Iranian nuclear specialists access to a Chinese-supplied pressurized water reactor (PWR) at Chashma, northeast of the Pakistani town, Faisalabad.[59] Iran also perceived how America was playing a double standard in its foreign policy. Israel was not pressured into joining the NPT, but Iran was expected to support the indefinite extension of the NPT. "If you are friends of America it seems that it is easier to have a nuclear program," stated Meir Javedanfar.[60] Iran feels that the asymmetry between Iran and US conflict becomes much more pronounced due to the US connection with Israel in the Middle East. While it is one thing for the US to be a global power and have regional interests, it is another to have a regional ally who can assist the global power in attaining its regional ambitions. Iran is prepared to work with the IAEA and all states concerned about promoting confidence in its fuel cycle program. Hassan Rohani, Iran's top nuclear negotiator, argued, "Iran cannot be expected to give in to United States' bullying and non-proliferation double standards."[61] Additionally, it is annoying for Iran to see how the US ignores what Israelis do in the realm of proliferation and how it vehemently opposes even the development of a civilian nuclear program in Iran that might have military applications. Hashemi Rafsanjani, the president of Iran from 1989 to 1997, stated on December 14, 2001 this was widely interpreted as indicating that Tehran was seeking nuclear weapons as a deterrent to Israel. He stated,

> If one day, the Islamic world is also equipped with weapons like those that Israel possesses now, then the imperialist's strategy will reach a standstill because the use of even one nuclear bomb inside Israel will destroy everything. However, it will only harm the Islamic world. It is not irrational to contemplate such an eventuality. Of course you can see that the Americans have kept their eyes peeled and they are carefully looking for even the slightest hint that technologically advances are being made by an independent Islamic country. If an independent Islamic country is thinking about acquiring other kinds of weaponry, then they will do their utmost to prevent it from acquiring them. Well, that is something that almost the entire world is discussing right now.[62]

Also, Iran and Israel are both highly concerned about the other's nuclear and missile programs. Israel sees Iran's potential nuclear program as one of the greatest threats to its security, particularly as Tehran had tested missiles that can reach Israeli territory.[63] Akbar Etemad stated in an interview,

> The way the west is isolating Iran leaves it no choice but to build nuclear weapons. Iran has nothing to lose and nothing to fear from sanctions anymore. When Israel threatens to attack Iran, it dares to do so because it has nuclear weapons and Iran does not. The Iranian government may now see them [nuclear weapons] as the only way they can defend themselves.[64]

Around the same time, Iran's ambassador to the NPT Review Conference in New York called for a nuclear-free Middle East and called for international pressure on Israel to give up its nuclear arms. "Every effort should be made," stated Ambassador Sirus Nasseri, "to implement the treaty in all its aspects to prevent proliferation of nuclear weapons. This, of course, should by no means hamper the peaceful use of nuclear energy."[65] Interestingly, the CIA Director James Woolsey reported during the same period that "Iran was also looking to purchase fully fabricated nuclear weapons in order to accelerate sharply its timetable."[66] By the following year it was reported by US Secretary of State Warren Christopher that Iran was undertaking a "crash effort to develop nuclear weapons." In reporting the fact he expressed his concerns that other countries were assisting Iran in developing nuclear technology. He believed that Russia was primarily assisting Iran in this regard since it had just recently concluded a contract with Iran for the completion of two nuclear reactors.[67] In fact, according to the IISS report, much unauthorized Russian assistance helped Iran in beginning construction of a heavy-water production plant at Arak.[68] In January 1996 Reza Amrollahi, head of the AEOI, stated that the country's first nuclear power plant [Bushehr] would become operational by 1999. At the same time, Iranian President Hashemi Rafsanjani said that work had begun on the Bushehr power plant, an area in which South Africa and Russia were known to have collaborated. He stated that "making use of nuclear technology for peaceful purposes is something without which a country could not find its real standing in the world."[69] By October 1996, according to an Iranian military source, Iran made a formal request to China regarding the dispatch of an Iranian observation team to China's next scheduled nuclear test. Iran also requested training for 10 or more Iranian personnel at Chinese nuclear weapon test sites.[70] In 1997, Iran hired several South African technicians whose jobs were eliminated following the demise of South Africa's nuclear weapons program. Iran also showed an interest in laser isotope separation.[71] All these prove how seriously Iran worked to build its nuclear program from the early 1990 and that no amount of pressure from the US kept Tehran from its determination to continue the nuclear weapons path.

The mid-to-late 1990s produced somewhat of a thaw in relations between Iran and the US as the regime seemed to be moderating and looking for overtures toward the West. That was especially true after the election of President Mohammed Khatami in 1997, who promised reforms even as he frequently asserted Iran's right to peaceful nuclear technology. Although leadership changed in Iran in 1997, President Mohammed Khatami did not bring about change in Tehran's nuclear program. This was for two reasons: First, the threat perception pertaining to the US did not change or even the regional security dynamics did not alter which would decrease its sense of insecurity, and second, the nuclear program was under the control of the Supreme Leader Khameini, who headed the Supreme National Security Council. Some argue that even though Ahmadinejad's foreign policies are aggressive, the reformists did become serious about the nuclear issue much before he came to power and that during Khatami's last few years, the dynamics of the nuclear program changed and suspension of uranium enrichment was removed.[72] Rather from 1997–2003 Pakistan's key nuclear scientist Abdul Qader Khan traveled extensively and made several visits to Iran along with other countries.[73] According to investigations, nuclear technologies, blueprints, and centrifuge parts were transferred to Iran through several middlemen including Malaysia, Turkey, Germany, Switzerland, and the UK.[74] By September 1997, *Jane's Intelligence Defense Review* reported that former US Secretary of State Warren Christopher said that, based on a variety of data, "we know that since the mid-1980s, Iran has had an organized structure dedicated to acquiring and developing nuclear weapons."[75] US State Department staff also stated then that there was evidence that Iran was engaged in nuclear activities "not conducive to [a] strictly peaceful program." Iran's nuclear industry is growing, with 3,000 personnel working at various sites in Isfahan. A second, top-secret weapons design center is near the Caspian Sea, at Moallem Kalayeh. Two other research sites are located at the Bushehr nuclear power plant and at Sharif University. A source at the Israeli Embassy in the US reported nuclear activities at the university were likely to have been moved since the university had been under western surveillance. Work continued at the Bushehr nuclear power plant, even though the plant was badly damaged during the 1980–88 War.[76] In 1998–99 the US government disclosed intelligence information that Russian entities had been involved in transferring WMD technology to Iran. The Russian government cracked down on the sources of information, thus preventing any further leaks about Russian–Iranian WMD activities. The Russian government's action almost stopped intelligence accumulation, especially in the years 1998 and 1999. These years are marked by intense Iranian activities in its WMD programs.[77] In 1999, Iran allocated $150 million for the year's work on building the Bushehr nuclear power plant, which was up from $100 million in 1998.[78] Throughout the late 1990s both Bush and Clinton administrations attempted to deter Russia from assisting Iran in its nuclear program "by means of warnings, selective sanctions, and promises of expanded economic ties."[79] However, it was hard to get the Russians on board because of how this trade provided the Russians more employment. The Russian economy was in shambles after the end of the cold war and the nuclear trade with Iran was useful in boosting the economy through employment and financial gains. Finally, by February 2000, the US CIA reported that Iran tried to acquire technology and equipment for weapons of mass destruction from Russia, China, and North Korea simultaneously. According to the CIA's Non-Proliferation Center reports, "Tehran is attempting to develop an indigenous capability to produce various types of weapons – nuclear, chemical and biological – and their delivery systems."[80] Iran's system of acquiring nuclear technology had become more efficient and modern, the CIA reported, and it may use such "guise to obtain whole facilities, such as a uranium conversion facility, that in fact could be used in any number of ways in support of efforts to produce fissile material needed for a nuclear weapon."[81] Thus, by 2000 Iran's nuclear program had already advanced a lot, enabling it to build a nuclear weapon in course of time.

Iran's nuclear program seemed to have dual purpose during the 1990s and asymmetry in the US–Iran relations triggered Tehran's effort to stay focused on the nuclear issue. Its concerted effort in this realm is noteworthy along with its attempts to oppose the indefinite extension of the NPT in 1995. Spector states that perhaps Iran's nuclear program received a new direction and momentum in 1995 and beyond because of the indefinite extension of the NPT.[82] Washington's double-standard in nuclear policy pertaining to Iran and Israel in the Middle East was also unacceptable to Iran because it made the Washington–Tehran conflict more asymmetric and threatening for Iran. The chapter that follows comprehends Iran's seemingly unrelenting nuclear drive since 2000.

6 Iran's fast-paced proliferation activity and hostile US policy since 2000

The aim of this chapter is to demonstrate that Iran's pace of proliferation activity became much faster since the end of 2000, which coincides with the change of American administration. Not only did Tehran's course of nuclear action change, but its ways of deceiving the international community and concealing nuclear activity had also altered. Unlike the previous periods, during this period, Iran almost came out in the open and bluntly claimed that it had the right to possess a comprehensive nuclear program and its enrichment activities were also revealed by the Iranian leadership. Although it can be argued that through some quarters this information had already been revealed at that time, it is still interesting to note that the administration did not deny those claims made by others or try to deceive the international community about its enrichment developments. Rather it claimed its rights pertaining to such developments. These new Iranian policies and nuclear developments can be associated with America's new foreign policies that pertains to Iran in the post-2000 period and, more specifically, after the 9/11 attacks.

Iran's nuclear program, 2000 and beyond

As discussed in Chapters 4 and 5, Iran's asymmetric conflict with America gave Iran enough incentive to seriously consider the nuclear weapons path and the desire was exacerbated because of having two other regional conflict adversaries. The nuclear program, however, was being developed incrementally, although with a strong focus on the dual component of it, in the midst of heavy and continuous sanctions and Tehran was still clandestinely enriching uranium for quite some time. The "denial and deception" strategy was pursued effectively by Iran, like the other regional proliferators such as Iraq and North Korea. That course of action changed by 2001. Although President Ahmadinejad and his firm speeches about the nuclear issue cannot be undermined, the pace of Iran's nuclear program became faster much before Ahmadinejad came to power. While Iran would have preferred to keep a low profile about its nuclear program until it was in a better position or almost close to building a bomb, the revelation of its nuclear weapons sites in 2002 changed its course of action and plan. The Iranian opposition group, the National Council of Resistance of Iran (NCRI), disclosed the two nuclear plants in Arak and Natanz that were developed in 1996 and 2000 respectively, which Iran kept as a secret from the

Case study: Iran

IAEA. Although it was no secret that Iran had a nuclear program, that it continued the development of its program after the Islamic Revolution and during Rafsanjani's presidency since 1989 was a matter of concern for the West. Instead of denying the revelations that were made in 2002, Iran made claims that its program remained within the parameters of the non-proliferation norms. Consequently, for the Iranians this revelation was not an embarrassment because they tried to argue that Iran complied with the norms of the NPT, according to which it needed to inform the IAEA if it intended to enrich uranium and after all preparations were completed to start enriching, which Iran was not doing at that point.[1] What needs to be underscored is that from 2000 to 2005 Iran made very serious efforts to build a nuclear weapon under the cover of a civilian nuclear program. Tehran's intention was to build it very fast as well. For example, according to NCRI, the construction of Natanz project began around 2000 'under the cover of cultivating desert' and it was scheduled for completion within three months.[2] Michale Levi states that in 2003 the acceleration of the nuclear program happened, which he believes was partly due to the fact that the program had already become public.[3] This relentless effort may be associated with America's foreign policy towards Iran in particular and the Islamic states in the Middle East in general. Ali Ansari states that "the growing confrontation over Iran's nuclear program could not be understood outside the general political malaise that characterized Iran–US relations."[4] Additionally, the war in Iraq in 2003 sent security threats to the Iranians that they were the next target of the Bush administration and only a nuclear deterrent capability could be instrumental in changing the American minds from attacking Iran to rid the country of non-democracy and proliferation activities. That Iran was the next target was not simply an Iranian illusion, but a strategy proposed by the neoconservatives in the Bush administration that echoed the Israeli interest too.[5] Nathan E. Busch states that Iran viewed nuclear weapons as a means of deterring US and Israeli attacks and this was a "major motivation after the US-led invasion of Iraq in 2003."[6] The international community watched America pursue its unilateral and aggressive foreign policy in Iraq and did nothing about it. Nuclear weapons seemed to be the answer to all this. Thus, after over three years of negotiations with Britain, France, and Germany, in 2005, Iran once again declared that it would never stop its uranium enrichment program.[7] Although in 2007 the American National Intelligence Estimate (NIE) reported that Iran had suspended its nuclear weapons program as early as 2003,[8] Iran did not declare it then or even in 2007 when the information was revealed. To comprehend the US intelligence report, Leonard Spector provides an analysis of the situation Iran may have been in during 2003. He states that there are several phases in the weapons program – designing the weapon, enriching uranium or plutonium, assembling the weapon, and possessing the delivery systems. According to him, Iran may have stopped the weaponization part – meaning designing the weapon – from 2003, even though enrichment of uranium was still going on. He further argues that no one really knows how far the bomb design was developed in Iran by 2003. Tehran may have developed it already by 2003 since the designing started in 1985.[9] In fact, even the NIE reports indicate that until fall 2003 "Iranian military entities were working under government direction to develop nuclear weapons."[10] While from 2002 onwards Iran allowed some inspections because disallowing it involved political costs, Spector argues that this may have been a function of the fact that it had finished the weapons designing work since Tehran received the blueprints from A. Q. Khan long ago.[11] Other reports suggest, in August 2004 after the suspension agreement with the European states broke down, Iran began a large trial run to convert 37 tons of U3O8 into Uranium Hexafluoride (UF) 6, and by October of that year, IAEA reported that Iran "had fed 22.5 tons of the 37 tons of yellowcake in the process line, producing approximately two tons of UF4 and 17.5 tons of intermediate uranium products and waste, without any UF6 production."[12] By 2006, Iran had appeared on a collision track with the US. In the same year the IAEA reported that Iran did not suspend its uranium enrichment program which could very well be used for making a bomb. Patrick Cronin states that

> Tehran's nuclear program, which had been dialed back during seesawing negotiations with the European states of Britain, France, and Germany, accelerated in 2006 and 2007, hastening the time when Iran would have to make a final decision – assuming it had not already done so – about whether to acquire a nuclear weapon.[13]

Iran has ignored UN Security Council sanctions, "responded with a rhetorical broadside, accompanied by steps to accelerate its uranium enrichment program."[14] Iran's new hardliner President Mahmoud Ahmadinejad who came to power in 2005 announced in April 2006 that Iran had developed the capability to enrich uranium.[15] The US–Iran relation saw a new setback after he took over the regime. His hard-line rhetoric against the US and Israel, along with his determination to move along with Tehran's nuclear activity, made Iran's relationship with the US even more hostile. While his anti-US attitude must be highlighted, as the evidence suggests Iran seemed bent on developing a fast-paced nuclear program well around the beginning of 2000 when actually a moderate leader, President Kahtami, was in power. Additionally, the person who decides to make nuclear weapons is not the president of Iran, but the Supreme leader, Khameini. So even if Ahmadinejad authorizes, the final approval comes from Khameini.[16] The Americans repeatedly warned Iran of military confrontation in the event that its resolve to build bombs continued. Today tension continues between them as Iran remains defiant with respect to the nuclear issue and America moves closer to much harsher sticks, even a military strike, against Iran. Interestingly, even with the change of the American administration in 2009, America is still not ruling out the military strike option to stop Iran from acquiring nuclear weapons, if other options – including direct talks – fail.[17] Iranian leadership still insists that America needs to address all issues[18] that led to this conflict in order to move on with talks to suspend Tehran's nuclear program.

US foreign and security policies since 2000 affecting Iran's nuclear decisions

Although Iran would have proliferated in the course of time due to its conflict engagements, unless of course conflicts were terminated, what is unfortunate is that the American administration's aggressive foreign policies since 2001 made Tehran's proliferation course more determined and faster. Most of the George W. Bush administration's security policies since 2001 were aggressive, threatening, and directed towards Iran, along with states like Iraq and North Korea. Thus, they directly impacted Iran's nuclear behavior.

The change of US administration in 2001

It is widely acknowledged by the war theorists that territorial conflict states are more war-prone compared to non-territorial ones.[19] Thus, there was no real reason for the US to wage a war on Iran in the 1990s because the Iran–US conflict was over non-territorial issues. With the change of the American administration in 2000, this line of thinking had changed. The Bush administration along with his neo-conservative policy-making circle viewed the world threats differently and, consequently, considered an entirely new line of responses that had to be taken to address them. Military strikes seemed to be the most effective strategy to combat rogue states and their proliferation proclivities. In 2003, the US sent signals to countries like Iran that it would wage wars on countries similar to Iraq – anti-western or trying to violate global security norms. Iran was obviously threatened with the possibility of being the next target in the region. In 2006, General Yahya Rahim Safavi the Islamic Revolution Guard Corps Commander-in-Chief stated,

> In the last 27 years the Islamic Republic of Iran has always been at the center point of the political, economic, and even military confrontations of the West and at present, Islamic Iran enjoys a geopolitical heavyweight [sic] in the region. . . . The current century is going to be the century of the nations overcoming dictatorial and dependent governments, and it will be the era of face to face clash with the global arrogance.[20]

These are interesting statements because they reflect on what unilateralism of the US has done to revolutionary countries such as Iran that want to stand up on their own and decide on their courses of action by themselves. A country that has hundreds of years of civilization is unlikely to tolerate humiliation and insult from a big power. Thus, Iranian leaderships argue that they want to relieve the nation of the burden of hundreds of years of humiliation. They contend that "this nation is proud and powerful but it has been kept behind."[21] This talk of humiliation and keeping them behind mostly come from the double standard US has proved in its foreign policy pertaining to Iran over the decades. More specifically, since 2001 Iran has been attacked by US foreign policy-makers from different fronts, which demonstrated one salient point: that Iran is an irresponsible and rogue state which is incapable of being a regional power. This has not only humiliated Iran, but has made it more adamant to confront the US and, as an extension, the rest of the international community that wants Iran to comply with its nuclear commitments. Ali Larijani stated,

The United States policy has consistently pursued a policy of denying Iran the chance to turn into a major power on the one hand and a regional power on the other. . . . The political backbone of these [European Union-3] demands deals with the fact that in the contemporary Middle Eastern political structure, Iran does not acquiesce to American wishes. . . . Iranian acquisition of power is related to the natural talent of Iranians in a fundamentally new way, an Islamic way of life and the logic of Iran's geo-politics and geo-economics.[22]

9/11 attacks and its aftermath

The 9/11 attacks were also responsible for the introduction of a new line of strategies to combat new and unknown threats. After the attacks, a paranoid US administration made efforts to find connection between Al Qaeda and every single state that was hostile to the Americans. Given the surprise and unacceptable terror attacks on the US, it was not unlikely on the part of the state to act aggressively and try to find ways to retaliate against the enemy at every opportune moment. Unfortunately, but as expected, such was the situation in the US administration. The already hawkish Republicans that doubted the Islamic fundamentalists from the start of this rule, decided not to leave any stone unturned where there was smell of a linkage with the terrorists. Even where there was no linkage, they tried to create and hypothetically assume one based on the level of hostility the state projected or was likely to have towards the US. Washington alleged that the Iranian regime had sponsored Middle Eastern terror and that it had connections with Al Qaeda.[23] Although this remained the American perspective, Roger Howard argues that right after the 9/11 attacks, Iranian authorities made serious efforts to clamp down on any Al Qaeda presence in the country and in early 2002 according to the Iranian Republic News Agency (IRNA) Tehran had arrested 150 people suspected of having connections to the Al Qaeda movement and just about two months later a senior intelligence officer of Iran went to West Europe to share information on Al Qaeda to his counterpart.[24] While this does not prove that Iran was a friendly country for the US in the Middle East, it highlights that even Iran tried to sympathize with the Americans on the 9/11 attacks and help them in any way possible to eradicate that kind of terrorism. However, this did not convince the Americans that the Iranians were not connected to Al Qaeda. America has always tried to see Iran using a different lens, that which portrays Iran as a state that sponsors terrorism. It is not unnatural for Washington to look at Iran that way, given Iran's connections with the Hezbollah, a Lebanon-based organization, supported financially, militarily, and morally by the Iranians, which orchestrates suicide bombings and terror attacks on Israeli and US targets. Thus, although to Tehran Hezbollah is a political movement enjoying respect within the Lebanese society, for Washington and Tel Aviv it is a terrorist organization. Also, because Iran supports this terrorist organization, in the eyes of Washington, Tehran is a state that supports terror activities.

There is no question that the 9/11 attacks on the US brought about a new urgency and readiness to take bigger risks by the administration pertaining to the rogue states. Immediately after the attacks, President Bush made decisions to focus American response to the attacks both on terrorism and those who harbor the terrorists.[25] Iran was automatically part of this thinking. Sverre Lodgaard states,

> The relationship between the US and Iran is highly politicized and adversarial. The animosity towards the Ayatollas is bi-partisan. No country is more difficult for the United States to engage diplomatically than Iran. Insert Iran's nuclear program into this adversarial relationship and it has turned even more confrontational – especially so since the program happened to surface in a fundamentally new international context driven by 9/11 and a much more assertive US policy. Nobody in Iran – and nobody else – could have envisaged that. It was a historical coincidence of sorts.[26]

Thus the conflict setting between Washington and Tehran became much more confrontational within the context of the new environment that 9/11 had created.

The anxiety for the American administration was that if the same terrorists who used planes to crash into the World Trade Center (WTC) and the Pentagon had hands on nuclear weapons, they would not hesitate to use them at any point in time. Thus, promoting non-proliferation policies more effectively became more important to the US at that juncture. Rogue states were of serious concern to the US since the 1990s because of their anti-western stance, non-democratic political institutions, and their inclination to possess WMDS including nuclear weapons and missiles and Iran was one of the declared rogue states as already discussed in the previous chapter. After 9/11, it was believed that rogue states would continue to proliferate and may help terrorists by providing them with nuclear weapons since both groups of state and non-state actors shared one common enemy – the US. It was also felt that democracy, which breeds peace, is ultimately the key to achieving the non-proliferation goals. Thus, the US administration was of the opinion that as a hegemonic state, which had major responsibilities toward maintaining peace and stability in the world and also wanted to eliminate its own enemies, it may need to wage wars on the rogue states that proliferate and do not change their dictatorial political institutions. Interestingly, it was never clear why the US singled out Iran's track record for condemnation when some of its regional allies such as Saudi Arabia allowed their citizens far less democratic freedom.[27] This clearly portrayed a double standard in the US foreign policy-making. Unconcerned about how the Iranians felt about such double standards, America went on with its new plans to democratize its non-allies in the Middle East, namely Iraq, Iran, and Syria, with whatever military strategy worked. Within this offing, Bush offended some of these rogue states with his "Axis of Evil" speech in 2002, which made the relationship between Iran and US even more confrontational. However, prior to that the US proposed means to combat rogue states and protect itself from rogue states' missile attacks.

Rogue states and the national missile defense program

In early 2000, the American administration focused on developing a missile shield to protect the Americans from rogue states' nuclear-tipped missile attacks. To this end in 2001 the US unilaterally abrogated the Anti-Ballistic Missile (ABM) Treaty of 1972, which was the cornerstone of nuclear deterrence between the two superpowers in the cold war years. The US needed a new threat to justify the development of its most advanced National Missile Defense system when the Soviet threat disappeared from the scene of international politics. The best way to deal with the issue was to identify some states as "rogues" that were not only violators of international norms, anti-western, and non-democratic, but were also developing their long-range missiles. To the American leadership the central point was that regional security concerns should not have driven the development of long-range missiles by these countries. Instead they should have been more interested in "quality development" of missiles. Given this, it was not hard on the part of the US to identify some states with the potential to target the US. It was believed to be their intention to hit the US and this apparently made sense in the context of the development of their long-range missiles and nuclear ambitions. The National Missile Defense (NMD) is a system that would protect the US from any external attack from states with long-range missiles. It was the intention of the US to protect all 50 states from a limited attack of the long-range missiles of the states of concern. The idea was that the attacks might consist of a couple of warheads, which could be supported by simple penetration aids. In order to counter such attacks the initial idea was that the system would have 100 ground-based interceptors stationed in Alaska. These ground-based and space-based interceptors would detect and track the incoming warheads.[28] Although the Clinton administration started this program, George W. Bush reaffirmed his commitment to the Missile Defense System during his first address to the nation immediately after taking the White House and said that he would make sure that the US was not weak in the face of its adversarial challenges.[29] His NMD program has been much more comprehensive, structured, and expensive. Interestingly, Iraq, Iran, and North Korea have been the target states due to their preoccupation with long-range missiles.

Iran's strategic ambitions and missile proliferation have raised new challenges for post-cold war US foreign policy. The Islamic Republic of Iran had started focusing on its long-range missiles in the mid-1990s, which are known as Shehab 3 and Shehab 4.[30] Its 1350 km range Shehab missile test in 1998 sent mixed signals to the West. It was believed then that Shehab 4 could have a range of 1940 km. The US has been concerned about the test but expected it nonetheless since it believed by then that the Iranians were going to develop missiles with even longer ranges and such tests proved that. This also gave Washington enough reason to focus on its own NMD program. Iran has received assistance from China, Russia, and North Korea for its long-range missile development. However, it is believed that Iran's missiles do not resemble the Chinese counterpart.[31] Iran possesses the 300 km range Scud-B and 500 km Scud-C missiles and is able to strike targets in Iraq and other Middle Eastern states. Its 1000 km *No-Dong* missile was acquired from North Korea which allowed it to target Israel for the first time.[32] The problem that Iran seems to have created, intentionally or not, is that it appears to be motivated to acquire long-range missiles more than anything else. Consequently, it can be argued that where

96 Case study: Iran

Iran seems less interested in improving the accuracy and numbers of its missiles and more focused on increasing their ranges, it must have something to do with its desire to target the West at some point in the life of the enduring rivalry. Thus, developing the NMD was the best solution to the problems these troubled states had created for the US.

Unfortunately, instead of decreasing the incentives to proliferate, NMD enhanced rogue states' propensity to proliferate. With NMD primarily focused on protecting the US from these states, the US has explicitly made itself an international enemy of these rogue states. Why should rogue states' incentives to proliferation be increased by NMD? First, these are states with strong reasons to acquire nuclear weapons in response to regional protracted conflicts, and in some cases, asymmetric conflicts with the US as well. Where the US believes that arms control cannot provide protection against actual threats, why should regional protracted conflict states believe in nuclear arms control which might cost them their regional security? Their past nuclear behaviors confirm this line of argument. Second, these states have been NPT violators; all are signatories, yet all made efforts to build nuclear weapons. NMD, a system that believes that these states will be potential proliferators, by default allows the rogues to acquire nuclear weapons. This does not mean that the US wants them to go nuclear, but that the NMD itself believes in the probability of their nuclear weapons acquisition. Third, the US, by not thinking about the nuclear arms race and focusing on strengthening its own security through NMD, had advocated realist belief in the present world. The non-proliferation agenda automatically lost its appeal where the world's only superpower was focusing on enhancing its own power and security in the otherwise peaceful and non-threatening world. States foreswear nuclear weapons when they see progress along the same lines at the superpower level. Finally, America's extensive unilateral economic, military, and diplomatic sanctions have already isolated the target countries from the US. NMD, by making a distinction between rogues and non-rogues, created additional inequality in the state system. The security needs of the rogue states increased due to this unequal treatment. The rogues became more anti-western, something that the US could avoid.[33]

It seemed obvious that a US NMD would provide additional impetus for Iran to refocus on its nuclear weapons program. Iran has expressed its dissatisfaction with the nuclear double standard of the West in general and the US in particular and it has tried to stand up to the US. The NPT proved to be weak due to the development of NMD, and Iran took advantage of this weakness. If the US can provide lip service to the world pertaining to nuclear disarmament and arms control, then why can Iran, a country threatened by regional and global power, not say one thing and do another? This was the opportune moment such countries have been waiting for. After all, the real world has always been about securing states and defending oneself from external aggression, being prepared for the next war. If the world's greatest power was securing itself from really no threat, why would Iran not imitate it when it had serious security concerns? Such strategic thinking shrouded Iran at the time, impacting the pace of proliferation.

The Axis of Evil

Unfortunately, the US's overt hostility towards the rogue states did not end with the decision to develop NMD. The antagonism between Washington and Tehran had increased since Iran was included as a member of an "Axis of Evil" states by President George W. Bush in his State of the Union address in January 2002.[34] In addition to his anti-Iran rhetoric, his infamous "Axis of Evil" speech made even moderate Iranian leaders like President Khatami furious. In this speech, Bush called Iran, Iraq, and North Korea the new "Axis of Evil" states, which were America's new concerns and needed addressing. America believed that these states were "arming to threaten the peace of the world" and thereby posed "a grave and growing danger to the United States."[35] At that time some in the American administration felt that the removal of the Iranian government should be prioritized over the toppling of Saddam's regime.[36] This obviously meant Washington was considering retaliation against Iran if it did not accept the dictates of the US. This was perceived by the Iranians as an antagonistic policy. In Afghanistan, Iranians used their good offices in relation to Northern Alliance, but it got nothing in return. The current Constitution in Afghanistan also got shape with the help of Iran. That cooperation, rather than bringing in American goodwill, brought the "Axis of Evil" speech in 2002, which the Iranians saw as a betrayal of Iranian goodwill.[37] This is typical in any intractable conflict relation, as stated in Chapter 2. The enemy image remains the same even when the enemy projects a different face. Although Iran was making an effort to help the US, America could not consider the Islamic Republic as a friendly state or change its policies overnight.

The Bush administration introduced the Nuclear Posture Review (NPR) in January 2002. NPR called for a triad which would include more offensive nuclear weapons, advanced conventional weapons, and anti-ballistic missile systems to better protect the US in the changed world environment.[38] One of the most controversial and debated parts of the triad was the development of mini-nuclear weapons or low-yield and "improved earth penetrating weapons to counter the increased use by potential adversaries of hardened and deeply buried facilities."[39] The Pentagon envisioned using these weapons in a preemptive attack to destroy hard bunkers of the sort used by Iraq and perhaps North Korea. It also planned on using nuclear weapons against a list of targeted states including North Korea, Iraq, and Iran – members of the Axis of Evil – along with Syria, Libya, Russia, and China. The situations when to use them were also specified: an Iraqi attack on Israel or its neighbors, a North Korean attack against South Korea, or a military confrontation over the status of Taiwan. It also proposed to use these weapons against chemical and biological weapons attacks. Bush's 2002 National Security Strategy (NSS) explicitly stated that the administration aims to establish military primacy: "Our forces will be strong enough to dissuade potential adversaries from pursuing a military buildup in hopes of surpassing, or equaling, the power of the United States."[40] The Bush administration had already started down this road by announcing its preemptive strike policy, incorporated into the NSS of the US in the fall of 2002. Additionally, the National Strategy to Combat Weapons of Mass Destruction

(NSWMD) which was issued in December 2002 noted that WMD in the hands of state and non-state actors posed the greatest threat to US national security and that an effective strategy to combat them was an integral component of the NSS of the US.[41] NPR, NSS, and NSWMD comprised the new US nuclear posture. The NPR also discussed "defeating hard and deeply buried targets" (HDBT) and stated, "Nuclear weapons could be employed against targets able to withstand non-nuclear attack (for example, deep underground bunkers or bio-weapon facilities)."[42] Defeating HDBT became an important mission of the Bush administration within the context of the terrorist attacks and also to justify the development and deployment of new nuclear weapons in an otherwise calm post-cold war world.

Scholars argue that the NSWMD announced in December of 2002 was "wise in some places" and "dangerously radical" in others. The radicals of the US administration believed that nuclear weapons possession was not the problem, but that the "bad guys" that possessed them were. As George Perkovich states,

> Rejecting the fundamental premise of the NPT, these officials seek not to create an equitable global regime that actively devalues nuclear weapons and creates conditions for their eventual elimination, but rather to eradicate the bad guys or their weapons while leaving the "good guys" free of nuclear constraints.[43]

He further argues that proliferation problem should stem from the possession of nuclear weapons, not from merely the intentions of the Axis of Evil states.[44] This clearly indicates that the states were discriminated against by the US. These were targeted not because they made efforts to acquire nuclear weapons or possessed ballistic missiles, but because they have been anti-western in their attitude and orientations. The radicals of the administration made matters worse by arguing that the rogue states and the terrorists cannot be contained or deterred, and thus they need to be eliminated. These sent alarming messages to states like Iran that have been anti-western and have supported the Islamic militants such as Hezbollah in Lebanon. Iran has vehemently protested against the new strategy of the US. In a letter to the United Nations Secretary General, the Iranian foreign ministry spokesman Hamid Reza Assefi quoted the foreign minister who stated that, "US threats are a flagrant violation of its commitments to the (nuclear) non-proliferation Treaty and go against the guarantees given by US officials."[45] Moreover, the administration's focus on tactical uses of nuclear weapons increased the motivations of the targeted states "to improve or extend their own force, or to get one if they don't have it."[46] A firm response to the NPR was given by Ali Akbar Hashemi Rafsanjani who accused the US of trying to frighten regional states into submission. He told the IRNA, "America thinks that if a military threat looms large over the head of these seven countries, they will give up their logical demands."[47] Iranians are proud as a nation and unlikely to accept unfair policies, especially from the US.

The US has contemplated attacking Iran for the suspicion that it is developing nuclear weapons. Iran is a signatory of the NPT and as of 2006 resumed developing its uranium enrichment program. While Iran claims that its nuclear program is exclusively for civilian energy purposes, which is permitted under article IV of the NPT, the US and some of its allies have been increasingly of the opinion that Iran's program is structured for a dual purpose. Even the European intelligence and the IAEA agreed that Iran is intent on developing the bombs. Iran has been a signatory to the NPT since 1968 which allows it to enrich uranium for civilian fuel programs only. However, from 2000 to 2002, for 18 months Iran concealed its enrichment activities from the IAEA inspectors, making the international community more suspicious of its real intentions pertaining to the enrichment programs. For an extended period it failed to meet the safeguard obligations with the IAEA and the US contends that Iran violated articles II and III of the NPT, which prohibit nuclear weapon states to transfer these weapons or components to non-nuclear weapon states and non-nuclear states to receive them in any manner respectively. In April 2006, Iran's controversial President Mahmoud Ahmadinejad announced that Iran joined "the club of nuclear countries" by mastering the entire nuclear fuel cycle and being able to enrich uranium for power stations.[48] The concern of the US is that if Iran can master enrichment to fuel grade, it can master enrichment to weapons grade because the processes of mastering are the same. Estimates on how long it would take for Iran to make a nuclear bomb range from a couple of years to a decade. According to the International Institute of Strategic Studies (IISS), Iran will be able to produce enough nuclear materials in three years. Just as there is disagreement between the US and its allies on the time that will be required for Iran to produce nuclear weapons, there is also disagreement between them with regard to what measures – diplomacy, sanctions, or military action – should be taken to prevent the country from acquiring the devastating weapons. Seymour Hersh wrote in 2006 that although publicly the Bush administration is focusing on diplomacy to resolve the issue, covertly it is planning a military attack on the country to not only crush its nuclear weapons program, but also to change the regime in power.[49] This news has been disappointing for the reformers in Iran because they feel that people in Iran can change the political system from within. Human rights journalist Akbar Ganji argues that the Iranian society will be able to have a peaceful transition to democracy. In fact, he is of the opinion that Iran is the only country in the Middle East that has the social fabric for democratization because moderation is there.[50]

Iran fits perfectly within the new nuclear posture framework of the US that laid out details of which countries need to be attacked preemptively with nuclear weapons and why. Both the NPR and NSWMD promise to respond to a WMD threat with nuclear weapons. Iran has been identified as an Axis of Evil state that was clandestinely building nuclear weapons and that was hostile towards the US, its interests, and its allies. The bipartisan 9/11 Commission also determined that Iran has connections with Al Qaeda. The fact that Iran had been declared in non-compliance with the NPT made it legal for the US to use nuclear weapons against Iran. Prior to the revelation of the new intelligence report in December 2007 that Iran had actually capped its nuclear weapons program in 2003,[51] the Bush administration was seriously contemplating a preemptive war against Iran with the usage of nuclear weapons.

100 Case study: Iran

Interestingly, Iran and Egypt were two key states that were against the indefinite renewal of NPT in 1995, as discussed in Chapter 5. To get them to support NPT's indefinite extension, during this intensive negotiation period prior to the NPT extension, the US reiterated its negative security assurance to the non-nuclear weapon states in 1995. The text of the 1995 negative security assurance of the US reads:

> The United States reaffirms that it will not use nuclear weapons against non-nuclear weapon states parties to the Treaty on the non-proliferation of nuclear weapons except in the case of an invasion or any other attack on the United States, its territories, its armed forces or other troops, its allies, or on a state towards which it has a security commitment, carried out or sustained by such a non-nuclear weapon state in association or alliance with a nuclear weapon state.[52]

Additionally, with respect to security assurance within the NPT, it was concluded in 1995 that "further steps should be considered to assure the non-nuclear weapon states party to the Treaty against the use or threat of use of nuclear weapons. These steps could take the form of an internationally legally binding instrument."[53] What is more intriguing is that the 1995 NPT extension also notes that

> attacks or threats of attack on nuclear facilities devoted to peaceful purposes jeopardize nuclear safety and raise serious concerns regarding the application of international law on the use of force in such cases, which could warrant appropriate action in accordance with the provisions of the Charter of the United Nations.[54]

Given this, no responsible state, not to speak of the US – a democracy and consequently a responsible actor – should contemplate launching a nuclear attack on a non-nuclear state. However, instead of abiding by these norms and respecting its own commitments, the US had decided to break the commitments, ignoring the ramifications of its decision for the Treaty or legal norms within that.

A revolutionary Iran is obviously unwilling to fulfill the commitments of a Treaty that is not respected by the world's greatest power. The faith in the Treaty along with the trust in the concept of the non-proliferation system was lacking after this. Iran understood that nuclear guarantees were false and that it had to protect its interests even if that meant defying the world and disrespecting the norms. As a result of this, its proliferation propensity became much more aggressive and it relentlessly pursued the program.

America's war on Iraq in 2003

The war on Iraq by the US removed Saddam Hussein from power, which was something the Iranians have been looking forward to since at least the Iran–Iraq War. The war and its consequence should have made the Iranians happy and secure, yet they seemed most disturbed with the situation in Iraq. Some points must be noted here. First, although the general conception is that with the removal of Saddam Hussein, Iran's security threats emanating from Iraq are over, in reality that is not the case. Iran's conflict with Iraq was not over who rules Iraq, the regime type, or with Saddam in particular – although Saddam's ruthless militant actions always made Iran insecure – but over territorial issues, which remain unresolved even though Iraq has a new regime now. Thus, the Iran–Iraq protracted conflict is far from over, although some argue that "conflict with Iraq is over" just because Saddam is out.[55] Second, the insecurity that the aftermath of the war presented in Iraq is more threatening for Iran than it was when Saddam was in power. This has more to do with the "transition to power stage" in Iraq than with other traditional conflict issues. Iran was particularly threatened because

> clashing forces challenge a fledging government whose future remains uncertain. Foreign forces are at once part of a solution and a problem in the eyes of Gulf States, which agree on the objectives but not necessarily the means of stabilizing Iraq. No one expects an early end to Iraq's insurgency or to sectarian political violence, whether because of a US "surge" or a potential US disengagement.[56]

Meir Javedanfar states that as far as Iranians are concerned, Saddam is gone, but pro-American government is in Iraq. Also Sunni militants and Al Qaeda view Iran as an enemy. Thus, if Al Qaeda wins in Iraq it will be more threatening for Iran.[57] Third, the presence of the US in Iraq and along Iran's border itself poses enormous threat to Tehran that has an enduring rivalry with Washington. While most of the Gulf States wanted the US to play a leading role in supporting and establishing the new Iraqi government, Iran called on the US to leave Iraq.[58] For Iran, the US was the greatest threat at the time and withdrawing US troops from Iraq became an important agenda. Because that was unlikely to happen in the very near future, deterring America from taking aggressive moves against Iran became important. The desire to acquire a nuclear weapon became much stronger as a result of this. Ray Takeyh states that

> with Saddam gone, America has emerged as the foremost strategic problem for Iran and the primary driver of its nuclear weapons policy. The Bush Doctrine, which pledges the pre-emptive use of force as a tool of counter-proliferation, combined with the substantial augmentation of American military power on Iran's periphery, has intensified Tehran's fears of "encirclement" by the United States – or even worse, of being its next target.[59]

Fourth, America's projection of power in Iraq and Afghanistan itself was extremely threatening for Iran. Washington proved that it was the dominant power in the world that could pursue aggressive foreign and security policies wherever it wished and other major powers in the world or the United Nations had no power to stop it from implementing its war plans. The powerlessness of the United Nations was

102 Case study: Iran

threatening to a weak regional state engaged in an enduring rivalry with the world's greatest power. After all, the United Nations is a security umbrella for the weaker states in the international system more than the stronger ones. The incapacity of the major powers in rallying around "a no-war idea" effectively also alarmed Iran that it was expected to be the next target of the Bush administration's war plans. America did what it wanted. Consequently, Iran had to prepare itself for an attack by its long-running adversary. Scholars argue that because of the "projection of US power in Afghanistan and Iraq, the case for achieving a nuclear deterrent has become measurably more compelling."[60] Reformist politician Mostafa Tajazadeh stated on the eve of the US invasion of Iraq, "It is a matter of equilibrium. If I don't have a nuclear bomb, I don't have security."[61] Although other forms of non-conventional weapons could act as deterrents against a possible attack from the US, Saddam's chemical weapons did not stop an adamant America from pursuing its war plans. Thus, chemical weapons are not effective deterrents when they have already been used. The taboo on the usage has been lifted as far as these weapons are concerned. Rather, "Operation Iraqi Freedom" has provided Iran with the necessary lessons. The Iranian leadership noticed "that Saddam's much-bruited repositories of chemical weapons did not prove a deterrent against an American president determined to effect regime change."[62] Therefore, the value attached to nuclear weapons could not be undermined. According to an Iranian official, "The fact that Saddam was toppled in twenty-one days is something that should concern all countries in the region."[63] Only the acquisition of nuclear weapons could deter the US from launching an attack against Iran in a similar way. Finally, the double standard in US foreign policy was unacceptable to the Iranians. While Iraq was a threat to Iran, it was unfair to allow Israel to acquire nuclear weapons capability and disallow the same to Iraq or Iran. Similarly, India and Pakistan got away with their nuclear proliferation yet Iraq was being attacked for making efforts to acquire the same capabilities. Some Iranians even argue that if Washington wants regional powers to not possess nuclear weapons, then it should forgo its own weapons. Amir Mohebian states, "The Americans say in order to preserve the peace for [their] children, [they] should have nuclear weapons and [we] should not."[64] Treaties and norms are for all to follow and no state should be privileged in the system of sovereign states. As George Perkovich states,

> real security against weapons of mass destruction requires all relevant states and individuals to enforce vigorously the treaties, rules, laws, and procedures that have been established to outlaw chemical and biological weapons and to contain, and ultimately eliminate, the threats posed by nuclear arsenals.[65]

These points need to be underscored to understand why Iran seemed more determined in enriching its uranium during this period and why the drive was so relentless. The other reason that may have motivated Iran more to acquire nuclear weapons in the post-2003 period is that Iran knew that in the absence of Saddam, if the Americans left, the Iranians would dominate Iraq and even the Arabs fear that.[66] Akbar Ganji argues that "empires of the past happened through expansion of territory; now it is with nuclear weapons."⁶⁷ In the regional context, Iran's unrelenting drive during this period could be associated with this.

Iran also fully understands how important the Gulf region is to the US for oil supplies and what the dominant power of the world can do to control this part of the world for its energy interests. The war on Iraq was primarily waged for that, which made Iran more apprehensive about the intentions of America. Another part of the explanation is physical control of oil supplies. One-third of the world's oil supplies flows through the Strait of Hormuz, and to keep it flowing has been the bedrock of US foreign policy for more than 50 years. Mossadeq was overthrown partly because of his affinity to the Iranian communist party (the Tudeh party), and partly because of his plans to nationalize the Iranian oil industry. The Shah's unswerving commitment to free flow of Iranian oil became a central pillar of the Nixon doctrine.⁶⁸ In his final State of the Union address, President Carter declared,

> Any attempt by any outside force to gain control of the Persian Gulf region will be regarded as an assault on the vital interests of the United States of America, and such an assault will be repelled by any means necessary, including military force.⁶⁹

The Reagan administration said the same thing and began establishing military establishments/bases in Saudi Arabia. In 1990, when Saddam had occupied Kuwait, Secretary of Defense Cheney stated, "We're there because the fact of the matter is that part of the world controls the world supply of oil, and whoever controls the supply of oil will have a stranglehold on the American economy."⁷⁰ In fact, today's geopolitics is primarily about energy supplies and energy security. The US has occupied Iraq and keeps a military presence in Afghanistan; has a number of bases in the Gulf region, including new ones in Iraq to replace those that were lost in Saudi Arabia; and deploys carrier groups in the vicinity of the Gulf. It holds the region in a tight military grip. A nuclear-armed Iran could question the credibility of that military dominance, however.⁷¹ Therein lies one of the greatest fears of the US, which Iran understands well. Consequently, it acts to undo such US hegemonic ambition in the region.

Tehran perceived acute security threats in the post-2000 period. Its fast-paced nuclear weapons program was a function of the adverse security environment it faced. Michael Levi argues that Iran "would not be where it is today" if 9/11, the war on Iraq, and the Axis of Evil speech never happened.⁷² From Tehran's perspective they helped the US in setting up the provisional Afghan government after the fall of Taliban, an assistance which even President Clinton admitted.⁷³ Unfortunately, soon after Iran was blamed for helping the terrorists and was called an Axis of Evil state, even though the Iranians were not creating trouble. Consequently, the Iranians felt that "America can't be trusted."⁷⁴ This deficit of trust is a typical attribute of a long-running conflict. Referring to the feelings and understandings of the Iranians, Shaul Bakhash states that on the nuclear issue they feel, "We suspended enrichment for two years – look what happened?"⁷⁵ No matter how hard they try, nothing will be enough as long as the US maintains a double standard in its foreign policy. The turbulent region also posed security predicaments as did the presence of the US along Iran's border. Spector states that the US presence in Iraq was extremely threatening to Iran and within that context he argues that it is difficult to believe that Iran halted its nuclear weapons program for the presence of US forces in Iraq. Rather, he believes that this could be a "tactical ploy to avoid the international pressure" to stop the program.[76] In fact, even before the US contemplated waging a war on Iran for continuing with its nuclear program, Iran was fearful of such a possibility. If the war in Iraq was successful and the US had planned an effective exit policy prior to getting engaged in the battle, the US would have moved towards Iran for regime change and non-proliferation purposes. After all, to the US Iran, Iraq, and North Korea all fell into the same category, which Iran was fully aware of. In fact, the updated version of the US NSS of March 2006 enhanced the focus on Iran as the next possible target of regime change. The document has a preface signed by the President, the first words of which are "America is at war." It names seven oppressive regimes: North Korea, Iran, Syria, Cuba, Belarus, Burma, and Zimbabwe. Out of these, two – Iran and Syria – are singled out because they continue to harbor terrorists at home and sponsor terrorist activities abroad. One of them – Iran – also tries to acquire nuclear weapons. However, the concerns with Iran are much broader: "It threatens Israel, seeks to thwart Middle East peace, disrupts democracy in Iraq, and denies the aspirations of its people for freedom. The conclusion is that Iran presents the single greatest threat to the United States."[77] The US forces were already stationed in the region and it would simply take a decision to wage another war in the region and nothing more to attack Iran. Gareth Porter argues that the Iranian leadership was convinced that the Bush administration was planning to move against Iran after toppling Saddam Hussein in Iraq, and thus proposed in April 2003 to negotiate with the US over the issues that according to the administration were the basis for its hostile attitude toward Tehran: "its nuclear program, its support for Hezbollah and other anti-Israeli armed groups, and its hostility to Israel's existence."[78] Tehran offered concrete, substantive concessions on those issues. But it is believed that on the advice of US Vice President Dick Cheney and Secretary of Defense Donald Rumsfeld, Bush refused to respond to the negotiating proposal. Nuclear weapons were not, seemingly, the primary US concern about Iran. In the hierarchy of the administration's interests, the denial of legitimacy to the Islamic Republic trumped a deal that could provide assurances against an Iranian nuclear weapon.

According to Iran, the US did not pursue its policy of engaging in wars to promote and proliferate democracy and non-proliferation ideals in Iran because the war in Iraq was highly unsuccessful from the very beginning and the US became unpopular in the world for that. Iranian journalist Najmeh Bozorgmehr asserted that the Iranians have been convinced that they have to do something to show the US "we can give you a hard time" to induce the Bush administration to negotiate.[79] Along the same lines, Trita Parsi argued that the prevailing view among Iranian officials after the 2003 US rejection of diplomacy was that they had to have the capability to inflict some pain on the US in order to get their attention.[80] Farideh Farhi argues that Iran "wants its strategic weight," "to enhance its status," and the US to "get off its back."⁸¹ Similarly, Bozorgmehr argues that "Iran wants to bargain with the United States on Iran's regional role," as well as on removal of sanctions and assurances against US attack. Tehran has been looking for any source of leverage with which to bargain with the US on those issues, she says, and "enrichment has become a big bargaining chip."⁸² How enrichment of uranium is connected to bargaining on these issues is explicated by Farhi. She states that Iran is a "virtual nuclear power" by enriching uranium because in three months' time it can be a nuclear weapons state if it wants to take that path – which, according to her, Iran is not interested in taking if the issues are resolved and Iran obtains what it wants.⁸³ Iran needs security assurances from the US. It needs to know that it will not be attacked like Iraq.⁸⁴ Charles Ferguson argues that if the US gives Iran better concessions – a major player status in the Gulf region – that may be enough incentive for Iran to halt its nuclear program. It is stated that

> For Iran, the fact that the United States has led an international campaign to halt its 35-year-old nuclear energy development program – a program started with American blessing – is an affront to national pride. Indeed, the specter of violent military attacks on Iran from the United States or Israel if Iran does not stop uranium enrichment is met by defiance from Iran, where the enrichment program continues unabated. As Iran's U.N. ambassador, Javad Zarif declared before the United Nations Security Council on March 29, "Pressures and threats do not work for Iran. Iran is allergic to pressure and threats and intimidation." Consistent reports from Iran state that even Iranians who are opposed to their own government support continued nuclear energy development.⁸⁵

Akbar Ganji, Iran's preeminent political dissident, stated, "This [nuclear issue] is the only issue they [Iranian leadership] can gather more people to agree on."⁸⁶ Iran is tired of America's coercive foreign policies and the Iranians rally around the nuclear issue. Farhi argues that the country has been sanctioned for more than 20 years – which is economic coercion. Additionally, in the context of Iran–US talks she argues that "suspension of enrichment must come after negotiations," which she believes is "imposition and coercion."⁸⁷ Moreover, it is important to note here that the word suspension was not clearly stated by the US. United Nations Security Council (UNSC) Resolution calls states to suspend or shut down enrichment programs – which would produce plutonium. Charles Ferguson contends that "these machines are delicate. If they are stopped, they can crash and Iran would incur financial cost. Who would bear the cost?"⁸⁸ All these are important to comprehend. Iranians always understood that to avoid such coercion they had to stand up on their own and a strategic weapon would aid them in that.

The possibility that war could be waged was not ruled out by the leadership in Tehran. Consequently, some argued that if Iran continued to perceive threats due to regional instability and "Washington's (and Israel's) open advocacy of regime change," it was likely to "veer in the direction of nuclearization."⁸⁹ Iran had to work harder to ensure that the enrichment work went on and disclose it so that the US was deterred. "The focus was simply on the US and they [the Iranians] were obsessed

106 Case study: Iran

with the US"[90] at that time. Chains of revelations about Iran's nuclear program were made in 2005 and 2006, which demonstrated that "the regime's nuclear weapons program has accelerated in recent years."[91] Iran announced in April 2007 that it had made more progress towards installing 3,000 centrifuges in the underground enrichment plant at Natanz. However, it was believed that Iran would not be able to build a bomb with that before 2008 or 2009 because once a 3000-centrifuge enrichment plant operates effectively, Iran could only make a weapon with highly enriched uranium (enriched over 90 percent) within 9–11 months.[92]

Potential for reversing Iran's nuclear program

It is interesting that although regional rivalry should have been the primary concern of Iran, Michael Levi argues that after the invasion of Iraq in 2003, as far as the enemy hierarchy is concerned Iraq comes after the US and Israel remains at the bottom.[93] Thus, America needs to comprehend this seriously. What Washington fails to understand is that Tehran may be willing to renounce its nuclear program if the former makes concessions and changes the course of its foreign policies pertaining to the Middle East in general and Iran in particular. There are decision-makers in Iran who advocate a less confrontational policy pertaining to the US. For example, some argue that although Akbar Hashemi Rafsanjani and Ali Larijani are in agreement with the Iranian leadership about acquiring a nuclear weapons capability, they are still "willing to negotiate over the timing and they realize the benefits of normal international intercourse, both for Iran's commercial interests and for its relations with its Sunni neighbors."[94] Roger Howard is of the opinion that America

> would need to fit the issue into a wider Middle East picture and find ways of making Iran feel less threatened. In return for cessation of uranium enrichment, or for more effective guarantees that it would not be used for a weapons program, Washington could offer not only to lift all sanctions but also to drop calls for regime change and undertake not to meddle in Iran's domestic affairs; pull back its military presence in the region; and pressure Israel into surrendering or scaling down its nuclear arsenal. Israel talks about its defense against annihilation, but it might be such wider consequences of an Iranian nuclear program that it really fears.[95]

Farhi asserts that the Islamic Revolution was popular in Iran, which was also anti-American. It is part of the Iranian history. People who want to side with the US would be treated as anti-nationalists. Given this, the US has no one to talk to in Iran and it cannot mobilize people there against the Islamic Revolution or the regime. Thus, the "regime change fantasy" should be given up by the US.[96] This will create a setting stage for conflict resolution. In addition to projecting itself as a friendly state to Iran, the US needs to avoid having double standards in its foreign policy-making. What is fair for Israel should be fair for Iran or any other state in the Middle East. No state in today's interdependent world wants to be treated unfairly and feel left out. It is the natural right of all states to protect its sovereignty, keeping in mind not to jeopardize international peace and stability. A simple example explicates the fact that unless the Iran–US conflict is terminated, no negotiation will soften Iran's attitude on nuclear weapons program. In 2003, when the international community was alarmed about Iran's nuclear drive after the revelations, the first phase of negotiations started between Iran on the one hand and Britain, France, and Germany on the other. Iran agreed to sign and ratify the Additional Protocol and to suspend enriching uranium pending more negotiations. Europe understood Iran's right to develop peaceful nuclear energy and it promised to have more dialogue on regional peace and security. However, the negotiators "neglected the political context and ignored the core of the problem: the lack of trust, a consequence of a bitter political malaise between Iran and the US. Without sorting this problem out, any settlement of the nuclear dispute could be only temporary.[97] By 2004, the Iranians realized that they could not ratify the Protocol in the absence of an American guarantee that this was worth it. This is because by this time the Americans had already lost confidence on their European counterparts to succeed in this negotiation and almost clearly pointed to the fact that they would not be happy unless Iran dismantled its nuclear weapons program and it implicated regime change in Iran, which made Iran more concerned about its domestic and regional security.[98] Coming under IAEA's threat in November 2004, Iran agreed to temporarily suspend the enrichment and in exchange the Europeans agreed to begin serious negotiations to bring an end to the nuclear crisis and give Iran the right to resume its nuclear program under "objective guarantees" that the program is peaceful.[99] The talks made little headway with Iran objecting to permanent cessation of enrichment and the Europeans disliking the Iranian idea of limited enrichment activities. During this period America was also heavily involved with Iraq and Iran lost no opportunity to resist the agreement. With Ahmadinejad's coming to power Iran's insecurity pertaining to the US increased and Iran became more focused on its nuclear program, alarming the world. Thus, Ahmadinejad stated his strategy, "if you pull back they will push ahead, but if you stand against them, because of this resistance they will back off."[100] Sverre Lodgaard eloquently puts it, "US threatens Iran and Iran pushes its nuclear program with a long-term view to keeping outside powers from dictating and attacking it; and the United States in turn uses this to put additional pressure on the regime."[101] If this strategy continues, then new sanctions, which the United Nations might impose against Iran soon, will also not make any difference in changing Tehran's nuclear policy. In fact, some argue that sanctions have not hurt Iran much in the realm of proliferation. The US has made the cost of transactions high by asking banks not to do business with Iran. However, Iran has borders with about 15 countries, meaning sanctions will not work. "The cat has many places to hide."[102]

It is important to bear in mind that even though the 30-year-old protracted conflict started over ideological and hostage issues, over the years the conflict continued on many other issues, namely, Iran's support for terror groups and terrorism, development of missiles and nuclear weapons, and regime type, among others. Some argue that Iranians have a series of grievances against the US which go back to 1953 when the US got involved in the coup to overthrow Mossadeq and includes events such as the shooting down of an Iranian airliner by a US warship in 1988 as well as America's support for Iraq in the Iran–Iraq War.[103] "History of a very troubled relationship between the two countries" is what is important to discuss when discussing the nuclear issue.[104] Given this, resolving the long-running conflict dramatically is not possible. Thus, the first step for both parties would be to build confidence and trust. Ferguson raises an interesting point that is relevant in this context. He believes that the Americans have "short-term memories" while people in the Middle East have a "longer-term memory."[105] He further states, "A lot of Iranians feel a hate relationship with the US. With history behind us, there is a big level of distrust between us."[106] Thus, Karim Sadjadpour stressed that

> due to deep-seated mutual mistrust and hostility, a "Grand Bargain" to resolve all issues in one fell swoop is unrealistic; rather, the United States should attempt to build confidence with Iran on areas of overlapping interest, such as Iraq and Afghanistan. It is essential for the next U.S. president to probe whether a different approach could beget constructive changes in Tehran's strategic outlook.[107]

Direct bilateral communication is essential in building trust and confidence between the two actors. As Ferguson puts it, "You can have someone as an enemy, but you can still talk to them. The problem is that the US does not recognize the Islamic Republic of Iran."[108] With direct talks trust can be built. Once the trust has been built to some extent and the atmosphere to have discussions over some central issues including the nuclear issues has been created, matters can be dealt with incrementally. With time and effort and good intentions it is not impossible to terminate the 30-year-old intractable conflict, which can ultimately help in rolling back Iran's nuclear weapons program.

With President Barak Obama in the White House, time is ripe for both conflict actors to explore opportunities to settle the longstanding disputes and end this alarming nuclear proliferation problem. For Obama it will be important to discontinue Washington's anti-Iran rhetoric and start on a new page to entertain bilateral discussions and stretch a real hand of friendship towards Iran. It is important to create a non-confrontational atmosphere for trust to build and then move on from there. There is huge amount of miscommunication between the two adversaries, which is a product of a lack of direct contact, according to Michael Levi.[109] Therefore, the two states need to have bilateral and direct talks. Levi further states that there is difference between "talking, engaging, and negotiating."[110] Direct engagement is necessary. Once that happens, negotiations can follow. However, for Iran this is the time when the world will test its true intentions. If the country has been concerned about US aggressiveness and that made it more proliferation prone, then now is the time to settle the issues with the US and once that is accomplished, it should reverse its nuclear program. No one in the world is concerned about its energy program, but the IAEA must be convinced that its intention is not to develop nuclear weapons and that it is not buying time or deceiving the world at this point. That can only be done if it allows full and unconditional inspections and comes out in the open and declares all it has as far as the nuclear program is concerned. If Iran truly wants that, it should allow the US to have direct contacts with it and start building confidence and finally resolve the issues over which the conflict protracts. Unless it shows that its intentions are good, the world will have reason to doubt its program and intentions. Thus, it is in Iran's interest to make use of the "window of opportunity" since President Obama is willing to discuss matters comprehensively.

Conclusion

Iran has been a proliferation aspirant for many decades. Since the 1990s the world has been keeping an eye on Iran's nuclear activity. From 2002, Iran's nuclear ambition has alarmed the international community because of some disclosures of its nuclear program with military applications and Iran's refusal to allow the IAEA full access to its nuclear sites. As a result of that, the subject matter has taken center stage in world politics. Iran's nuclear program became a controversial topic in international security studies in general and proliferation studies in particular. While the Iranian government insisted that its program was peaceful, it seemed difficult to comprehend why the country was enriching uranium, in addition to conducting other activities that demonstrated its interest to pursue the weapons path. Understanding what Iran possesses in the nuclear realm and whether or not the Islamic Republic was and is deceiving the international community became pertinent. The world could not afford a proliferator in the Middle East, especially after Saddam Hussein was gone and the region could be proliferation-free, with the exception of Israel being an opaque proliferator. Scholars and policy-makers made efforts to understand, like all other proliferating states, what drives Iran to acquire nuclear weapons. More specifically, why does the Islamic Republic of Iran want to go nuclear? What purposes do nuclear weapons serve for Tehran? Although a lot has been written on the case, as expected, and a number of factors – security, domestic politics, prestige, and bargaining motivations – have been identified as some of the salient reasons for Iran's need to possess nuclear weapons, such studies have been mostly descriptive and analytical, which nonetheless contributed to the understanding of Iran's proliferation ambition. These earlier studies have failed to provide a theoretical account of Iran's nuclear weapons aspiration. In other words, a causal explanation of the drive has mostly been absent. The connection between conflicts and proliferation, which is most salient in this case, is also missing. Most importantly, the association between conflict asymmetry and proliferation, which primarily explains Iran's nuclear weapons ambition, has not been dealt with by scholars and policy-makers. Studies also do not examine what makes a proliferator relentless in its proliferation drive and under what conditions does the pace of proliferation become faster. In other words, what affects a would-be proliferator's pace of proliferation? The purpose of this book is to deviate from the descriptive and analytical work and develop a theoretical framework to comprehend the proliferation dynamics of states engaged in intractable conflicts. Iran, a case that has been engaged in PCs, is investigated to understand the applicability of the theory. Thus, the study examines Iran's proliferation drive by using theoretical constructs.

The book provides a theoretical framework which connects conflicts with proliferation propensities of states. It argues that variables such as conflict types – protracted/non-protracted, territorial/non-territorial, dyadic/non-dyadic, proximate/non-proximate, and asymmetric/symmetric – the number of conflict involvements, the regional or global status of the rival state, the opponent's nuclear and non-nuclear status, and whether or not a state's conflict rivals are allies shape or determine proliferation decisions. Although proliferation is generally a function of states engaged in conflicts, meaning due to states having acute security threats, not all conflict states proliferate. Although states may proliferate to obtain security, for prestige enhancement, and to acquire bargaining leverage, these variables are shaped by a state's engagement in PC. Some that are determined to proliferate are generally engaged in intractable territorial conflicts, involved in multiple conflicts simultaneously, face asymmetric conflicts, are regional states in conflict with global power, have dyadic, proximate, and nuclear adversaries, and have adversaries that are sometimes allies. Where all of these conditions are present, a state is likely to be the most determined proliferator.

PC states proliferate because war probability is higher in such conflict settings. However, states that are engaged in territorial conflicts are most likely to proliferate because territorial conflicts easily trigger wars. Deterrence is the most attractive strategy for such states that are both weary and fearful of war probability in the conflict setting. With the acquisition of a deterrent capability a state is able to dissuade its adversary from initiating an attack. Nuclear weapons are assumed to deter wars because they are the ultimate weapons. A general deterrent capability is possessed by states to regulate their adversarial relationships when neither of the opponents is seriously contemplating an attack. Possession of a bomb is generally expected to make resorting to force unattractive to the adversary. Where war remains a higher-than-normal probability, states in intractable conflicts are inclined to acquire means to avoid wars in their conflict setting. Since nuclear weapons are ideal war-deterrants because of their devastating nature, they are naturally factored into these states' strategic calculation. However, conflicts between global power and regional power, even if it is not over territorial issues, may have more probability of wars since one state has much more power to wage a war on the weaker state. Such conflicts – whether territorial or not – are thus more war-prone, unless non-conventional weapons, especially nuclear weapons, are possessed by the weaker power. To the weaker power, the presence of a hegemonic power rival is threatening. The global power possesses the power to bully the weaker state and can conveniently impose its terms on the regional power. This bullying becomes a more common phenomenon when the international system is unipolar, such as the present one. Where the system is unipolar and the rival is the hegemonic power, the weaker regional state is invariably threatened. This becomes a "structurally-determined rivalry" for the weak state. The global power is considered by the regional state as more of a threat if the systemic power structure has one superpower only. This essentially means that in a unipolar international system, this feeling of threat for the weaker party is exacerbated. There is no other power that is equal to the global power that could defend or protect the weaker power in times of a military confrontation with the global power. Rather, all states – weak or not, major power or minor power – are somewhat allied to the global power. The absence of other powers to protect it combined with the power of the global power to impose its terms on the weaker state with the usage of coercive mechanisms trigger acute insecurity for the weaker state. Given this, the environment becomes more confrontational to the weaker state which perceives the need for some quick addressing mechanism to compensate for the insecurity faced by it. Within this offing, the weak power strives to acquire a nuclear capability to address its security situation, counter bullying of the global power, and even to bargain better, where possible. This tendency to proliferate exacerbates where a state's conflict rival has nuclear weapons because first, there is a natural tendency to close the gap and reach parity with the rival state at the strategic level and, second, unless the state has similar weapons, the conflict turns into an asymmetric one where wars can be easily waged on it due to the absence of nuclear weapons and it is unable to use the same war strategy against its rival state due to the possession of such weapons by that state. This applies against regional and global adversaries. However, if a global rival has nuclear weapons, the regional rival has more of a tendency to acquire a similar capability because on other levels it is unable to be at par with the global power. With nuclear weapons the game is quite simple – one weapon is enough of a deterrent for a weaker state, which is not the case with conventional weapons. The weaker power also makes nuclear weapons fungible. Where one power is weaker than the other, the weaker power will have a natural propensity to proliferate to address its weakness. Nuclear weapons provide security, prestige, and a bargaining chip simultaneously for weaker states in the conflict where other means of competing with the adversary are unavailable, unaffordable, and useless. Therefore, for such states, although security and survival are the most important reasons for proliferation, they are also inclined to obtain prestige through the possession of nuclear capability and bargain effectively in an asymmetric conflict. The problem of status inconsistency, power, and prestige become blurred with security motivation. The situation becomes even worse when the global power pursues aggressive foreign and security policies. The weaker regional state pursues a fast-track proliferation activity. Assuming the worst about the intentions of an adversary means exaggerating the hostility of the opponent, which drives decision-makers into making wrong decisions based on poor judgments in the realm of security. The weaker party to a conflict functions on the basis of a preconceived evil image and notion of its stronger adversary. Misperceptions of intentions and capabilities work both ways in an asymmetric conflict which leads to additional complexity in an already problematic enduring rivalry relationship. This incentive to proliferate naturally increases when states are engaged in multiple PCs simultaneously. The more conflicts it has, the more likely it will want to obtain nuclear weapons because once possessed, these ultimate weapons can protect the state against all sorts of enemies – regional or global, weak or strong, and proximate or non-proximate. If states are involved in dyadic conflicts the chances are more that nuclear weapons will be desired because wars are more likely in dyadic conflicts and there is no one to depend on for security purposes in dyadic conflicts unlike non-dyadic conflicts where responsibilities can be shared, formally or informally. Proximate rivals are the most dangerous ones to compete with and war is always a probability because borders can flare up at any time which might be potentially disturbing and dangerous for escalation possibilities. If one state has multiple rivals and the rivals – all or even two – of them are allies, the situation becomes more hostile for the state because it can be attacked from different fronts by enemies who are allies. The feeling of isolation and insecurity dictates its security, defense, and foreign policies. Miscalculations of intentions of adversaries are evident. Adversaries are seen as very aggressive. Aggressive intentions of the adversary are overinflated. Trust deficit is a common characteristic of such conflicting states. Nuclear weapons are sought desperately if all of the conditions discussed earlier exist in conflict relations.

The aforementioned theoretical framework was used to understand Iran's nuclear weapons ambition and why it has been relentless in building a bomb in the absence of a hostile Iraq after Saddam's rule. The study found that although security threats emanating from Iraq, with whom it had a proximate and dyadic territorial conflict, was the primary reason for Iran's quest for nuclear weapons when Iran started its comprehensive nuclear program and Israel has been a matter of serious security concern for Iran since the 1980s, after the Lebanon war and Iran's support for Hezbollah, since 1990, Iran's nuclear ambition had mostly to do with its conflict with the US. From 2000, Iran has been more focused on its weapons program because of the aggressive foreign policies the US has pursued against the country. Its unrelenting pace of proliferation has been a function of conflict asymmetry with the US and America's aggressive policies targeting Iran.

While Iran started its nuclear program during the Shah's rule, the Islamic leaders continued building the program even though some leaders, especially Ayatollah Khomeini, after the Islamic Revolution have been reluctant to continue with it for religious reasons. Iran's triple protracted conflict explains why it has had to build a comprehensive nuclear weapons program with military component. Thus, the study reveals that protracted conflicts are connected to proliferation. Iran's nuclear ambition initially was a function of its twin protracted conflicts – Iran–Iraq and Iran–Israel – from 1947–79. The nuclear program received a momentum for its twin intractable conflicts at the time. Iran is engaged in both conflicts till today. The two conflicts and their ramifications in the nuclear realm have been grave. During the specified period, Iran was engaged in a territorial, dyadic, and protracted conflict with Iraq, a proximate rival that was also suspected of clandestinely developing nuclear weapons capabilities, and a non-dyadic protracted conflict with Israel that had nuclear weapons capability ready of assembly on short notice since the 1960s. However, it was a blessing for Iran that its enemies were not allies of each other. Thus, although the drive and resolve to acquire nuclear weapons were present, this was still the setting stage of the nuclear program and the pace of proliferation was not noticeably fast. Iraq was its principal enemy in the region with whom

114 Conclusion

it fought a protracted war from 1980 to 1988 and Baghdad used non-conventional weapons against Tehran in the war. During the war Iraq not only used chemical weapons repeatedly against the Iranian people, but the international community did not do anything to defend Iran or to condemn Iraq. The war had tremendous impact on Iran's proliferation activities in the aftermath. Iranian leadership became more serious about acquiring a deterrent capability to avoid another war in the dyadic relationship. Although Iran was a stronger power in the asymmetric conflict with Iraq, the latter's decision to wage a war against Iran proved that weaker states in a conflict have a great propensity to wage wars when they see a window of opportunity. This was extremely threatening to Iran. Additionally, Iraq also made efforts to build nuclear weapons since the 1970s and the Osiraq destruction proved that. This was more alarming for Iran, which was a victim of Saddam Hussein's invasion in 1980. It was obvious on the part of Iran to perceive security threats due to these and desire to obtain a deterrent capability. The study demonstrated the connection between territorial, dyadic, and proximate long-running conflicts and proliferation propensity. It also proved that if conflict adversaries have nuclear weapons, states have the desire to match the capability, which is more pronounced in a dyadic conflict where others' deterrent capabilities cannot deter a state's adversary. Iran's engagement with Iraq in a PC made it insecure and it became proliferation prone to address that insecurity.

Iran's security concern vis-à-vis Israel was also another motivating factor in its nuclear decision-making. Israel did not become as important an enemy as Iraq to Tehran before 1982 even though the conflict started much earlier. Iran was not a direct party to the Arab–Israeli conflict, but it wanted Israel to be wiped out of the Middle East because of religious reasons. However, that was not a strong reason for Iran to go nuclear. Also, this was a non-dyadic conflict and Arab states were there to address Israeli security threats. That situation changed in 1982 when Iran created Hezbollah and started using it as its proxy in Lebanon. Israel considered these as terror activities and thus the problem became more acute. Iran's support for Hezbollah and Hamas has been the principal cause of concern for Israel. Israel threatens Iran not only with military retaliation, but because it has always been an ally of the superpower, the US. Consequently, Iran's security threats emanating from Israel had a different logic and dynamic. Additionally, Israel has been an opaque nuclear state since the 1960s which has always been a concern for Iran, but became more of a threat after relations between the two deteriorated in the aftermath of the 1982 war over Lebanon and military encounters.

While Israel was an opaque nuclear state, Iraq was also trying to build nuclear bombs since the 1970s. If the Osiraq facility was not destroyed by Israel in the early 1980s, Iraq would have been a nuclear state a long time ago. Both countries were the protracted conflict rivals of Iran – Iraq being a rival in a dyadic conflict since the 1950s and Israel in a non-dyadic Arab–Israeli conflict since 1947. It was pertinent for Iran to have a deterrent capability to avoid strategic imbalance with its rivals and avoid wars in the conflict settings.

Since 1979 Iran became engaged in another protracted conflict, but this time with a superpower, the US, that was not only a nuclear state, but its global status made this conflict asymmetric, making Iran an extremely vulnerable state in the conflict setting. From 1979 to 1990, Iran had three serious security concerns to deal with and two of its rivals, Israel and the US, have been allies. While Iraq was not an ally of the US, it has been hard for Iran to overlook the fact that during the Gulf War, Iraq's usage of chemical weapons was not dealt with seriously by the US and the latter supplied weapons to Iraq despite its war initiation and usage of non-conventional weapons against Iran. However, this was a period when Iran was still in the midst of developing its nuclear program, but was not relentlessly pursuing the option to develop nuclear weapons. The study finds reasons for this, but the most important reason was that this was also a period in the cold war when the US was not the only superpower and it did not pursue very aggressive foreign policies towards Iran, even though the US was constantly watching Iran and its nuclear weapons desire. Additionally, the Iran–US PC was getting consolidated by this period. After the end of the cold war the international system changed from bipolarity to unipolarity and the US became a hegemonic power in the world with global reach, trying to interfere in the internal affairs of states that it believed were antiwestern and to impose its terms on those states. Targeting the Middle East became its obsession, and it made its first strategic move against Iraq. The 1990–91 Gulf War brought with it American presence in the region and the war that the US waged on Iraq after more than a decade in 2003 institutionalized that presence in Iraq, a bordering country of Iran. The relations with Iran following the first Gulf War were hostile which were projected by the US's labeling of Iran as a rogue state trying to develop illicit WMDs and missiles and being anti-western due to its non-democratic political institution. Iran was humiliated and offended by such labeling and felt threatened since it was clear that the US would target these states one after the other. That impacted Iran's nuclear program during the period. Iran was also worried about the asymmetric conflict it was engaged in with the global power. It needed to acquire a strategic capability as well as elevate its status and close the gap with its global adversary on the nuclear level. This corroborates the proposition that weak states in asymmetric conflicts want to acquire nuclear weapons more for deterrence and status reasons. From 1990 to 2000 Iran focused on its nuclear program with military applications in it. It looked outside for materials and went to the nuclear black market for obtaining these. The A.Q. Khan connection was made during this period. Iran also emphasized on its missile program during the period and tested its long-range missiles during the end of the period. However, even during this period, Iran's threat perception from the US was not as high as it has been since 2000. Since 2000, the US and Iran's relationship has been extremely antagonistic. It was at an all time low since the conflict between them started. The US placed Iran in the club of the "Axis of Evil" states that had to be contained to secure the world. The US strategic and security policies including the development of the National Missile Defense System and Nuclear Posture Review have all been designed to combat countries like Iran. Regime change has been a serious goal of the Bush administration. Iran was on the one hand extremely humiliated, on the other hand threatened. For humiliation, it needed to strengthen its position and for threat it had to secure itself from attack by the US. The war on Iraq in 2003 demonstrated the

116 *Conclusion*

US's willingness to attack these states for its own security and economic interests. While Saddam was gone, US presence in the Gulf was more permanent than in the 1990s. Additionally, the conflict with Iraq had not ended for Iran. Neither did the one with Israel. Rather Israel and the US became the greatest concerns for Iran. Since then the US has had access to the region through Israel and Iraq. Iran could not wait any longer for the international community to defend it and the NPT was no assurance anymore once the US decided to develop new nuclear weapons to use against regional targets. Iran had to move forward with its weapons program fast. Informing the US about its enrichment was also a function of its need to prove that it had a deterrent capability of some sorts. Iran wanted its fate not to be like Iraq and also intended to use its nuclear capacity to elevate its status and negotiate effectively with the US on issues and obtain concessions. Given all this, Tehran was even more propelled to try and build the bomb at the shortest possible time to feel secure in the relationship and not give in to the pressures and domination of Washington. Multiple conflicts made Iran naturally proliferation prone, but a conflict with the global power that had nuclear weapons and that which pursued aggressive policies towards Iran made it a determined proliferator and the pace of its proliferation faster than previous times. Iran faces all conditions of a determined proliferator and consequently seems to have been one.

Theoretical implications

The study has some major theoretical implications. Dominant theories of International Relations that focus on power and military capabilities such as Realism and its variant Neorealism are unable to explain Iran's propensity to acquire nuclear weapons simply by focusing on the structure of the International system, which is anarchic, or by security motivations. If anarchy caused proliferation, then all states in the international system would have proliferated. That is obviously not the case. Also, if simple security drives compelled states to acquire nuclear weapons then many states would have nuclear weapons because most states in the international system are insecure because of power disparity between states. That is not the case either. Just because some states have nuclear weapons other do not follow suit. A sweeping generalization cannot be made. While conflicts trigger proliferation, all conflicts do not do so. Conflict typology, numbers, as well as nuclear or non-nuclear status of the rivals determine proliferation proclivity. Thus, it is important to restructure the theoretical paradigms along these lines for them to be better applicable against cases.

Although the study focuses on military power politics, which does not generally fall under the category of the critical perspectives in International Relations that primarily focus on human emancipation, the findings of the study have major implications for a central strand of the critical approach, namely Constructivism. Constructivists claim that "anarchy is what states make of it." The "structure of identity and interest" is important in understanding the dynamics of anarchy. This plays a crucial role in mediating anarchy's explanatory role. Thus, simply by concentrating on anarchy one cannot explain why the US military power is perceived

Conclusion 117

differently by different states. Why does Canada not feel threatened by the US but Iran does? These are important questions to ask before sweeping generalizations are made about anarchy and its consequences in the realm of power politics. Constructivists argue that such perceptions of threat depend on friendship and knowledge. While these theorists do not go beyond this, the present study builds on that line of argument. It demonstrates that this is why conflicts need to be factored into understanding arms race or weapons proliferation. Friendship and knowledge – good or bad of each other – are functions of conflict or non-conflict relations. Where states are in conflicts, anarchy gets a different meaning because conflicting states are not friends but rivals and no power above the state level is there to aid them in case of attacks. Power parity is focused on by such states. Anarchy becomes salient when states are engaged in intractable conflicts. Anarchy becomes a matter of concern when states are engaged in asymmetric conflicts. Anarchy also becomes a cause of apprehension when states are involved in asymmetric conflicts with global powers. Anarchy triggers acute arms race when rivals pursue aggressive policies. Anarchy impacts military decisions when a state cannot defend itself from different fronts for being engaged in multiple conflicts and when conflict rivals help each other. Thus, the study portrays the power of the Constructivist's perspectives in International Relations in explaining proliferation in regional states afflicted with conflicts.

In the realm of proliferation, the implications of the study are salient. While proliferation has always been understood by theorists as functions of security, prestige, or to bargain better, under what conditions these incentives would be more attractive to states have been ignored by them. Instead of considering these as independent variables that impact the dependent variable, proliferation, these should be examined as intervening variables that are shaped by conflicts and their typologies. Simple causal connection between independent and dependent variables could be spurious and may provide unreliable conclusions and findings. Integrating the independent, intervening, and dependent variables are important in proliferation studies.

Policy implications

The study has major policy implications. As long as the US does not fashion a different style of foreign policy pertaining to Iran and terminate the PC with Tehran, it is unlikely for Iran to relinquish its nuclear weapons program. While Iran may be compelled to suspend its program due to international pressure and for the fear of being subjected to more serious sanctions that might affect the civilians, such suspension will only be temporary and a permanent solution to this problem will only be a function of the termination of the Iran–US PC. The US policies need to be restructured based on this notion.

Before any reconciliation can be made it is important for the US to stretch the hand of friendship towards Iran so that a thaw in the relationship can be created. Conflict thaws do not produce automatic resolution to the issues, but they definitely create an environment which is conducive to the settlement of issues. The perception factor is important in this context. Iran must feel that the US is genuinely interested in talking with Tehran. This can only happen if signals of friendship are given. Additionally, wanting to talk directly would mean some degree of recognition of the Islamic Republic by the US, which has been Iran's demand for a long time. That itself will stabilize the relationship somewhat. Just as conflicts need to be institutionalized before proliferation decisions are taken based on that, similarly thaws need to be consolidated before issues can be settled. Building trust is important within this context. Confidence-building measures must be taken. This can only happen if policies are consistent and warlike policies are not in the conflict offing. After all, no positive result can come out of an antagonistic environment.

There is no point putting pressure on Iran to suspend the program. Neither is it a good idea to threaten Iran with war, which the Bush administration was doing and which President Barak Obama has not ruled out as one of the options in dealing with Iran. Instead, a congenial atmosphere must be created to have bilateral discussions between the two states to attain the non-proliferation goals and in exchange Iran must get security assurance from the US, stipulating that the Americans have no intention of attacking the Republic or imposing Washington's terms on Tehran's ideologically-driven government. These things can only happen if the US gives the Iranians a sense of security through changing its hostile policies. Times have changed and the US policy-makers must understand that sticks may not be the answer to some of the security problems in today's world.

One interesting policy implication of the study is that Iran is a unique proliferator because of the asymmetric conflict it has been engaged in with the US and, given this, if the US provides security guarantee to Iran, it is a likely candidate to relinquish its nuclear weapons program. Other regional states have regional conflicts and they proliferate for their regional counterparts' nuclear weapons acquisition or security problems in the regions; those cases are much more complicated because regional disputes that are intractable are difficult to settle. Additionally, regional states may acquire nuclear weapons for regional dominance and in such cases renouncing nuclear weapons may be difficult. Also, the US may not have direct influence in any of those states or may not be interested in settling the conflicts where its interests are not directly at stake. In this case, because the US is directly involved in the conflict, it has more reason to provide security and concessions and create an environment where Iran will not be able to say "no" to undertake the non-proliferation path. If the US provides security then other regional problems that Iran faces will not compel it to acquire nuclear weapons. Iraq is already a less-hostile state in the region which has a pro-American government and Israel is an ally of the US. So, if the conflict with this rival is settled and Tehran feels secure, its conflict with the regional rivals will also be muted and in the course of time may be settled with the help of Washington, since both of its regional rivals are now allies of the US. Under the circumstances, Tehran may be in a good position to renounce its nuclear weapons program.

Ultimately, this is also a test for Iran. If Iran really means what it says, now will be the time to prove it. If Washington offers friendship and Tehran refuses to reciprocate, it will be one of the most isolated countries in the world because it will lose all sympathies that those countries have had for it for a long time. Unless Iran proves that it has not deceived the international community for the wrong reasons, it will be hard on its part to obtain any amount of support from regional states or the major powers of the international system. Iran must work diligently this time if it is invited by the US to come to the negotiating table and prove that its intentions are not to destabilize the international system.

Further research

More research can be done to understand the applicability of the theoretical framework of the study. The theory can be tested against other cases that have had or still have asymmetric conflict with a global power. North Korea and Iraq in the Saddam era can be two cases that can be used to test the theory this study introduces. The validity of the theory will be tested more rigorously once other cases have been tested. The theory will be more robust once that is done because one case study is often not enough to test the power of a theory, although teasing out relationships between variables in a detailed manner is easier in a single-case study.

Notes

Introduction

1 Alexander Wendt, "Anarchy is What States Make of It," in Robert J. Art and Robert Jervis, eds., *International Politics: Enduring Concepts and Contemporary Issues*, 8th edition, (New York: Longman, 2006); Richard Wyn Jones, ed., *Critical Theory and World Politics*, (Boulder and London: Lynne Rienner Publishers, 2001).
2 Ibid.

1 Factors utilized to comprehend Iran's nuclear weapons aspiration

1 See, among others, Leonard S. Spector with Jacqueline R. Smith, *Nuclear Ambitions: The Spread of Nuclear Weapons 1989–1990*, (Boulder, Oxford: Westview Press, 1990); Kenneth R. Timmerman, *Weapons of Mass Destruction: The Cases of Iran, Syria, and Libya*, (Los Angeles: Simon Wiesenthal Center Report for Middle East Defence News, Middle East Defence News, 1992); Anthony Cordesman, *Iran and Iraq*, (Boulder, Colorado: Westview Press, 1994); Shai Feldman, *Nuclear Weapons and Arms Control in the Middle East*, (Cambridge, Mass.: The MIT Press, 1997); Anthony Cordesman and Ahmed Hashim, *Iran: Dilemmas of Dual Containment*, (Boulder, Colorado: Westview Press, 1997); Saideh Lotfian, "Threat Perception and Military Planning in Iran: Credible Scenarios of Conflict and Opportunities for Confidence Building," in Eric Arnett, ed., *Military Capacity and the Risk of War*, (New York and Oxford: Oxford University Press, 1997); Fredrick R. Strain, "Iran's Nuclear Strategy: Discerning Motivations, Strategic Culture, and Rationality," (*Institute for National Strategic Studies*, 1998); Haleh Vazri, "Iran's Nuclear Quest: Motivations and Consequences," in Raju G. Thomas, ed., *The Nuclear Non-proliferation Regime: Prospects for the 21st Century*, (New York: St. Martin's Press, 1998).
2 Leonard Spector, *Going Nuclear: The Spread of Nuclear Weapons 1986–1987*, (Cambridge, Mass.: Ballinger, 1987), pp. 50–51.
3 Etel Solingen, *Nuclear Logics: Contrasting Paths in East Asia and the Middle East*, (Princeton: Princeton University Press, 2007), p. 164.
4 Ibid., p. 164.
5 Paula A. DeSutter, *Denial and Jeopardy: Deterring Iranian Use of NBC Weapons*, (Washington D.C.: National Defense University Press, 1997).
6 PBS, *Frontline*, April 13, 1993.
7 Etel Solingen, *Nuclear Logics*, p. 164.
8 Peter Herby, *The Chemical Weapons Convention and Arms Control in the Middle East*, (Oslo: International Peace Research Institute, 1992), p. 42.
9 Speech by Ali Akbar Hashemi Rafsanjani, Tehran Domestic Service, 19.35 GMT, October 6, 1988, Translation in FBIS-NES, October 7, 1988, p. 2. Also, quoted by

Leonard Spector, "Nuclear Proliferation in the Middle East: The Next Chapter Begins," in Efraim Karsh, Martin S. Navias, and Philip Sabin, eds., *Non-Conventional Weapons Proliferation in the Middle East*, (New York: Oxford University Press, 1993), p. 143.
10. Mark Gasiorowski, "Iranian Politics after the 2004 Parliamentary Elections," *Strategic Insights*, vol. 3, issue 6, June 2004.
11. William J. Broad and Elaine Sciolino, "Iran's Secrecy Widens Gap in Nuclear Intelligence," *The New York Times*, May 19, 2006.
12. See, IAEA reports at http://www.iaea.org/NewsCenter/Focus/IaeaIran/index.shtml
13. Ali Akbar Dareini, "Iran Will Pursue Nuclear Program," *Associated Press*, September 21, 2004.
14. See, "Iranian Nuclear Chief Ali Larijani: The West Should Learn the Lesson of North Korea," *IRINN TV*, September 20, 2005 at http://memri.org/. Also see, http://www.iaea.org/Publications/Documents/Board/2005/gov2005-67.pdf
15. "Khatami: Iran Entitled to Nuclear Energy," *Iran-UN Politics*, August 25, 2006. http://www.arabicnews.com/ansub/Daily/Day/060825/2006082502.html
16. Mark Hitchcock, *The Apocalypse of Ahmadinejad: The Revelation of Iran's Nuclear Prophet*, (New York: The Doubleday Religious Publishing Group, 2007).
17. Emirates Centre for Strategic Studies, *Iran's Nuclear Program*, (New York: Palgrave, Macmillan, 2007).
18. Therese Delpech, *Iran and the Bomb: The Abdication of International Responsibility*, (London: Hurst & Company, 2006), p. 91.
19. Ibid., p. 37.
20. Etel Solingen, *Nuclear Logics*, p. 180.
21. Ibid., p. 183.
22. Nazila Fathi and Michael Slackman, "Rebuke in Iran to Its President on Nuclear Role," *The New York Times*, January 19, 2007.
23. Jacques E.C. Hymans, *The Psychology of Nuclear Proliferation: Identity, Emotions, and Foreign Policy*, (Cambridge: Cambridge University Press, 2006), p. 42.
24. Papers presented at "Making Big Choices: Individual Opinion Formation and Societal Choice," conference at the Weatherhead Center for International Affairs, Harvard University, May 25–26, 2000.
25. Jacques E.C. Hymans, *The Psychology of Nuclear Proliferation*, pp. 10–11.
26. Ibid., p. 11.
27. Ibid., p. 13.
28. Ibid., p. 206.
29. Anne Hessing Cahn, "Determinants of the Nuclear Option: The Case of Iran," in Onkar Marwah and Ann Schultz, eds., *Nuclear Proliferation and the Near-Nuclear Countries*, (Cambridge, Mass.: Ballinger Publishing Company, 1975), p. 198.
30. Ray Takeyh, "Iran at the Strategic Crossroads," in James A Russell, ed., *Proliferation of Weapons of Mass Destruction in the Middle East: Directions and Policy Options*, (New York: Palgrave Macmillan, 2006), p. 55.
31. Shahram Chubin, "Understanding Iran's Nuclear Ambitions," in Patrick M. Cronin, ed., *Double Trouble: Iran and North Korea as Challenges To International Security*, (Westport, Connecticut and London: Praeger Security International, 2008), p. 57.
32. See, Ray Takeyh, "Iran's Populace Largely Opposes Nuclear Program," Interview by Bernard Gwertzman, March 2, 2005, *CFR Online* March 7, 2005; Michael Herzog, "Iranian Public Opinion on the Nuclear Program," *Policy Focus* no. 56, (Washington Institute, June 2006); Mahan Abdin, "Public Opinion and the Nuclear Standoff," *Mid East Mirror*, no. 1, vol. 2, April/May 2006. http://www.mideastmonitor.org/issues/0604/0604_3.htm
33. Shahram Chubin, "Understanding Iran's Nuclear Ambitions," p. 48.
34. Dr Hossein Faqihiyan, Director General of Nuclear Fuel Production Co., and Deputy of

the Atomic Energy Organization (AEO), in Daily Newspaper, *Farhang-e-Ashti*, May 4, 2006; in BBC Online, May 10, 2006.
35 Ray Takeyh, "Iran at the Strategic Crossroads," p. 52.
36 "Iranians Defend Nuclear Rights," *Los Angeles Times*, March 7, 2006.
37 Shahram Chubin, "Understanding Iran's Nuclear Ambitions," p. 54.
38 Ibid., pp. 54–55.
39 Ibid., pp. 52–53.
40 Patrick M. Cronin, "Introduction: The Dual Challenge of Iran and North Korea," in Patrick M. Cronin, ed., *Double Trouble: Iran and North Korea as Challenges To International Security*, (Westport, Connecticut and London: Praeger Security International, 2008), p. 6.
41 Shahram Chubin, *Iran's Nuclear Ambitions*, (Washington D. C.: Carnegie Endowment for International Peace, 2006).
42 Etel Solingen, *Nuclear Logics*, p. 177.
43 Shahram Chubin, *Iran's Nuclear Ambitions*.
44 Ray Takeyh, "Iran at the Strategic Crossroads," p. 57.
45 Leonard Spector, *Regional Orders at Century's Dawn*, (Princeton: Princeton University Press, 1998), p. 208.
46 Gareth Smyth, "Iran's Intellectuals Left in Cold by Populist President," *The Financial Times*, June 21, 2006.
47 Etel Solingen, *Nuclear Logics*, p. 181.
48 Nathan E. Busch, *No End in Sight: The Continuing Menace of Nuclear Proliferation*, (Kentucky: The University Press of Kentucky, 2004), p. 273.
49 Etel Solingen, *Nuclear Logics*, p. 186.
50 See, Ahmed S. Hashim, "Iranian Science and Technology Capacity: Implications of Ideology and the Experience of War for Military Research and Development," in Eric Arnett, ed., *Military Capacity and the Risk of War*, (New York, Oxford: Oxford University Press, 1997), p. 219; IISS, *The Military Balance*, 1998–99, p. 127.
51 Patrick M. Cronin, "The Trouble with Iran," in Patrick M. Cronin, ed., *Double Trouble: Iran and North Korea as Challenges To International Security*, (Westport, Connecticut and London: Praeger Security International, 2008), p. 12.
52 "Iranians Defend Nuclear Rights," *Los Angeles Times*, March 7, 2006.
53 Ray Takeyh, "Iran at the Strategic Crossroads," in James A Russell, ed., (2006), p. 52.
54 Shahram Chubin, "Understanding Iran's Nuclear Ambitions," in Patrick M. Cronin, ed., (2008), p. 57.
55 Daniel Byman, et al., *Iran's Security Policy in the Post-Revolutionary Era*, (Santa Monica: RAND, 2001), p. 9.
56 Chuck Freilich, "The United States, Israel, and Iran: Defusing an 'Existential Threat,'" *Arms Control Today*, November 2008. http://www.armscontrol.org/act/2008_11/freilich
57 Ibid.
58 Robert E. Hunter, "The Iran Case: Addressing Why Countries Want Nuclear Weapons," *Arms Control Today*, vol. 34, December 2004. http://www.armscontrol.org/act/2004_12/Hunter
59 Daniel Byman, et al., *Iran's Security Policy*, p. 8.
60 Robert E. Hunter, "The Iran Case: Addressing Why Countries Want Nuclear Weapons."
61 Sverre Lodgaard, "Iran's Uncertain Nuclear Ambitions," in Morten Bremer Maerli and Sverre Lodgaard, eds., *Nuclear Proliferation and International Security*, (London and New York: Routledge, 2007), p. 101.
62 Nathan E. Busch, *No End in Sight: The Continuing Menace of Nuclear Proliferation*, (Kentucky: The University Press of Kentucky, 2004), p. 31.
63 Gregory F. Giles, "The Islamic Republic of Iran and Nuclear, Biological, and Chemical Weapons," in Peter R. Lavoy, Scott D. Sagan, and James J. Wirtz, eds., *Planning the*

Unthinkable: How New Powers Will Use Nuclear, Biological, and Chemical Weapons, (Ithaca and London: Cornell University Press, 2000), p. 84.
64 Chuck Freilich, "The United States, Israel, and Iran: Defusing an 'Existential Threat,'" *Arms Control Today*, November 2008. http://www.armscontrol.org/act/2008_11/freilich
65 See, Hooshang Amirahmadi, ed., *Revisiting Iran's Strategic Significance in the Emerging Regional Order*, (New Brunswick, New Jersey: US–Iran Conference, 1995).
66 Ray Takeyh, "Iran at the Strategic Crossroads," in James A. Russell, ed., p. 57.
67 Therese Delpech, *Iran and the Bomb: The Abdication of International Responsibility*, (London: Hurst & Company, 2006), p. 13.
68 Shahram Chubin, *Eliminating Weapons of Mass Destruction: The Persian Gulf Case*, Henry Stimson Occasional paper 33, (Washington D. C.: Henry Stimson Center, 1997), p. 25.
69 Anthony Cordesman, *Iran and Iraq*, (Boulder, Colorado: Westview Press, 1994), p. 2.
70 Gregory F. Giles, "The Islamic Republic of Iran and Nuclear, Biological, and Chemical Weapons," in Peter R. Lavoy, Scott D. Sagan, and James J. Wirtz, eds., *Planning the Unthinkable*, p. 86.
71 Ibid., p. 85.
72 Shai Feldman, *Nuclear Weapons and Arms Control in the Middle East*, (Cambridge, Mass.: MIT Press, 1997), p. 137, fn48.
73 Shahram Chubin, *Iran's Nuclear Ambitions*, (Washington D.C.: Carnegie Endowment for International Peace, 2006), Al Venter, *Iran's Nuclear Option: Tehran's Quest for the Atomic Bomb*, (Drexel Hill, PA: Casemate Publishers, 2004), and Emirates Centre for Strategic Studies, *Iran's Nuclear Program*, (New York: Palgrave Macmillan, 2007).
74 Ray Takeyh, *Hidden Iran: Paradox and Power in the Islamic Republic*, (Times Books, 2007).
75 Alexander George and Andrew Bennett, *Case Studies and Theory Development in Social Sciences*, (Cambridge, Mass.: MIT Press, 2005), p. 25.

2 Proliferation proclivities of protracted conflict states

1 Kenneth N. Waltz, *Theory of International Politics*, (New York: Random House, 1979), p. 188.
2 Kenneth N. Waltz, "Origins of War in Neorealist Theory," in Robert I. Rotberg and Theodore K. Rabb, eds., *The Origin and Prevention of Major Wars*, (Cambridge: Cambridge University Press, 1988), pp. 50–51.
3 Among others, John Lewis Gaddis, "Great Illusions, the Long Peace, and the Future of the International System," in Charles W. Kegley, ed., *The Long PostWar Peace*, (New York: HarperCollins, 1991), Chapter 2.
4 Edward E. Azar, *et al.*, "Protracted Social Conflict: Theory and Practice in the Middle East," *Journal of Palestine Studies*, vol.8, no.1, 1978, p. 50.
5 See Saira Khan, *Nuclear Proliferation Dynamics in Protracted Conflict Regions: A Comparative Study of South Asia and the Middle East*, (Aldershot and Vermont: Ashgate Publishing Ltd., 2002), p. 42.
6 Michael Brecher and Jonathan Wilkenfeld, "Interstates Crises and Violence," in Manus I. Midlarsky, ed., *Handbook of War Studies II*, (Ann Arbor: The University of Michigan Press, 2002), p. 288.
7 Ibid., p. 288.
8 Michael Brecher and Jonathan Wilkenfeld, *A Study of Crisis*, (Ann Arbor: The University of Michigan Press, 1997), pp. 3–4, 8–11; Michael Brecher, *Crises in World Politics*, (Oxford: Pergamon Press, 1993), p. 3; Glenn Snyder and Paul Diesing, *Conflict Among Nations: Bargaining, Decision-Making and System Structure in*

124 *Notes*

      International Crises, (Princeton, New Jersey: Princeton University Press, 1977), p. 7; Glenn H. Snyder, "Crisis Bargaining," in Charles F. Hermann, ed., *International Crises: Insights from Behavioral Research*, (New York: Free Press, 1972), p. 217.
9. Michael Brecher, *Crises in World Politics*, (1993), p. 3; Michael Brecher and Jonathan Wilkenfeld, *Crisis, Conflict, and Instability*, (Oxford: Pergamon Press, 1989), pp. 5 and 19.
10. Glenn Snyder and Paul Diesing, *Conflict Among Nations*, p. 7.
11. Michael Brecher and Jonathan Wilkenfeld, *A Study of Crisis*, (1997), p. 3.
12. David J. Singer and Melvin Small, *The Wages of War 1816–1965: A Statistical Handbook*, (New York: John Wiley, 1972), p. 381.
13. See Saira Khan, *Nuclear Weapons and Conflict Transformation: The Case of India-Pakistan*, (London and New York: Routledge, 2009).
14. Interestingly there is another theory of war weariness by Arnold Toynbee that suggests that political leaders who have experienced repeated wars and devastation of wars have a strong aversion towards wars. Also, at the nation-state level, war weariness becomes part of the national character or political culture. In other words, the feeling is shared by the population as well. This essentially means that such states are not expected to have the need to make use of the deterrence strategy because they are deterred from waging wars due to being war-weary. See, Arnold Toynbee, *A Study of History*, vol. 9, (London: Oxford University Press, 1954).
15. Patick Morgan, *Deterrence: A Conceptual Analysis*, (Beverly Hills, London: Sage Publishers, 1977), pp. 40–43.
16. Saira Khan, *Nuclear Proliferation Dynamics in Protracted Conflict Regions: A Comparative Study of South Asia and the Middle East*, (Aldershot and Vermont: Ashgate Publishing Ltd., 2002), p. 40.
17. Hans J. Morgenthau, *Politics Among Nations: The Struggle for Power and Peace*, (New York: Knopf, 1956), pp. 102–137.
18. Kalevi J. Holsti, *Peace and War: Armed Conflicts and International Order, 1648–1989* (Cambridge: Cambridge University Press, 1991) pp. 218–219, 280–282.
19. Definition of hegemony provided by Wikipedia. See, http://en.wikipedia.org/wiki/Hegemony
20. See, Samuel P. Huntington, "The Lonely Superpower," *Foreign Affairs*, March/April 1999, pp. 35–49.
21. Ibid., pp. 35–49.
22. Damon Coletta, "Unipolarity, Globalization, and the War on Terror: Why Security Studies Should Refocus on Comparative Defense," *International Studies Review*, vol.9, no. 3, Fall 2007, p. 390.
23. Joseph S. Nye, *Bound to Lead: The Changing Nature of American Power*, (New York: Basic Books, 1990), p. 188.
24. T.V. Paul, *Asymmetric Conflicts: War Initiation by Weaker Powers*, (New York: Cambridge University Press, 1994), p. 35.
25. Ibid., p. 35.
26. Kenneth N. Waltz, "Nuclear Myth and Political Reality," *American Political Science Review*, 84, 1990, p. 740.
27. A. F. K. Organski, *World Politics*, (New York: Alfred A. Knopf, 1968), p. 343.
28. See, Samuel P. Huntington, "The Lonely Superpower," *Foreign Affairs*, March/April 1999, pp. 35–49.
29. Robert Gilpin, *War and Change in World Politics*, (Cambridge: Cambridge University Press, 1981), p. 28; William C. Wohlforth, *The Elusive Balance: Power and Perceptions During the Cold War*, (Ithaca, NY: Cornell University Press, 1993), pp. 12–14.
30. John J. Mearsheimer, *Conventional Deterrence*, (Ithaca: Cornell University Press, 1983), p. 25.

31 Arie M. Kacowicz and Yaacov Bar-Siman-Tov, "Stable Peace: A Conceptual Framework," in Arie M. Kacowicz and Yaacov Bar-Siman-Tov, *et al.*, *Stable Peace among Nations*, (New York, Oxford: Rowman and Littlefield Publishers Ltd., 2000), p. 20.
32 T. V. Paul, *Power Versus Prudence: Why Nations Forgo Nuclear Weapons*, (Montreal & Kingston: McGill-Queen's University Press, 2000), p. 6.
33 John J. Mearsheimer, *Tragedy of Great Power Politics*, (New York and London: W.W. Norton and Company, 2001), p. 345.
34 David A. Baldwn, "Neoliberalism, Neorealism, and World Politics," in David A. Baldwin, ed., *Neorealism and Neoliberalism: The Contemporary Debate*, (New York: Columbia University Press, 1993), p. 20.
35 Stephen Van Evera, *Causes of War*, (Ithaca: Cornell University Press, 1999), p. 135.
36 Daniel L. Byman and Mathew C. Waxman, *Confronting Iraq: U.S. Policy and the Use of Force Since the Gulf War*, (Santa Monica, CA: RAND, 2000), p. 5.
37 John J. Mearsheimer, *Tragedy of Great Power Politics*, (New York and London: W.W. Norton and Company, 2001), p. 345.
38 Jack S. Levy, "Misperceptions and the Causes of War: Theoretical Linkages and Analytical Problems," *World Politics*, vol. 36, 1983, p. 88.
39 Janice Gross Stein, "Image, Identity, and Conflict Resolution," in Chester A. Crocker, *et al.*, eds., *Managing Global Chaos: Sources of and Responses to International Conflict*, (Washington D.C.: US Institute of Peace Press, 1996), p. 93.
40 Jack S. Levy, "Misperceptions and the Causes of War," 1983, p. 88.
41 Stephen Van Evera, *Causes of War*, p. 135.
42 Saira Khan, *Nuclear Proliferation Dynamics in Protracted Conflict Regions*, p. 46.
43 Stephen M. Meyer, *The Dynamics of Nuclear Proliferation*, (Chicago: University of Chicago Press, 1984), p. 65.
44 George Quester, "Reducing the Incentives to Proliferation," *Annals*, 430, March 1977, p. 71.
45 For more information on value/norm-driven and interest-driven behaviors between allies, see, Thomas Risse-Kappen, *Cooperation Among Democracies*, (Princeton: Princeton University Press, 1997), chapter 2 and p. 34.
46 *A Report on the International Control of Atomic Energy*. Prepared for the Secretary of State's Committee on Atomic Energy, Washington, D.C., U.S. Government Printing Office, March 16, 1946. Department of State Publication 2498. http://www.learn-world.com/ZNW/LWText.Acheson-Lilienthal.html

3 Iran's nuclear ambition and twin protracted conflicts between 1947 and 1979

1 *Iran's Strategic Weapons Programs*, An IISS Strategic Dossier, (London: Routledge, 2005), p. 10.
2 Ibid., p. 10.
3 Ibid., p. 10.
4 Leslie H. Gelb, "U.S. Nuclear Deal with Iran Delayed," *The New York Times*, March 8, 1975, p. 2.
5 "Iran: Atomic Energy Program," A report by United States Energy Research and Development Administration, October 1976, p. 3.
6 Leonard S. Spector with Jacqueline R. Smith, *Nuclear Ambitions: The Spread of Nuclear Weapons, 1989–1990* (Boulder, Oxford: Westview Press, 1990), p. 205.
7 Richard Kessler, "Argentina's Invap to Supply Iran Fuel for Research Reactor," *Nucleonics Week*, May 14, 1987, p. 2.
8 "US, Iran Resume Atom Power Talks," *The Washington Post*, August 9, 1977.

Notes

9. Leonard S. Spector, *Going Nuclear: The Spread of Nuclear Weapons 1986–1987*, (Cambridge, Mass.: Ballinger Publishing Company, 1987), pp. 50–51.
10. Ibid., pp. 50–51.
11. Ibid., p. 45.
12. *Iran's Strategic Weapons Programs*, An IISS Strategic Dossier, (London: Routledge, 2005), p. 11.
13. "Report of the NSSM 219 Working Group, Nuclear Cooperation Agreement with Iran," March 19, 1975, Digital National Security Archive. Available online at http://nsarchive.chadwych.com/
14. *Iran's Strategic Weapons Programs*, An IISS Strategic Dossier, (London: Routledge, 2005), p. 11.
15. Anthony Cordesman, *Iran and Iraq*, (Boulder: Westview, 1994), p. 104.
16. Leonard Spector and Jacqueline R. Smith, *Nuclear Ambitions*, (Boulder, Colorado: Westview Press, 1990), p. 204.
17. IAEA, *Implementation*, GOV/2003/6, September 12, 2003, p. 2.
18. Nathan E. Busch, *No End in Sight: The Continuing Menace of Nuclear Proliferation*, (Kentucky: The University Press of Kentucky, 2004), p. 265.
19. *Iran's Strategic Weapons Programs*, The International Institute for Strategic Studies, (London and New York: Routledge, 2005), p.79 fn 19.
20. Saira Khan, *Nuclear Proliferation Dynamics in Protracted Conflict Regions: A Comparative Study of South Asia and the Middle East*, (Aldershot and Vermant: Ashgate Publishing Ltd., 2002), pp. 241–42.
21. Pierre Goldschmidt and George Perkovich, "Iran Nuclear Showdown," *Transcript of Briefing*. Washington D.C. and Vermont: Carnegie Endowment for International Peace, January 18, 2006, p. 3. http://www.carnegieendowment.org/files/iran2006–01–18.pdf
22. *Iran's Strategic Weapons Programs*, The International Institute for Strategic Studies, (London and New York: Routledge, 2005), p.87
23. Ibid., p.89.
24. Ibid., p. 109.
25. Ibid., p. 109.
26. Tim Weiner, "Iran Said to Test Missile Able to Hit Israel and Saudis," *The New York Times*, July 23, 1998.
27. *Iran's Strategic Weapons Programs*, The International Institute for Strategic Studies, p. 109.
28. "Iran's Nuclear Program," *The Guardian*, April 28, 2006.
29. Interview with Meir Javedanfar, November 12, 2007.
30. Interview with Meir Javedanfar, November 12, 2007.
31. The International Institute for Strategic Studies, *The Military Balance 2009*, (Abingdon, Oxon: Taylor and Francis, 2009).
32. Ibid.
33. Seymour M. Hersh, "The Iran Plans: Would President Bush go to War to Stop Iran from Getting the Bomb?," *The New Yorker*, April 17, 2006.
34. Roger Howard, "Neither Sanctions nor Bombs will End the Iran Nuclear Crisis," *The Guardian*, January 11, 2007.
35. Alidad Mafinezam and Aria Mehrabi, *Iran and Its Place among Nations*, (Westport, Connecticut, London: Praeger, 2008), p. 63.
36. Speech by Hashemi Rafsanjani, *Tehran Domestic Service*, 19:35 GMT, October 6, 1988, Translation. In FBIS-NES, October 7, 1988, p. 2. Also, quoted by Leonard Spector, "Nuclear Proliferation in the Middle East: The Next Chapter Begins," in Efraim Karsh, Martin S. Navias, and Philip Sabin, eds., *Non-Conventional Weapons Proliferation in the Middle East*, (New York: Oxford University Press, 1993), p. 143.
37. *Der Spiegel*, February 8, 1975; Anne Hessing Cahn, "Determinants of the Nuclear Option: The Case of Iran," in Onkar Marwah and Ann Schultz, eds., *Nuclear*

Proliferation in the Near-Nuclear Countries, (Cambridge, Mass.: Ballinger Publishing Company, 1975).
38 Steve Weissman and Herbert Krosney, *The Islamic Bomb*, (New York: Times Books, 1981), p.89.
39 Statement made by H.E. Manouchehr Mottaki, Foreign Minister of the Islamic Republic of Iran before the United Nations Security Council, UN Press Release, March 23, 2007.
40 Alireza Jafarzadeh, *The Iran Threat: President Ahmadinejad and the Coming Nuclear Crisis*, (New York: Palgrave Macmillan, 2007), p. 132.
41 Ibid., p. 132.
42 Alidad Mafinezam and Aria Mehrabi, *Iran and Its Place among Nations*, (Westport, Connecticut, London: Praeger, 2008), p. 36.
43 "Iran Profile: Nuclear Chronology, 1957–85," Nuclear Threat Initiative, (NTI), www.nti.org/e_research/profiles/Iran/1825_1826.html
44 Alireza Jafarzadeh, *The Iran Threat: President Ahmadinejad and the Coming Nuclear Crisis*, p. 132.
45 Kenneth R. Timmerman, "Weapons of Mass Destruction: The Cases of Iran, Syria and Libya," A Simon Wiesenthal Center Special Report, August 1992, p. 41–42.
46 Alireza Jafarzadeh, *The Iran Threat*, p. 132.
47 "Nuclear Facilities," *Middle East Defense News*, June 8, 1992.
48 "Paper Reports Uranium Sales," *Worldwide Report*, July 13, 1987, p. 40.
49 Edward J Perkins, "Nuclear News from South Africa," Secret Cable [US Embassy in South Africa], July 29, 1987, in Digital National Security Archive, http://nsarchive.chadwyck.com/
50 Safa Ha'iri, "Secrets of Iran's Nuclear Program and a Map of Its Secret Factories," *Al Watan Al Arabi*, January 20, 1995, pp. 18–19.
51 D. Segal, "Atomic Ayatollahs," *The Washington Post*, April 12, 1987.
52 Statement from Kenneth R. Timmerman, "Iran's Nuclear Program: Myth or Reality," *The Middle East Data Project Inc.*, 1995. Also paper presented at the USPID Sixth International Castiglioncello Conference, Castiglioncello, Italy, September 30, 1995.
53 Kenneth R. Timmerman, "Weapons of Mass Destruction: The Cases of Iran, Syria, and Libya," *A Simon Wiesenthal Center Special Report from Middle East Defense News*, August 1992, p. 42; Warren H. Donnelly and Zachary S. Davis, "Iran's Nuclear Activities and the Congressional Response," *CRS Issue Brief*, Congressional Research Service, The Library of Congress, May 20, 1992, p. 10.
54 David Albright and Mark Hibbs, "Spotlight shifts to Iran" *The Bulletin of Atomic Scientists*, March 1992, pp. 9–11.
55 Mark Hibbs, "Bonn Will Decline Tehran Bid to Resuscitate Bushehr Project," *Neocleonics Week*, May 2, 1991, p. 17.
56 Saddam Hussein's Cabinet Statement, June 23, 1981 (FBIS, June 24, 1981, p. E-3); see Shai Feldman, *Nuclear Weapons and Arms Control in the Middle East*, (Cambridge, Mass.: The MIT Press, 1997), chapter 4, note 46.
57 Shai Feldman, *Nuclear Weapons*, p. 136.
58 Saideh Lotfian, "Threat Perception and Military Planning in Iran: Credible Scenarios of Conflict and Opportunities for Confidence Building," in Eric Arnett, ed., *Military Capacity and Risk of War*, (New York, Oxford: Oxford University Press, 1997), p. 197.
59 Ibid., p. 199.
60 Ray Takeyh, "Iran at the Strategic Crossroads," in James A. Russell, ed., *Proliferation of Weapons of Mass Destruction in the Middle East: Directions and Policy Options in the New Century*, (New York: Palgrave Macmillan, 2006), p. 53.
61 Michael Brecher and Jonathan Wilkenfeld, *A Study of Crisis*, (Ann Arbor: The University of Michigan Press, 1997), pp. 268–269.
62 Robert Harkavy, *Spectre of a Middle Eastern Holocaust: The Strategic and Diplomatic*

Implications of the Israeli Nuclear Weapons Program, Monograph Series in World Affairs, vol. 14, (Denver: University of Denver Press, 1977), pp. 70–71.
63 Rodney W. Jones, *et al.*, *Tracking Nuclear Proliferation*, (Washington D.C.: Brookings Institution Press, 1998), p. 208.
64 Seymour M. Hersh, *The Samson Option*, (New York: Random House, 1991), pp. 291, 312, 319.
65 George Perkovich and James M. Action, *Abolishing Nuclear Weapons*, Adelphi Paper 396, (New York: Routledge, 2008), p. 24.
66 Daniel Byman, *et al.*, *Iran's Security Policy: In the Post-Revolutionary Era*, (Santa Monica: RAND, 2001), p. 85.
67 Ibid., p. 85.
68 Michael D. Evans and Jerome R. Corsi, *Showdown with Nuclear Iran: Radical Islam's Messianic Mission to Destroy Israel and Cripple The United States*, (Nashville, Tennessee: Nelson Current, 2006), p. 80.
69 Farhad Pouladi, "Iran's Ahmadinejad Attacks Israel at Iraq Conference," *Agence-France Presse via Middle East Times*, July 9, 2006. http://www.metimes.com/storyview.php?StoryID+20060709-014952-3804r
70 Michael D. Evans and Jerome R. Corsi, *Showdown with Nuclear Iran*, p. 80.
71 Ibid., p. 81.
72 See, among others, Avner Cohen, *Israel and the Bomb*, (New York: Columbia University Press, 1998).
73 Michael D. Evans and Jerome R. Corsi, *Showdown with Nuclear Iran*, p. 152.
74 Ibid., p. 152.
75 Michael D. Evans and Jerome R. Corsi, *Showdown with Nuclear Iran*, p. 11.
76 George Perkovich and James M. Action, *Abolishing Nuclear Weapons*, p. 24.
77 Ray Takeyh, "Iran at the Strategic Crossroads," p. 53.
78 Michael D. Evans and Jerome R. Corsi, *Showdown with Nuclear Iran*, p. 152.
79 Shahram Chubin, "Understanding Iran's Nuclear Ambition," in Patrick M. Cronin, ed., *Double Trouble: Iran and North Korea as Challenges To International Security*, (Westport, Connecticut, London: Praeger, 2008), p. 50.
80 Ibid., p. 50.

4 Iran's nuclear program and triple protracted conflicts from 1979 onwards

1 Saira Khan, *Nuclear Proliferation Dynamics in Protracted Conflict Regions: A Comparative Study of South Asia and the Middle East*, (Aldershot and Vermont: Ashgate Publishing Ltd., 2002), p. 238.
2 John L. Esposito, "Introduction: From Khomeini to Khatami," in John L. Esposito and R. K. Ramazani, ed., *Iran at the Crossroads*, (New York: Palgrave, 2001), p. 1.
3 "Chronology of US–Iran Relations, 1906–2002," *Frontline*. http://www.pbs.org/wgbh/pages/frontline/shows/tehran/etc/cron.html
4 Ayaz Ahmed Khan, "Plans to Attack Iran," *Defense Journal*, April 2007, p. 11.
5 "Chronology of US–Iran Relations, 1906–2002," *Frontline*. http://www.pbs.org/wgbh/pages/frontline/shows/tehran/etc/cron.html
6 Yonah Alexander and Milton Hoenig, *The New Iranian Leadership: Ahmadinejad, Terrorism, Nuclear Ambition, and the Middle East*, (Westport, Connecticut: Praeger Security International, 2008), p. 5.
7 Ibid., p. 5.
8 Ayaz Ahmed Khan, "Plans to Attack Iran," p. 11.
9 "The Mystic Who Lit the Fires of Hatred," *Time Magazine*, January 7, 1980.
10 Ibid.
11 Ibid.
12 Ibid.

13 Curtis H. Martin, "'Good Cop/Bad Cop' as a Model for Nonproliferation Diplomacy Toward North Korea and Iran," *Nonproliferation Review*, vol.14, no.1, March 2007, p. 70.
14 Yonah Alexander and Milton Hoenig, *The New Iranian Leadership*, p. 5.
15 Ibid., p. 6.
16 Ali. M. Ansari, *Confronting Iran: The Failure of American Foreign Policy and the Next Crisis in the Middle East*, (New York: Basic Books, 2006), pp. 71–72.
17 Ibid., p. 90.
18 *Iran's Strategic Weapons Programs*, The International Institute for Strategic Studies, p. 111.
19 George A Lopez and David Cortright, "The Smarter US Option: A Full Summit with Iran," *Policy Brief*, The Joan B. Kroc Institute for International Peace Studies, no.11, June 2006.
20 George Perkovich, "Dealing with Iran's Nuclear Challenge," *Carnegie Endowment for International Peace*, April 28, 2003, p. 3.
21 Gary Sick, "A Selective Partnership: Getting US–Iranian Relations Right," *Foreign Affairs*, November/December 2006, p. 1.
22 Ibid., p. 1.
23 Kenneth Katzman, "Iran: US Concerns and Policy Responses," *CRS Report for Congress*, July 31, 2006, p. 28.
24 "Chronology US–Iran Relations, 1906–2002," *Frontline* p. 4. http://www.pbs.org/wgbh/pages/frontline/shows/tehran/etc/cron.html
25 Kenneth Katzman, "Iran," p. 23.
26 Ayaz Ahmed Khan, "Plans to Attack Iran," p. 11.
27 Kenneth Katzman, "Iran," p. 35.
28 "With Release of Terry Anderson, US Hostage Ordeal Ended in Lebanon," *Washington Report on Middle East Affairs*, December 1995, pp. 79–80.
29 "Iran Depicts Bush Plea as 'Arrogant,'" *The Washington Post*, January 28, 1989, p. A15.
30 Kenneth Katzman, "Iran," p. 27.
31 Alireza Jafarzadeh, *The Iran Threat: President Ahmadinejad and the Coming Nuclear Crisis*, (New York: Palgrave Macmillan, 2007), p. 70.
32 Daniel Byman, et al., *Iran's Security Policy: In the Post-Revolutionary Era*, (Santa Monica: RAND, 2001), p. 84.
33 Ibid., p. 84.
34 Sciolino Elaine, *The Outlaw State: Saddam Hussein's Quest for Power and the Gulf Crisis*, (New York: John Wiley and Sons, 1991), p.168.
35 Kenneth Katzman, "Iran," p. 27.
36 Bernard Gwertzman, "US Said to Favor Sale of F-16 Jets to the Jordanians," *The New York Times*, February 27, 1982, p. 1.
37 Ali. M. Ansari, *Confronting Iran*, p. 106.
38 Interview with Shaul Bakhash, November 28, 2007.
39 "President Mahmoud Ahmadinejad's UN Address," IRNA, September 17, 2005.
40 Statement of Ray Takeyh on "Iran: Briefing and Hearing before the Committee on Foreign Affairs," *House of Representatives*, January 11 and 31, 2007, Serial no. 110–113, p. 77.
41 Ibid., Serial no. 110–113, p. 77.
42 Statement of Enders Wimbush on "Iran: Briefing and Hearing before the Committee on Foreign Affairs," *House of Representatives*, January 11 and 31, 2007, Serial no. 110–113, p. 87.
43 Michael D. Evans and Jerome R. Corsi, *Showdown with Nuclear Iran*, (Tennessee: Nelson Current, 2006), p. 80.
44 Bernard Reich, "Reassessing the United States–Israeli Special Relationship," *Israel Affairs*, 1, 1994, p. 69.

45 Abraham Ben-Zvi, *Alliance Politics and the Limits of Influence: The Case of the US and Israel, 1975–1983*, (Jerusalem, Israel: Jaffee Center for Strategic Studies, 1984), p. 38.
46 Avner Cohen, *Israel and the Bomb*, (New York: Columbia University Press, 1998), pp. 323–338.
47 Patrick M. Cronin, "The Trouble with Iran," in Patrick M. Cronin, ed., *Double Trouble: Iran and North Korea as Challenges to International Security*, (Westport Connecticut: Praeger Security International, 2008), p. 14.
48 Rachel Bzostek and Samuel B. Robison, "US Policy toward Israel, Iraq, and Saudi Arabia: An Integrated Analysis, 1981–2004," *International Studies Perspectives*, vol. 9, November 4, 2008, p. 369.
49 Daniel Byman, et al., *Iran's Security Policy in the Post-Revolutionary Era*, (Santa Monica: RAND, 2001), p. 2.
50 Ibid., p. 85.
51 Interview with Shaul Bakhash, November 28, 2007.
52 Ibid.
53 Tony Karon, "Why Iran Will Go Nuclear," *Time*, February 12, 2005, p. 5.
54 Peter R. Lavoy, "Nuclear Proliferations Over the Next Decade: Causes, Warning Signs, and Policy Responses," *Nonproliferation Review*, vol. 13, no. 3, November 2006, p. 441.
55 Perkovich, George and James M. Action, *Abolishing Nuclear Weapons*, Adelphi Paper 396, (New York: Routledge, 2008), p. 86, fn. 5.
56 Colin Dueck and Ray Takeyh, "Iran's Nuclear Challenge," *Political Science Quarterly*, vol. 122, no. 2, 2007, p. 193.
57 Ibid., p. 193.
58 Interview with Farideh Farhi, December 3, 2007.
59 "Anti-Arrogance Campaign Becomes Necessary," *Jumhuri-ye-Islami*, November 3, 2004.
60 Colin Dueck and Ray Takeyh, "Iran's Nuclear Challenge," p. 193.
61 Ibid.
62 Statement of Enders Wimbush, Serial no. 110–113, p. 87.
63 Interview with Shaul Bakhash, November 28, 2007.
64 Ilan Berman, Interview by Dimitri Neos, Foreign Affairs Forum Interview, March 20, 2006.
65 Patrick M. Cronin, "The Trouble with Iran," p. 14.
66 Alireza Jafarzadeh, *The Iran Threat*, p. 131.
67 Tony Karon, "Why Iran Will Go Nuclear," p. 5
68 Andrew Kich and Jeanette Wolf, "Iran's Nuclear Facilities: A Profile," *Center for Nonproliferation Studies*, 1998.
69 Iran's Strategic Weapons Program: A Net Assessment, IISS London: Routledge, 2005, p. 12.
70 IAEA Director General's Report, "Implementation of the NPT Safeguards Agreement in the Islamic Republic of Iran," November 10, 2003. www.iaea.org/Publications/Documents/Board/2003/gov2003-75.pdf
71 "Implementation of the NPT Safeguards Agreement in the Islamic Republic of Iran," November 10, 2003.
72 "Iran Profile: Nuclear Chronology, 1957–1985," Nuclear Threat Initiative (NTI). ww.nti.org/e_research/profiles/Iran/1825_1826.html
73 "A. Q. Khan & Iran," *Global Security.Org* http://www.globalsecurity.org/wmd/world/iran/khan-iran.htm
74 Shahram Chubin, "Understanding Iran's Nuclear Ambitions," in Patrick M. Cronin, ed., *Double Trouble: Iran and North Korea as Challenges to International Security*, (Westport Connecticut and London: Praeger Security International, 2008), p. 50.
75 Ibid., p. 50.

76 Interview with Leonard Spector, December 7, 2007.
77 Ibid.

5 The ramifications of the asymmetric Iran–US protracted conflict from 1990 to 2000 in Iran's nuclear domain

1. President George H. W. Bush, "Address Before a Joint Session of the Congress on the Persian Gulf Crisis and the Federal Budget Deficit," September 11, 1990. http://bushlibrary.tamu.edu/research/papers/1990/90091101.html
2. See, Michael Klare, *Rogue States and Nuclear Outlaws*, (New York: Hill and Wang, 1995).
3. Ibid., pp. 27–28.
4. Paul Hoyt, "The Rogue States Image in American Foreign Policy," *Global Society*, no. 14, 2000, pp. 297–310.
5. See, Miroslav Nincic, *Renegade Regimes: Confronting Deviant Behavior in World Politics*, (New York: Columbia University Press, 2005).
6. K. P. O'Reilly, "Perceiving Rogue States: The Use of the 'Rogue State' Concept by US Foreign Policy Elites," *Foreign Policy Analysis*, vol. 3, issue 4, October 2007, p. 297.
7. Miroslav Nincic, *Renegade Regimes*.
8. K. P. O'Reilly, "Perceiving Rogue States: The Use of the 'Rogue State' Concept by US Foreign Policy Elites," p. 297.
9. Michael Klare, *Rogue States and Nuclear Outlaws*, p. 134.
10. K. P. O'Reilly, "Perceiving Rogue States: The Use of the 'Rogue State' Concept by US Foreign Policy Elites," p. 305
11. See, Paul Hoyt, "The Rogue States Image in American Foreign Policy," *Global Society*, no. 14, 2000.
12. K. P. O'Reilly, "Perceiving Rogue States: The Use of the 'Rogue State' Concept by US Foreign Policy Elites," p. 304.
13. Ibid., p. 311.
14. Michael Klare, *Rogue States and Nuclear Outlaws*, (New York: Hill and Wang, 1995), p. 132.
15. Testimony before House Banking Committee, May 8, 1992, p. 9.
16. Elaine Sciolino, "CIA Says Iran Makes Progress on Atom Arms," *The New York Times*, November 30, 1992; R. Jeffrey Smith, "Officials Say Iran is Seeking Nuclear Weapons Capability," *The Washington Post*, October 31, 1991
17. Akbar Ganji, Talk on "Human Rights and Democracy," *Simon Centre*, University of British Columbia, November 29, 2007.
18. Michael Klare, *Rogue States and Nuclear Outlaws*, p. 205.
19. K. P. O'Reilly, "Perceiving Rogue States: The Use of the 'Rogue State' Concept by US Foreign Policy Elites," p. 301.
20. Kunhui Cai, Madan Chauhan, Jim Jacaruso, Manoj Pant, Vinay Srivastava, and Yoji Tsubaki, *Asymmetric Conflict*, PPA601, spring 2007.
21. Interview with Shaul Bakhash, November 28, 2007.
22. Samuel P. Huntington, "The Lonely Superpower," in G. John Ikenberry, ed., *American Foreign Policy: Theoretical Essays*, 5th edition, (New York: Pearson Education, 2005), pp. 540–550.
23. Ibid.
24. Interview with Leonard Spector, December 7, 2007.
25. Interview with Michael Levi, November 23, 2007.
26. Interview with Meir Javedanfar, November 12, 2007.
27. Ibid.
28. Samuel P. Huntington, "The Clash of Civilizations," in Robert J. Art and Robert Jervis, eds., *International Politics: Enduring Concepts and Contemporary Issues*, 6th edition, (New York: Longman, 2003), pp. 411–425.

29 Samuel P. Huntington, "The Lonely Superpower," pp. 540–550.
30 Michael J. Mazarr, "The Folly of 'Asymmetric War'," *Washington Quarterly*, vol. 31, no.3, Summer 2008, p. 46.
31 Interview with Leonard Spector, December 7, 2007.
32 Interview with Shaul Bakhash, November 28, 2007.
33 Ibid.
34 Kunhui Cai, Madan Chauhan, Jim Jacaruso, Manoj Pant, Vinay Srivastava, and Yoji Tsubaki, *Asymmetric Conflict*, PPA601, Spring 2007.
35 *Iran's Strategic Weapons Programs*, an IISS Strategic Dossier, (London: Routledge, 2005), p. 12.
36 Interview with Leonard Spector, December 7, 2007.
37 Interview with Shaul Bakhash, November 28, 2007.
38 Ibid.
39 "Iran Reject NPT Unless all Nuclear Weapons are Scrapped," *Deutsche Presse-Agentur*, April 21, 1995; in Lexis-Nexis, http://www.lexis-nexis.com/
40 Kunhui Cai, Madan Chauhan, Jim Jacaruso, Manoj Pant, Vinay Srivastava, and Yoji Tsubaki, *Asymmetric Conflict*, PPA601, spring 2007.
41 *Iran's Strategic Weapons Programs*, an IISS Strategic Dossier, (London: Routledge, 2005), p. 12.
42 Ibid.
43 Interview with Meir Javedanfar, November 12, 2007.
44 "Iran Profile: Nuclear Chronology, 1991," *Nuclear Threat Initiative*, (NTI), www.nti.org/e_research/profiles/Iran/1825_1826.html
45 Leonard Spector, "Islamic Bomb West's Long-Term Nightmare," *Washington Times*, January 19, 1994, p. A19.
46 *Iran's Strategic Weapons Programs*, an IISS Strategic Dossier, (London: Routledge, 2005), p. 13.
47 Mark Hibbs, "Bonn Will Decline Teheran Bid To Resuscitate Bushehr Project," *Nucleonics Week*, May 2, 1991, pp. 17–18.
48 "Iran Profile: Nuclear Chronology, 1991," Nuclear Threat Initiative, (NTI), www.nti.org/e_research/profiles/Iran/1825_1826.html
49 Mary Curtius, "Dissidents Say Tehran Is Pursuing Nuclear Arms," *The Boston Globe*, June 30, 1991; in Lexis-Nexis, http://www.lexis-nexis.com/.
50 Ibid.
51 "The China–Iran Nuclear Cloud," *Middle East Defense News*, July 22, 1991; in Lexis-Nexis, http://www.lexis-nexis.com/.
52 Yonah Alexander and Milton Hoenig, *The New Iranian Leadership: Ahmedinejad, Terrorism, Nuclear Ambition, and the Middle East*, (Westport, Connecticut: Praeger Security International, 2008), p. 121.
53 *Iran's Strategic Weapons Programs*, an IISS Strategic Dossier, (London: Routledge, 2005), p. 13.
54 Ibid., p. 13.
55 "Iranian Diplomats On Nuclear Warhead Purchases," *Proliferation Issues*, March 5 1993, pp. 14–16; Paul Beaver Flash Points Update, *Jane's Defense Weekly*, April 3, 1993, pp. 20–21.
56 Kenneth R. Timmerman, "Weapons of Mass Destruction: The Cases of Iran, Syria, and Libya," A Simon Wiesenthal Center Special Report from Middle East Defense News, *Middle East Defense News*, August 1992, p. 43.
57 Steve Coll, "U.S. Halted Nuclear Bid By Iran; China, Argentina, Agreed to Cancel Technology Transfers," *The Washington Post*, 17 November 1992; in Lexis-Nexis, http://www.lexis-nexis.com/.
58 "Middle East," *International Security Digest*, January 1995.
59 Mark Hibbs, "Iran May Withdraw From NPT Over Western Trade Barriers," *Nucleonics Week*, September 22, 1994, pp. 1, 8–9; Mark Hibbs, "Western Group

Battles Iran at Third NPT PrepCom Session" *Nucleonics Week*, September 22, 1994, pp. 9–10; Mark Hibbs, "It's 'Too Early' For Tehran To Leave NPT, Delegates Say," *NuclearFuel*, September 26, 1994, pp. 9–10.
60 Interview with Meir Javedanfar, November 12, 2007.
61 Hassan Rohini, "Iran's Nuclear Program: The Way Out," *Time*, May 9, 2006.
62 "Nuclear Weapons-Iranian Statements" http://www.globalsecurity.org/wmd/world/iran/nuke2.htm
63 Daniel Byman, Shahram Chubin, Anoushiravan Ehteshami, and Jerrold Green, *Iran's Security Policy: In the Post-Revolutionary Era*, (Santa Monica: RAND, 2001), p. 85.
64 Maziar Bahari, "Isolating or Attacking Iran Won't Work," *The Washington Post*, September 18, 2008. http://newsweek.washingtonpost.com/postglobal/needtoknow/2008/09/iran_does_not_trust_the_west_a.html
65 "Naseri Address UN Conference on NPT Issues," *IRNA* (Tehran), May 12, 1995; in FBIS Document FTS19950512000507, May 12, 1995.
66 James Woolsey, "Challenges to Peace," speech before the Washington Institute for Near East Policy, 23 September 1994 (mimeo); Anthony H. Cordesman, "Threats and Non-Threats From Iran," Center for Strategic and International Studies, January 26, 1995.
67 Steven Greenhouse, "US Seeks To Deny A-Plants To Iran," *The New York Times*, January 24, 1995, p. A4; Daniel Williams and Thomas W. Lippman, "Christopher Charges Iran Continues Nuclear Program," *The Washington Post*, January 21, 1995, p. A11.
68 Iran's Strategic Weapons Programs, an *IISS Strategic Dossier*, (London: Routledge, 2005), p. 13.
69 "President Inaugurates New Nuclear Research Facility," *IRNA* (Tehran) January 2, 1996; in FBIS Document FTS 19960102000243, January 2, 1996; "President on Peaceful Use of Nuclear Power," *IRNA* (Tehran) January 2, 1996; in FBIS Document FTS 19960102000270, January 2, 1996.
70 "Iran's Chinese Shopping List," *Iran Brief*, October 1, 1996, pp. 4–5.
71 Marina Bidoli, "Atomic Energy Corp In Danger Of Being Vaporized," *Financial Mail*, August 15, 1997; Inigo Gilmore, "Daily On Iranian Nuclear 'Shopping List' in South Africa," *The Times* (London), August 18, 1997; Mathew Campbell and Uzi Mahnami, "Iran's Mullahs On Brink Of A Nuclear Bomb," *The Times* (London), December 21, 1997; G.N. Markov, V.N. Lokhman, and E. Ronanader, "Multiple Photoionization of 169Yb in a Three-Level Atomic Medium by the Collinear Propagation of Laser Pulses," *Journal of Physics*, Section B, 1995, vol. 28, pp. 215–220; Ann MacLachlan and Michael Knapik, "South Africa to End MIS SWU Project," *Nuclear Fuel*, December 12, 1997.
72 Interview with Farideh Fardi, December 3, 2007.
73 Pierre Goldschmidt and George Perkovich, "Iran's Nuclear Showdown," *Transcript of Briefing*, Washington D.C. Carnegie Endowment for International Peace, January 18, 2006, p. 9. http://www.carnegieendowment.org/files/iran2006-01-18.pdf
74 Yonah Alexander and Milton Hoenig, *The New Iranian Leadership: Ahmedinejad, Terrorism, Nuclear Ambition, and the Middle East*, (Westport, Connecticut: Praeger Security International, 2008), p. 117.
75 Al J. Venter, "Iran's Nuclear Ambition: Innocuous Illusion Or Ominous Truth?," *Jane's International Defense Review*, September 1997, pp. 29–31.
76 Ibid., pp. 29–31.
77 "US Sent Data To Russia on Iran WMD," *Middle East Newsline*, vol. 4, no. 199, May 29, 2002, http://www.menl.com/
78 "Iranians To Learn In Russia How To Operate Nuclear Power Plant," *Middle East News Items*, February 4, 1999; in Lexis-Nexis, http://www.lexis-nexis.com/
79 Ray Takeyh, "Iran at the Strategic Crossroads," in James A. Russell, ed., *Proliferation*

of *Weapons of Mass Destruction in the Middle East: Directions and Policy Options in the New Century*, (New York: Palgrave, Macmillan, 2006), p. 59.
80 Jim Mannion, "Iran Tapped Russia, China for Weapons of Mass Destruction Technology: CIA," *Agence France Presse*, February 2, 2000, in Lexis-Nexis, http://www.lexis-nexis.com/
81 Ibid.
82 Interview with Leonard Spector, December 7, 2007.

6 Iran's fast-paced proliferation activity and hostile US policy since 2000

1 Ali M. Ansari, *Confronting Iran: The Failure of American Foreign Policy and the Next Crisis in the Middle East*, (New York: Basic Books, 2006), pp. 199–201.
2 *Iran's Strategic Weapons Programs*, The International Institute for Strategic Studies, p. 16.
3 Interview with Michael Levi, November 23, 2007.
4 *Iran's Strategic Weapons Programs*, The International Institute for Strategic Studies, p. 201.
5 Roger Howard, *Iran in Crisis: Nuclear Ambitions and the American Response*, (London, New York: Zed Books, 2004), pp. 18–19.
6 Nathan E. Busch, *No End in Sight: The Continuing Menace of Nuclear Proliferation*, (Kentucky: The University Press of Kentucky, 2004), p. 264.
7 George Perkovich, "Iran Says No-Now What?," *Carnegie Endowment for International Peace*, Policy Brief, no. 63, September 2008, p. 1.
8 "Iran: Nuclear Intentions and Capabilities," *National Intelligence Estimate*, November 2007. http://www.dni.gov/press_releases/20071203_release.pdf
9 Interview with Leonard Spector, December 7, 2007.
10 "Iran: Nuclear Intentions and Capabilities."
11 Interview with Leonard Spector, December 7, 2007.
12 *Iran's Strategic Weapons Programs*, The International Institute for Strategic Studies, p. 42.
13 Patrick M. Cronin, "The Trouble with Iran," in Patrick M. Cronin, ed., *Double Trouble: Iran and North Korea As Challenges to International Security*, (Westport, Connecticut: Praeger Security International, 2008), p. 12.
14 Ibid., p. 19.
15 "In the Club," *The Economist*, vol. 378, no. 8473, London, April 15, 2006.
16 Interview with Meir Javedanfar, November 12, 2007.
17 "First Iran Meeting of Obama Presidency Planned," *Berlin: Associated Free Press*, January 29, 2009.
18 Iran's President wants the US to apologize to Iran. He believes that US should change its attitude towards Iran. He states, "Change means that they should apologize to the Iranian nation and try to make up for their dark background and the crimes they have committed against the Iranian nation." He said this in a speech in the western city of Kermanshah which was broadcast live on Iranian television. For more information on this, see, Nazila Fathi and Alan Cowell, "After Obama Overture, Iran's Leader Seeks US Apology," *The New York Times*, January 28, 2009.
19 Saira Khan, *Nuclear Proliferation Dynamics in Protracted Conflict Regions: A Comparative Study of South Asia and the Middle East*, (Aldershot and Vermont: Ashgate Publishing Ltd., 2002), pp. 42–43.
20 General Yahya Rahim Safavi the Islamic Revolution Guard Corps Commander-in-Chief, *Iran Web site*, May 9, 2006, p. 1, in *BBC Online*, May 11, 2006.
21 Ayatollah Ali Khameini's Speech Islamic Republic of Iran News Network, June 4, 2006, in *BBC Online*, June 5, 2006.
22 Ali Larijini, Speech at Middle East Center, Tehran, October 27, 2005, Reprinted in *Journal of European Society for European Studies*, 2006, pp. 125–131.

Notes   135

23 Roger Howard, *Iran in Crisis*, p. 58.
24 Ibid., p. 59.
25 Bob Woodward, *Bush at War*, (New York: Simon and Schuster, 2002), p. 30.
26 Sverre Lodgaard, "Iran's Uncertain Nuclear Ambitions," in Morten Bremer Maerli and Sverre Lodgaard, eds., *Nuclear Proliferation and International Security*, (London and New York: Routledge, 2007), p. 105.
27 Roger Howard, *Iran in Crisis*, p. 13.
28 Charles D. Ferguson and John E. Pike, "National Missile Defense: Developing Disaster," *Disarmament Diplomacy*, issue no. 44, 2000.
29 "Bush Reaffirms Support for Missile Defense System," *Daily Star*, January 10, 2001.
30 Barbara Opall, "Israelis Say Russia Aids Iran's Quest for Missiles," *Defense News*, February 10, 1997, p. 1.
31 Aaron Karp, "Lessons of Iranian Missile Programs for US Non-proliferation Policy," *The Non-proliferation Review*, vol. 5, no. 3, spring–summer 1998.
32 Rodney W. Jones, et al., *Tracking Nuclear Proliferation*, (Washington D.C.: Brookings Institution Press, 1998), p. 169.
33 Saira Khan, "Targeting the Rogue States: The US National Missile Defense System and Nuclear Proliferation," Paper presented at the International Studies Association Annual Convention, Chicago, February 20–24, 2001.
34 Graeme A. M. Davies, "Inside Out or Outside In: Domestic and International Factors Affecting Iranian Foreign Policy Towards the United States 1990–2004," *Foreign Policy Analysis*, vol. 4, no. 3, July 2008, p. 211.
35 Roger Howard, *Iran in Crisis*, p. 9.
36 Ibid., p. 9.
37 Interview with Farideh Farhi, December 3, 2007.
38 William M. Arkin, "Secret Plan Outlines the Unthinkable," *Los Angeles Times*, March 10, 2002.
39 Excerpts from the Nuclear Posture Review, J. D. Crouch, Assistant Secretary of Defense for International Security Policy, Special Briefing on the Nuclear Posture Review, Department of Defense, January 9, 2002.
40 Keir A. Lieber and Daryl G. Press, "The Rise of US Nuclear Primacy," *Foreign Affairs*, vol. 85, no.2, March/April 2006, p. 52.
41 US Office of the President, National Strategy to Combat Weapons of Mass Destruction, The White House, December 2002, http://www.whitehouse.gov/news/releases/2002/12/WMDStrategy.pdf
42 See, Defense Link, US Department of Defense: www.defenselink.mil/news/Jan2002.d/20020109npr.pdf
43 George Perkovich, "Bush's Nuclear Revolution: A Regime Change in Non-proliferation," *Foreign Affairs*, vol. 82, no.2, March/April 2003, p. 3.
44 Ibid., p. 4.
45 "Iranian Foreign Ministry spokesman's letter to the UN Secretary General," *Agence France-Presse*, March 18, 2002.
46 George Perkovich, "Bush's Nuclear Revolution: A Regime Change in Nonproliferation," p. 5.
47 Sharon LaFraniere, "Allies Unperturbed by US Nuclear List: Iranians, Russians Criticize Report," *The Washington Post*, March 11, 2002.
48 "Iran's Nuclear Program," *The Guardian*, April 28, 2006.
49 Seymour M. Hersh, "The Iran Plans: Would President Bush go to War to stop Iran from getting the Bomb?," *The New Yorker*, April 17, 2006.
50 Akbar Ganji, Talk on "Human Rights and Democracy," Simon Centre, The University of British Columbia, November 29, 2007.
51 "US Report: Iran Stopped Nuclear Weapons Work in 2003," *CNN*, December 3, 2007.
52 http://disarmament.un.org/wmd/npt/1995dec2.htm; S/1995/263
53 http://disarmament.un.org/wmd/npt/1995dec2.htm; NPT/CONF.1995/32(Part I), Annex

54 Ibid.
55 Interview with Akbar Ganji, November 29, 2007.
56 Patrick M. Cronin, "The Trouble with Iran," p. 20.
57 Interview with Meir Javedanfar, November 12, 2007.
58 Patrick M. Cronin, "The Trouble with Iran," p. 20.
59 Ray Takeyh, "Iran at the Strategic Crossroads," in James A Russell, ed., *Proliferation of Weapons of Mass Destruction in the Middle East: Directions and Policy Options in the New Century*, (New York: Palgrave Macmillan, 2006), p. 54.
60 Ibid., p. 56.
61 Karl Vick, "Iranians Assert Right to Nuclear Weapons," *The Washington Post*, March 11, 2003.
62 Ray Takeyh, "Iran at the Strategic Crossroads," p. 55.
63 *Reuters*, April 19, 2003.
64 Karl Vick, "Iranians Assert Right to Nuclear Weapons."
65 George Perkovich, "Bush's Nuclear Revolution: A Regime Change in Nonproliferation."
66 Interview with Akbar Ganji, November 29, 2007.
67 Ibid., 2007.
68 Sverre Lodgaard, "Iran's Uncertain Nuclear Ambitions," in Morten Bremer Maerli and Sverre Lodgaard, eds., *Nuclear Proliferation and International Security*, (London and New York: Routledge, 2007), p. 105.
69 "State of the Union Address by Jimmy Carter 1980." Available online at www.thisnation.com/library/sotu/1980jc.html; American Government and Politics Online.
70 Ibid.
71 Sverre Lodgaard, "Iran's Uncertain Nuclear Ambitions," pp. 105–106.
72 Interview with Michael Levi, November 23, 2007.
73 Interview with Shaul Bakhash, November 28, 2007.
74 Ibid.
75 Ibid.
76 Interview with Leonard Spector, December 7, 2007.
77 Sverre Lodgaard, "Iran's Uncertain Nuclear Ambitions," in Morten Bremer Maerli and Sverre Lodgaard, eds., *Nuclear Proliferation and International Security*, (London and New York: Routledge, 2007), p. 105.
78 Gareth Porter, "Iran Nuclear Conflict is about US Dominance," *Antiwar.com*, May 12, 2006. http://www.antiwar.com/orig/porter.php?articleid=8982
79 Ibid.
80 Ibid.
81 Interview with Farideh Farhi, December 3, 2007.
82 Gareth Porter, "Iran Nuclear Conflict is about US Dominance."
83 Interview with Farideh Farhi, December 3, 2007.
84 Interview with Michael Levi, November 23, 2007.
85 William O. Beeman, "Iran and US Locked into Spiral Conflict – Last Refuge of Weak Leaders," *New America Media*, April 13, 2006.
86 Interview with Akbar Ganji, November 29, 2007.
87 Interview with Farideh Farhi, December 3, 2007.
88 Interview with Charles Ferguson, November 20, 2007.
89 Kaveh L. Afrasiabi and Pirouz Mojtahedzadeh, "Iran's Nuclear Program: Threats are not the Way to Influence Tehran," *International Herald Tribune*, July 2, 2004.
90 Interview with Shaul Bakhash, November 28, 2007.
91 Alireza Jafarzadeh, *The Iran Threat: President Ahmadinejad and the Coming Nuclear Crisis*, (New York: Palgrave Macmillan, 2007), p. 140.
92 *Iran's Strategic Weapons Programs: A Net Assessment*, (Abingdon: Routledge for the IISS, 2005), p. 54.
93 Interview with Michael Levi, November 23, 2007.

94 Mark Fitzpatrick, "Is Iran's Nuclear Capability Inevitable?," in Patrick M. Cronin, ed., *Double Trouble: Iran and North Korea As Challenges to International Security*, (Westport, Connecticut: Praeger Security International, 2008), p. 29.
95 Roger Howard, "Neither Sanctions nor Bombs will end the Iran Nuclear Crisis," *The Guardian*, January 11, 2007.
96 Interview with Farideh Farhi, December 3, 2007.
97 Ali. M. Ansari, *Confronting Iran: The Failure of American Foreign Policy and the Next Crisis in the Middle East*, (New York: Basic Books, 2006), p. 205.
98 Ibid., p. 223.
99 Iran's Strategic Weapons Program, IISS, p. 110.
100 "Iran Complains of Nuclear Bullying," *CNN,* February 23, 2007.
101 Sverre Lodgaard, "Iran's Uncertain Nuclear Ambitions," p. 106.
102 Interview with Farideh Farhi, December 3, 2007.
103 Meghan L. O'Sullivan, *Shrewd Sanctions: Statecraft and State Sponsors of Terrorism*, (Washington D.C.: Brookings Institution Press, 2003).
104 Interview with Farideh Farhi, December 3, 2007.
105 Interview with Charles Ferguson, November 20, 2007.
106 Ibid.
107 George Perkovich and Karim Sadjadpour, "Strategic Engagement with Iran: Steps for the Next U.S. President," *Carnegie Endowment for International Peace*, October 16, 2008.
108 Interview with Charles Ferguson, November 20, 2007.
109 Interview with Michael Levi, November 23, 2007.
110 Ibid.

Bibliography

Books and articles

Abdin, Mahan, "Public Opinion and the Nuclear Standoff," *Mid East Mirror*, vol. 2, no. 1, April/May 2006. http://www.mideastmonitor.org/issues/0604/0604_3.htm

Afrasiabi, Kaveh L. and Pirouz Mojtahedzadeh, "Iran's Nuclear Program: Threats are not the Way to Influence Tehran," *International Herald Tribune*, July 2, 2004.

Albright, David and Mark Hibbs, "Spotlight Shifts to Iran," *The Bulletin of Atomic Scientists*, March 1992.

Alexander, Yonah and Milton Hoenig, *The New Iranian Leadership: Ahmedinejad, Terrorism, Nuclear Ambition, and the Middle East*, (Westport, Connecticut: Praeger Security International, 2008).

Allison, Graham, *Nuclear Terrorism: The Ultimate Preventable Catastrophe*, (New York: Henry Holt Times Books, 2004).

Amirahmadi, Hooshang, ed., *Revisiting Iran's Strategic Significance in the Emerging Regional Order*, (New Brunswick, New Jersey: US–Iran Conference, 1995).

Ansari, Ali M., *Confronting Iran: The Failure of American Foreign Policy and the Next Crisis in the Middle East*, (New York: Basic Books, 2006).

Arkin, William M., "Secret Plan Outlines the Unthinkable," *Los Angeles Times*, March 10, 2002.

Azar, Edward E., Paul Jureidini and Ronald McLaurin, "Protracted Social Conflict: Theory and Practice in the Middle East," *Journal of Palestine Studies*, vol.8, no.1, 1978.

Bahari, Maziar, "Isolating or Attacking Iran Won't Work," *The Washington Post*, September 18, 2008.

Bahgat, Gawdat, "Iran, the United States, and the War on Terrorism," *Studies in Conflict and Terrorism*, vol. 26, no.3, 2003.

—— "Nuclear Proliferation: The Islamic Republic of Iran," *Iranian Studies*, vol. 39, no.3, 2006.

Baldwin, David A., "Neoliberalism, Neorealism, and World Politics," in David A. Baldwin, ed., *Neorealism and Neoliberalism: The Contemporary Debate*, (New York: Columbia University Press, 1993).

Beaver, Paul, "Flash Points Update," *Jane's Defense Weekly*, April 3, 1993, pp. 20–21.

Beeman, William O., "What is (Iranian) 'National Character'?," *Iranian Studies*, vol.9, no.1, 1976.

—— "Iran and the United States: Postmodern Culture Conflict in Action," *Anthropology Quarterly*, vol. 76, no.4, 2003.

—— "After Ahmedinejad: The Prospects for US–Iranian Relations," in *Iranian Challenges:*

Chaillot Paper, no. 89, edited by P. Walker, (Paris: Paris Institute for Security Studies, 2006).

—— "Iran and US Locked into Spiral Conflict – Last Refuge of Weak Leaders," *New America Media*, April 13, 2006.

Ben-Yahuda, Hemda, "Territoriality and War in International Crises: Theory and Findings, 1918–2001," *International Studies Review*, vol. 6, no. 4, December 2004.

Ben-Zvi, Abraham, *Alliance Politics and the Limits of Influence: The Case of the US and Israel, 1975–1983*, (Jerusalem, Israel: Jaffee Center for Strategic Studies, 1984).

Bernstein, Jeremy, *Nuclear Weapons: What You Need To Know*, (Cambridge Mass.: Cambridge University Press, 2008).

Bertsch, Gary K. and William C. Potter, "Conclusion," in Gary K. Bertsch and William C. Potter, eds., *Dangerous Weapons, Desperate States: Russia, Belarus, Kazakstan, and Ukraine*, (New York and London: Routledge, 1999).

—— "Introduction: The Challenge of NIS Export Control Developments," in Gary K. Bertsch and William C. Potter, eds., *Dangerous Weapons*, (New York and London: Routledge, 1999).

Bidoli, Marina, "Atomic Energy Corp In Danger Of Being Vaporized," *Financial Mail*, August 15, 1997.

Bloomfield, D., and Ben Reilly, "The Changing Nature of Conflict and Conflict Management," in Peter Harris and Ben Reilly, eds., *Democracy and Deep-rooted Conflict*, (Stockholm: Institute for Democracy and Electoral Assistance, IDEA, 1998).

Blum, Gabriella, *Islands of Agreement: Managing Enduring Armed Rivalries*, (Cambridge, Mass.: Harvard University Press, 2007).

Booth, Ken, "War, Security and Strategy: Toward a Doctrine for Stable Peace," in Ken Booth, ed., *New Thinking about Strategy and International Security*, (London: HarperCollins, 1991).

Boulding, K., *The Image*, (Ann Arbor: The University of Michigan Press, 1961).

Brecher, Michael, *Crises in World Politics*, (Oxford: Pergamon Press, 1993).

Brecher, Michael and Jonathan Wilkenfeld, *Crisis, Conflict and Instability*, (Oxford: Pergamon Press, 1989).

—— *A Study of Crisis*, (Ann Arbor: The University of Michigan Press, 1997).

—— "Interstates Crises and Violence," in Manus I. Midlarsky, ed., *Handbook of War Studies II*, (Ann Arbor: The University of Michigan Press, 2002).

Broad, William J. and Elaine Sciolino, "Iran's Secrecy Widens Gap in Nuclear Intelligence," *The New York Times*, May 19, 2006.

Brodie, Bernard, ed., *The Absolute Weapon*, (New York: Harcourt Brace, 1946).

Burton, John, *Conflict: Resolution and Provention*, (New York: St. Martin's Press, 1990).

Busch, Nathan E., *No End in Sight: The Continuing Menace of Nuclear Proliferation*, (Kentucky: The University Press of Kentucky, 2004).

Butfoy, Andy, *Disarming Proposals: Controlling Nuclear, Biological and Chemical Weapons*, (Sydney: UNSW Press, 2005).

Butler, Richard, *The Greatest Threat: Iraq, Weapons of Mass Destruction, and the Growing Crisis of Global Security*, (New York: Public Affairs, 2000).

Byman, Daniel L. and Mathew C. Waxman, *Confronting Iraq: U.S. Policy and the Use of Force Since the Gulf War*, (Santa Monica, CA: RAND, 2000).

Byman, Daniel, Shahram Chubin, Anoushiravan Ehteshami, and Jerrold Green, *Iran's Security Policy in the Post-Revolutionary Era*, (Santa Monica, CA.: RAND, 2001).

Bzostek, Rachel and Samuel B. Robison, "US Policy toward Israel, Iraq, and Saudi Arabia:

An Integrated Analysis, 1981–2004," *International Studies Perspectives*, vol. 9, issue 4, November 2008.

Cadwell, Dan and Robert E. Williams Jr., *Seeking Security in an Insecure World*, (Boulder, New York, Oxford: Rowman & Littlefield Publishers, 2006).

Cahn, Anne Hessing, "Determinants of the Nuclear Option: The Case of Iran," in Onkar Marwah and Ann Schultz, eds., *Nuclear Proliferation and the Near-Nuclear Countries*, (Cambridge, Mass.: Ballinger Publishing Company, 1975).

Cai, Kunhui, Madan Chauhan, Jim Jacaruso, Manoj Pant, Vinay Srivastava, and Yoji Tsubaki, *Asymmetric Conflict*, PPA601, Spring 2007.

Campbell, Mathew and Uzi Mahnami, "Iran's Mullahs On Brink Of A Nuclear Bomb," *The Times* (London), December 21, 1997.

Carpenter, Ted Galen, "Iran's Nuclear Program: America's Policy Options," *Policy Analysis*, no.578, September 2006.

Chubin, Shahram, *Eliminating Weapons of Mass Destruction: The Persian Gulf Case*, Henry Stimson Occasional paper 33, (Washington D.C.: Henry Stimson Center, 1997).

—— *Wither Iran? Reform, Domestic Politics, and National Security*, (Oxford, New York: Oxford University Press, 2002).

—— *Iran's Nuclear Ambitions*, (Washington D.C.: Carnegie Endowment for International Peace, 2006).

—— "Understanding Iran's Nuclear Ambitions," in Patrick M. Cronin, ed., *Double Trouble: Iran and North Korea as Challenges To International Security*, (Westport, Connecticut and London: Praeger Security International, 2008).

Cimbala, Stephen J., *Nuclear Weapons and Strategy: U.S. Nuclear Policy for the Twenty-First Century*, (London and New York: Routledge, 2005).

Cirincione, Joseph, *Bomb Scare: The History and Future of Nuclear Weapons*, (New York: Columbia University Press, 2007).

Clad, James C., "An Unexpected Chance to Get Down to the Fundamentals," *Non-Proliferation Project: Global Policy Program*, May 27, 2002.

Clarke, Richard, *Against All Enemies: Inside America's War on Terror*, (New York: Free Press, 2004).

Cohen, Avner, *Israel and the Bomb*, (New York: Columbia University Press, 1998).

Coletta, Damon, "Unipolarity, Globalization, and the War on Terror: Why Security Studies Should Refocus on Comparative Defense," *International Studies Review*, vol.9, no. 3, Fall 2007.

Coll, Steve, "U.S. Halted Nuclear Bid By Iran; China, Argentina, Agreed to Cancel Technology Transfers," *The Washington Post*, November 17, 1992, in Lexis-Nexis, http://www.lexis-nexis.com

Cordesman, Anthony, *Iran and Iraq*, (Boulder, Colorado: Westview Press, 1994).

Cordesman, Anthony H., "Threats and Non-Threats From Iran," *Center for Strategic and International Studies*, January 26, 1995.

Cordesman, Anthony and Ahmed Hashim, *Iran: Dilemmas of Dual Containment*, (Boulder, Colorado: Westview Press, 1997).

Corsi, Jerome, *Atomic Iran: How the Terrorist Regime Bought the Bomb and American Politicians*, (Nashville, TN: Cumberland House Publishing, 2005).

Cronin, Patrick M., "Introduction: The Dual Challenge of Iran and North Korea," in Patrick M. Cronin, ed., *Double Trouble: Iran and North Korea as Challenges To International Security*, (Westport, Connecticut and London: Praeger Security International, 2008).

—— "The Trouble with Iran," in Patrick M. Cronin, ed., *Double Trouble* (2008).

Curtius, Mary, "Dissidents Say Tehran Is Pursuing Nuclear Arms," *The Boston Globe*, June 30, 1991, in Lexis-Nexis, http://www.lexis-nexis.com/

Dareini, Ali Akbar, "Iran Will Pursue Nuclear Program," *Associated Press*, September 21, 2004.

Delpech, Therese, *Iran and the Bomb: The Abdication of International Responsibility*, (London: Hurst & Company, 2006).

DeSutter, Paula A., *Denial and Jeopardy: Deterring Iranian Use of NBC Weapons*, (Washington D.C.: National Defense University Press, 1997).

Donnelly, Warren H. and Zachary S. Davis, "Iran's Nuclear Activities and the Congressional Response," *CRS Issue Brief*, Congressional Research Service, The Library of Congress, May 20, 1992.

Drell, Sidney D. and James E. Goodby, *The Gravest Danger: Nuclear Weapons*, (Stanford, California: Hoover Institution Press, 2003).

Dueck, Colin and Ray Takeyh, "Iran's Nuclear Challenge," *Political Science Quarterly*, vol. 122, no. 2, 2007.

Dunn, Lewis A., "Nuclear Proliferation and World Politics," *Annals of the American Academy of Political and Social Science*, no. 430, March 1977.

—— "Containing Nuclear Proliferation," *Adelphi Paper*, no. 263, (London: International Institute of Strategic Studies, 1991).

—— "Countering Proliferation: Insights from Past 'Wins, Losses, and Draws'," *Nonproliferation Review*, vol.13, no. 3, November 2006.

Ehteshami, Anoushiravan, "Iran's International Posture after the Fall of Baghdad," *Middle East Journal*, vol. 58, no. 2, 2004.

Elaine, Sciolino, *The Outlaw State: Saddam Hussein's Quest for Power and the Gulf Crisis*, (New York: John Wiley and Sons, 1991).

Emirates Centre for Strategic Studies, *Iran's Nuclear Program*, (New York: Palgrave, Macmillan, 2007).

Esposito, John L., "Introduction: From Khomeini to Khatami," in John L. Esposito and R. K. Ramazani, ed., *Iran at the Crossroads*, (New York: Palgrave, 2001).

Evans, Michael D. and Jerome R. Corsi, *Showdown with Nuclear Iran: Radical Islam's Messianic Mission to Destroy Israel and Cripple the United States*, (Nashville, Tennessee: Nelson Current, 2006).

Falkenrath, Richard A., "Confronting Nuclear, Biological, and Chemical Terrorism," *Survival*, vol. 40, no.3, Autumn 1998.

Fathi, Nazila and Michael Slackman, "Rebuke in Iran to Its President on Nuclear Role," *The New York Times*, January 19, 2007.

Fathi, Nazila and Alan Cowell, "After Obama Overture, Iran's Leader Seeks US Apology," *The New York Times*, January 28, 2009.

Feldman, Shai, *Nuclear Weapons and Arms Control in the Middle East*, (Cambridge, Mass.: The MIT Press, 1997).

Ferguson, Charles D. and John E. Pike, "National Missile Defense: Developing Disaster," *Disarmament Diplomacy*, no. 44, 2000.

Fever, Peter D. and Scott D. Sagan, "Proliferation Pessimism and Emerging Nuclear Powers," *International Security*, vol. 22, no. 2, Fall 1997.

Fitzpatrick, Mark, "Assessing Iran's Nuclear Program," *Survival*, vol.48, no.3, 2006.

—— "Is Iran's Nuclear Capability Inevitable?," in Patrick M. Cronin, ed., *Double Trouble: Iran and North Korea As Challenges to International Security*, (Westport, Connecticut: Praeger Security International, 2008).

Freilich, Chuck, "The United States, Israel, and Iran: Defusing an 'Existential Threat',"

142 Bibliography

Arms Control Today, November 2008. http://www.armscontrol.org/act/2008_11/freilich.

Gaddis, John Lewis, "Great Illusions, the Long Peace, and the Future of the International System," in Charles W. Kegley, ed., *The Long Post-War Peace*, (New York: HarperCollins, 1991).

Garver, John W., *China and Iran: Ancient Partners in a Post-Imperial World*, (Washington D.C.: University of Washington Press, 2006).

Gasiorowski, Mark, "Iranian Politics after the 2004 Parliamentary Elections," *Strategic Insights*, vol. 3, no. 6, June 2004.

Gelb, Leslie H., "U.S. Nuclear Deal with Iran Delayed," *The New York Times*, March 8, 1975.

George, Alexander and Andrew Bennett, *Case Studies and Theory Development in Social Sciences*, (Cambridge Mass.: MIT Press, 2005).

Giles, Gregory F., "The Islamic Republic of Iran and Nuclear, Biological, and Chemical Weapons," in Peter R. Lavoy, Scott D. Sagan, and James J. Wirtz, eds., *Planning the Unthinkable: How New Powers Will Use Nuclear, Biological, and Chemical Weapons*, (Ithaca and London: Cornell University Press, 2000).

Gilmore, Inigo, "Daily On Iranian Nuclear 'Shopping List' in South Africa," *The Times* (London), August 18, 1997.

Gilpin, Robert, *War and Change in World Politics*, (Cambridge Mass.: Cambridge University Press, 1981).

Goldschmidt, Pierre and George Perkovich, "Iran Nuclear Showdown," *Transcript of Briefing*. (Washington D.C.: Carnegie Endowment for International Peace, January 18, 2006).

Gordon, Corera, *Shopping for Bombs: Nuclear Proliferation, Global Insecurity, and the Rise and Fall of the A.Q. Khan Network*, (Oxford, New York: Oxford University Press, 2006).

Graeme, Davies A. M., "Inside Out or Outside In: Domestic and International Factors Affecting Iranian Foreign Policy Towards the United States 1990–2004," *Foreign Policy Analysis*, vol. 4, no. 3, July 2008.

Greenhouse, Steven, "US Seeks To Deny A-Plants To Iran," *The New York Times*, January 24, 1995.

Greenwood, Ted, *Nuclear Proliferation: Motivations, Capabilities and Strategies for Control*, (New York: McGraw Hill, 1977).

Gwertzman, Bernard, "US Said to Favor Sale of F-16 Jets to the Jordanians," *The New York Times*, February 27, 1982.

Ha'iri, Safa, "Secrets of Iran's Nuclear Program and a Map of Its Secret Factories," *Al Watan Al Arabi*, January 20, 1995.

Harkavy, Robert, *Spectre of a Middle Eastern Holocaust: The Strategic and Diplomatic Implications of the Israeli Nuclear Weapons Program*, Monograph Series in World Affairs, vol. 14, (Denver: University of Denver Press, 1977).

Hashim, Ahmed S., "Iranian Science and Technology Capacity: Implications of Ideology and the Experience of War for Military Research and Development," in Eric Arnett, ed., *Military Capacity and the Risk of War*, (New York, Oxford: Oxford University Press, 1997).

Herby, Peter, *The Chemical Weapons Convention and Arms Control in the Middle East*, (Oslo: International Peace Research Institute, 1992).

Herring, Eric, "Rogue Rage: Can We Prevent Mass Destruction," in Eric Herring, ed., *Preventing the Use of Weapons of Mass Destruction*, (London: Frank Cass Publishers, 2000).

Hersh, Seymour M., *The Samson Option*, (New York: Random House, 1991).

Hersh, Seymour M., "The Iran Plans: Would President Bush go to War to stop Iran from Getting the Bomb?," *The New Yorker*, April 17, 2006.

Herzog, Michael, "Iranian Public Opinion on the Nuclear Program," *Policy Focus*, no. 56, (Washington D.C.: The Washington Institute for Near East Policy, June 2006).

Hibbs, Mark, "Bonn Will Decline Teheran Bid To Resuscitate Bushehr Project," *Nucleonics Week*, May 2, 1991.

—— "Iran May Withdraw From NPT Over Western Trade Barriers," *Nucleonics Week*, September 22, 1994.

—— "Western Group Battles Iran at Third NPT Prepcom Session" *Nucleonics Week*, September 22, 1994.

—— "It's 'Too Early' For Tehran To Leave NPT, Delegates Say," *NuclearFuel*, September 26, 1994.

Hitchcock, Mark, *The Apocalypse of Ahmedinejad: The Revelation of Iran's Nuclear Prophet*, (New York: The Doubleday Religious Publishing Group, 2007).

Holsti, Kalevi J., *Peace and War: Armed Conflicts and International Order, 1648–1989* (Cambridge: Cambridge University Press, 1991).

Howard, Roger, *Iran in Crisis: Nuclear Ambitions and the American Response*, (London, New York: Zed Books, 2004).

—— "Neither Sanctions nor Bombs will End the Iran Nuclear Crisis," *The Guardian*, January 11, 2007.

Hoyt, Paul, "The Rogue States Image in American Foreign Policy," *Global Society*, no. 14, 2000.

Hunter, Robert E., "The Iran Case: Addressing Why Countries Want Nuclear Weapons," *Arms Control Today*, vol. 34, December 2004. http://www.armscontrol.org/act/2004_12/Hunter

Huntington, Samuel P., "The Lonely Superpower," *Foreign Affairs*, March/April 1999.

—— "The Clash of Civilizations," in Robert J. Art and Robert Jervis, eds., *International Politics: Enduring Concepts and Contemporary Issues*, 6th edition, (New York: Longman, 2003).

—— "The Lonely Superpower," in G. John Ikenberry, ed., *American Foreign Policy: Theoretical Essays*, 5th edition, (New York: Pearson Education, 2005).

Hymans, Jacques E.C., *The Psychology of Nuclear Proliferation: Identity, Emotions, and Foreign Policy*, (Cambridge: Cambridge University Press, 2006).

Iran's Strategic Weapons Programs, An IISS Strategic Dossier, (London and New York: Routledge, 2005).

Iran's Strategic Weapons Programs, A Net Assessment (Abingdon: Routledge for the IISS, 2005).

Jafarzadeh, Alireza, *The Iran Threat: President Ahmadinejad and the Coming Nuclear Crisis*, (New York: Palgrave Macmillan, 2007).

James, Carolyn C., "Iran and Iraq as Rational Crisis Actors: Dangers and Dynamics of Survivable Nuclear War," in Eric Herring, ed., *Preventing the Use of Weapons of Mass Destruction*, (London: Frank Cass Publishers, 2000).

Jones, Richard Wyn, ed., *Critical Theory and World Politics*, (Boulder and London: Lynne Rienner Publishers, 2001).

Jones, Rodney W. and Mark. G. McDonough with Toby F. Dalton and Gregory D. Koblentz, *Tracking Nuclear Proliferation*, (Washington D.C.: Brookings Institution Press, 1998).

Kacowicz, Arie M., Yaacov Bar-Siman-Tov, Ole Elgstrom and Magnus Jerneck, *Stable*

Peace among Nations, (New York, Oxford: Rowman and Littlefield Publishers Ltd., 2000).

Karl, David J., "Proliferation Pessimism and Emerging Nuclear Powers," *International Security*, vol. 21(3), Winter 1996/97.

Karon, Tony, "Why Iran Will Go Nuclear," *Time*, February 12, 2005.

Karp, Aaron, "Lessons of Iranian Missile Programs for US Nonproliferation Policy," *The Nonproliferation Review*, vol. 5, no. 3, Spring–Summer 1998.

Katz, Mark N., "Iran and America: Is Rapprochement Finally Possible?," *Middle East Policy*, vol.12, no. 4, 2005.

Katzman, Kenneth, "Iran: US Concerns and Policy Responses," *CRS Report for Congress*, July 31, 2006.

Kessler, Richard, "Argentina's Invap to Supply Iran Fuel for Research Reactor," *Nucleonics Week*, May 14, 1987.

Khan, Ayaz Ahmed, "Plans to Attack Iran," *Defense Journal*, April 2007.

Khan, Saira, "Targeting the Rogue States: The US National Missile Defense System and Nuclear Proliferation," Paper presented at the International Studies Association Annual Convention, Chicago, February 20–24, 2001.

——— *Nuclear Proliferation Dynamics in Protracted Conflict Regions: A Comparative Study of South Asia and the Middle East*, (Aldershot and Vermont: Ashgate Publishing Ltd., 2002).

——— *Nuclear Weapons and Conflict Transformation: The Case of India-Pakistan*, (London and New York: Routledge, 2009).

Kich, Andrew and Jeanette Wolf, "Iran's Nuclear Facilities: A Profile," (Monterey, CA: Center for Nonproliferation Studies, 1998).

Kile, Shannon N., ed., *Europe and Iran: Perspectives on Nonproliferation*, (Oxford: Oxford University Press, 2005).

Klare, Michael, *Rogue States and Nuclear Outlaws*, (New York: Hill and Wang, 1995).

Knopf, Jeffrey W., "Recasting the Optimism-Pessimism Debate," *Security Studies*, vol.12, no.1, Autumn 2002.

LaFraniere, Sharon, "Allies Unperturbed by US Nuclear List: Iranians, Russians Criticize Report," *The Washington Post*, March 11, 2002.

Larijini, Ali, Speech at Middle East Center, Tehran, October 27, 2005, Reprinted in *Journal of European Society for European Studies*, 2006.

Lavoy, Peter R., "Nuclear Proliferations Over the Next Decade: Causes, Warning Signs, and Policy Responses," *Nonproliferation Review*, vol.13, no. 3, November 2006.

Levy, Jack S., "Misperceptions and the Causes of War: Theoretical Linkages and Analytical Problems," *World Politics*, vol. 36, 1983.

Lieber, Keir A. and Daryl G. Press, "The Rise of US Nuclear Primacy," *Foreign Affairs*, vol. 85, no. 2, March/April 2006.

Litwak, Richard, *Rogue States and US Foreign Policy: Containment After the Cold War*, (Washington D.C.: The Woodrow Wilson Center Press, 2000).

Lodgaard, Sverre, "Iran's Uncertain Nuclear Ambitions," in Morten Bremer Maerli and Sverre Lodgaard, eds., *Nuclear Proliferation and International Security*, (London and New York: Routledge, 2007).

Lopez, George A. and David Cortright, "The Smarter US Option: A Full Summit with Iran," *Policy Brief*, The Joan B. Kroc Institute for International Peace Studies, no.11, June 2006.

Lotfian, Saideh, "Threat Perception and Military Planning in Iran: Credible Scenarios of Conflict and Opportunities for Confidence Building," in Eric Arnett, ed., *Military Capacity and the Risk of War*, (New York, Oxford: Oxford University Press, 1997).

MacLachlan, Ann and Michael Knapik, "South Africa to End MIS SWU Project," *Nuclear Fuel,* December 12, 1997.

Mafinezam, Alidad and Aria Mehrabi, *Iran and Its Place among Nations*, (Westport, Connecticut, London: Praeger Security International, 2008).

Mannion, Jim, "Iran Tapped Russia, China for Weapons of Mass Destruction Technology: CIA," *Agence France Presse*, February 2, 2000, in Lexis-Nexis, http://www.lexis-nexis.com/.

Markov, G.N., V.N. Lokhman, and E. Ronanader, "Multiple Photoionization of 169Yb in a Three-Level Atomic Medium by the Collinear Propagation of Laser Pulses," *Journal of Physics,* section B, vol. 28, 1995.

Martin, Curtis H., "'Good Cop/Bad Cop' as a Model for Nonproliferation Diplomacy Toward North Korea and Iran," *Nonproliferation Review*, vol.14, no.1, March 2007.

Mazarr, Michael J., "The Folly of 'Asymmetric War'," *Washington Quarterly*, vol. 31, no. 3, Summer 2008.

Mearsheimer, John J., *Conventional Deterrence*, (Ithaca: Cornell University Press, 1983).

—— *Tragedy of Great Power Politics*, (New York and London: W. W. Norton and Company, 2001), p. 345.

Mesquitta, Bruce Bueno De, and William H. Riker, "An Assessment of the Merits of Selective Nuclear Proliferation," *Journal of Conflict Resolution*, vol. 26, no. 2, June 1982.

Meyer, Stephen M., *The Dynamics of Nuclear Proliferation*, (Chicago: University of Chicago Press, 1984).

Morgan, Patrick, *Deterrence: A Conceptual Analysis*, (Beverly Hills, London: Sage Publishers, 1977).

Morgenthau, Hans J., *Politics Among Nations: The Struggle for Power and Peace*, (New York: Alfred A. Knopf, 1956).

—— *Politics Among Nations: The Struggle for Power and Peace*, sixth edition, Revised by Kenneth W. Thompson, (New York: Alfred A.Knopf, 1985).

Mueller, John, and Karl Mueller, "The Methodology of Mass Destruction: Assessing Threats in the New World Order," in Eric Herring, ed., *Preventing the Use of Weapons of Mass Destruction*, (London: Frank Cass Publishers, 2000).

Mutimer, David, *The Weapons State: Proliferation and the Framing of Security*, (Boulder, London: Lynne Rienner, 2000).

Nincic, Miroslav, *Renegade Regimes: Confronting Deviant Behavior in World Politics*, (New York: Columbia University Press, 2005).

Nye, Joseph S., *Bound to Lead: The Changing Nature of American Power*, (New York: Basic Books, 1990).

O'Reilly, K. P., "Perceiving Rogue States: The Use of the 'Rogue State' Concept by US Foreign Policy Elites," *Foreign Policy Analysis*, vol. 3, issue 4, October 2007.

O'Sullivan, Meghan L., *Shrewd Sanctions: Statecraft and State Sponsors of Terrorism*, (Washington D.C.: Brookings Institution Press, 2003).

Opall, Barbara, "Israelis Say Russia Aids Iran's Quest for Missiles," *Defense News*, February 10, 1997.

Organski, A. F. K., *World Politics*, (New York: Alfred A. Knopf, 1968).

Paul, T.V., *Asymmetric Conflicts: War Initiation by Weaker Powers*, (New York: Cambridge University Press, 1994).

—— *Power Versus Prudence: Why Nations Forgo Nuclear Weapons*, (Montreal & Kingston: McGill-Queen's University Press, 2000).

Perkins, Edward J., "Nuclear News from South Africa," Secret Cable [US Embassy in South

Africa], July 29, 1987, in Digital National Security Archive, http://nsarchive.chadwyck.com/

Perkovich, George, "Bush's Nuclear Revolution: A Regime Change in Nonproliferation," *Foreign Affairs*, vol. 82, no. 2, March/April 2003.

——— "Dealing with Iran's Nuclear Challenge," *Carnegie Endowment for International Peace*, April 28, 2003.

——— "Iran Says No-Now What?," *Carnegie Endowment for International Peace*, Policy Brief, no. 63, September 2008.

Perkovich, George and James M. Action, *Abolishing Nuclear Weapons*, Adelphi Paper 396, (New York: Routledge, 2008).

Perkovich, George and Karim Sadjadpour, "Strategic Engagement with Iran: Steps for the Next U.S. President," *Carnegie Endowment for International Peace*, October 16, 2008.

Pollack, Kenneth, *The Persian Puzzle: The Conflict Between Iran and America*, (New York: Random House, 2003).

Pollack, Kenneth and Ray Takeyh, "Taking on Tehran," *Foreign Affairs*, March/April 2005.

Porter, Gareth, "Iran Nuclear Conflict is about US Dominance," Antiwar.com, May 12, 2006. http://www.antiwar.com/orig/porter.php?articleid=8962

Potter, William C., *Nuclear Power and Nonproliferation: An Interdisciplinary Perspective*, (Cambridge, Mass.: Gunn and Hain, 1982).

Pouladi, Farhad, "Iran's Ahmadinejad Attacks Israel at Iraq Conference," *Agence-France Presse via Middle East Times*, July 9, 2006. http://www.metimes.com/storyview.php?StoryID+20060709-014952-3804r.

Quester, George, *The Politics of Nuclear Proliferation*, (Baltimore: Johns Hopkins University Press, 1973).

——— "Reducing the Incentives to Proliferation," *Annals* 4, March 30, 1977.

Reich, Bernard, "Reassessing the United States–Israeli Special Relationship," *Israel Affairs*, vol. 1, issue 1, 1994.

Reiss, Mitchell, *Without the Bomb: The Politics of Nuclear Non-Proliferation*, (New York: Columbia University Press, 1988).

——— *Bridled Ambition: Why Countries Constrain Their Nuclear Capabilities*, (Washington D.C.: Woodrow Wilson Center Press, 1995).

Rennack, Dianne E., *Nuclear, Biological, Chemical, and Missile Proliferation Sanctions: Selected Current Law*, (Hauppage, NY: Novinka Books, 2004).

Richelson, Jeffrey, *Spying on the Bomb: American Nuclear Intelligence from Nazi Germany to Iran and North Korea*, (New York: Norton, 2006).

Risse-Kappen, Thomas, *Cooperation Among Democracies*, (Princeton: Princeton University Press, 1997).

Ritter, Scott, *Target Iran: The Truth about the White House's Plans for Regime Change*, (New York: Nation Books, 2006).

Rohini, Hassan, "Iran's Nuclear Program: The Way Out," *Time*, May 9, 2006.

Russell, James A., *Proliferation of Weapons of Mass Destruction in the Middle East: Directions and Policy Options in the New Century*, (New York: Palgrave Macmillan, 2006).

Russell, Richard L., *Weapons Proliferation and the War in the Greater Middle East: Strategic Contest*, (New York: Routledge, 2005).

Sagan, Scott D., "Why Do States Build Nuclear Weapons?: Three Models in Search of a Bomb," *International Security*, vol. 21, no. 3, Winter 1996/97.

Sagan, Scott D. and Kenneth N. Waltz, *The Spread of Nuclear Weapons: A Debate Renewed*, (New York: W.W. Norton & Company, 2003).

Saikal, Amin, "The Iran Nuclear Dispute," *Australian Journal of International Affairs*, vol. 60, no. 2, 2006.

Sciolino, Elaine, "CIA Says Iran Makes Progress on Atom Arms," *The New York Times*, November 30, 1992.

Segal, D., "Atomic Ayatollahs," *The Washington Post*, April 12, 1987.

Sick, Gary, "A Selective Partnership: Getting US–Iranian Relations Right," *Foreign Affairs*, vol. 85, no. 6, November/December 2006.

Singer, David J. and Melvin Small, *The Wages of War 1816–1965: A Statistical Handbook*, (New York: John Wiley, 1972).

Smith, Derek D., *Deterring America: Rogue States and the Proliferation of Weapons of Mass Destruction*, (Cambridge, UK: Cambridge University Press, 2006).

Smith, R. Jeffrey, "Officials Say Iran is Seeking Nuclear Weapons Capability," *The Washington Post*, October 31, 1991.

Smyth, Gareth, "Iran's Intellectuals Left in Cold by Populist President," *The Financial Times*, June 21, 2006.

Snyder, Glenn H., "Crisis Bargaining," in Charles F. Hermann, ed., *International Crises: Insights from Behavioral Research*, (New York: Free Press, 1972).

Snyder, Glenn and Paul Diesing, *Conflict Among Nations: Bargaining, Decision-Making and System Structure in International Crises*, (Princeton, New Jersey: Princeton University Press, 1977).

Sokolski, Henry and Patrick Clawson, eds., *Checking Iran's Nuclear Ambitions*, (Honolulu: Hawaii: University Press of the Pacific, 2004).

Solingen, Etel, *Nuclear Logics: Contrasting Paths in East Asia and the Middle East*, (Princeton: Princeton University Press, 2007).

Spector, Leonard, *Going Nuclear: The Spread of Nuclear Weapons 1986–1987*, (Cambridge, Mass.: Ballinger, 1987).

—— "Nuclear Proliferation in the Middle East: The Next Chapter Begins," in Efraim Karsh, Martin S. Navias, and Philip Sabin, eds., *Non-Conventional Weapons Proliferation in the Middle East*, (New York: Oxford University Press, 1993).

—— "Islamic Bomb West's Long-Term Nightmare," *The Washington Times*, January 19, 1994.

—— *Regional Orders at Century's Dawn*, (Princeton: Princeton University Press, 1998).

Spector, Leonard S. with Jacqueline R. Smith, *Nuclear Ambitions: The Spread of Nuclear Weapons 1989–1990*, (Boulder, Colorado: Westview Press, 1990).

Spiegel, Steven L., Jennifer D. Kibbe, and Elizabeth G. Matthews, eds., *The Dynamics of Middle Nuclear Proliferation*, (Lewiston NY: E. Mellen Press, 2001).

Stein, Janice Gross, "Image, Identity, and Conflict Resolution," in Chester A. Crocker, and Fen Oster Hampson with Pamela Aall, eds., *Managing Global Chaos: Sources of and Responses to International Conflict*, (Washington D.C.: US Institute of Peace Press, 1996).

Strain, Fredrick R., "Iran's Nuclear Strategy: Discerning Motivations, Strategic Culture, and Rationality," *Institute for National Strategic Studies*, (*Essays of Strategy* 14, 1998).

Takeyh, Ray, "Iran's Populace Largely Opposes Nuclear Program," Interview by Bernard Gwertzman, March 2, 2005, Council on Foreign Relations *CFR Online* March 7, 2005. http://www.cfr.org/publication/publication_list.html?groupby=4&type=interview&page=25

—— "Iran at the Strategic Crossroads," in James A Russell, ed., *Proliferation of Weapons of Mass Destruction in the Middle East: Directions and Policy Options in the New Century* (New York: Palgrave Macmillan, 2006).

―― *Hidden Iran: Paradox and Power in the Islamic Republic*, (New York: Times Books, 2007).
Tarock, Adam, "Iran's Nuclear Program and the West," *Third World Quarterly*, vol. 27, no. 4, 2006.
The International Institute for Strategic Studies (IISS), *The Military Balance 2009*, (Abingdon, Oxon: Taylor and Francis, 2009).
Timmerman, Kenneth R., *Weapons of Mass Destruction: The Cases of Iran, Syria, and Libya*, Los Angeles: A Simon Wiesenthal Center Special Report from Middle East Defense News, *Middle East Defense News*, August 1992.
―― "Iran's Nuclear Program: Myth or Reality," *The Middle East Data Project Inc.*, 1995.
―― *Countdown to Crisis: The Coming Nuclear Showdown with Iran*, (New York: Three Rivers Press, 2006).
Toynbee, Arnold, *A Study of History*, vol. 9, (London: Oxford University Press, 1954).
Van Evera, Stephen, *Causes of War*, (Ithaca: Cornell University Press, 1999).
Vazri, Haleh, "Iran's Nuclear Quest: Motivations and Consequences," in Raju G. Thomas, ed., *The Nuclear Non-proliferation Regime: Prospects for the 21st Century*, (New York: St. Martin's Press, 1998).
Venter, Al J., "Iran's Nuclear Ambition: Innocuous Illusion Or Ominous Truth?," *Jane's International Defense Review*, September 1997.
―― *Iran's Nuclear Option: Tehran's Quest for the Atomic Bomb*, (Drexel Hill, PA: Casemate Publishers, 2004).
Vick, Karl, "Iranians Assert Right to Nuclear Weapons," *The Washington Post*, March 11, 2003.
Walker, Graham F., *The Search for WMD: Nonproliferation, Intelligence, and Preemption in the New Security Environment*, (Halifax NS: Centre for Foreign Policy Studies, Dalhousie University, 2006).
Walt, Stephen M., "Containing Rogues and Renegades: Coalition Strategies and Counterproliferation," in Victor A. Utgoff, ed., *The Coming Crisis: Nuclear Proliferation, US Interests, and World Order*, (Cambridge, Mass.: MIT Press, 2000).
Waltz, Kenneth N., *Theory of International Politics*, (New York: Random House, 1979).
―― "Origins of War in Neorealist Theory," in Robert I. Rotberg and Theodore K. Rabb, eds., *The Origin and Prevention of Major Wars*, (Cambridge: Cambridge University Press, 1988).
―― "Nuclear Myth and Political Reality," *American Political Science Review*, vol. 84, 1990.
Weiner, Tim, "Iran Said to Test Missile Able to Hit Israel and Saudis," *The New York Times*, July 23, 1998.
Weissman, Steve and Herbert Krosney, *The Islamic Bomb*, (New York: Times Books, 1981).
Weltman, John J., "Nuclear Devolution and World Order," *World Politics*, vol. 32, no. 2, January 1980.
Wendt, Alexander, "Anarchy is What States Make of It," in Robert J. Art and Robert Jervis, eds., *International Politics: Enduring Concepts and Contemporary Issues*, 8th edition, (New York: Longman, 2006).
Williams, Daniel and Thomas W. Lippman, "Christopher Charges Iran Continues Nuclear Program," *The Washington Post*, January 21, 1995.
Wohlforth, William C., *The Elusive Balance: Power and Perceptions during the Cold War*, (Ithaca, NY: Cornell University Press, 1993).
Woodward, Bob, *Bush at War*, (New York: Simon and Schuster, 2002).

Zak, Chen, "Iran's Nuclear Policy and the IAEA: An Evaluation of Program 93+2", no. 3, Washington D.C.: *Washington Institute for Near East Policy*, 2002.

Other documents

"A. Q. Khan & Iran," *Global Security.Org.*
"Anti-Arrogance Campaign Becomes Necessary," *Jumhuri-ye-Islami*, November 3, 2004.
"Bush Reaffirms Support for Missile Defense System," *Daily Star*, January 10, 2001.
Bush, George H. W., "Address Before a Joint Session of the Congress on the Persian Gulf Crisis and the Federal Budget Deficit," September 11, 1990.
"Chronology of US–Iran Relations, 1906–2002," *Frontline*. http://www.pbs.org/wgbh/pages/frontline/shows tehran/etc/cron.html
Defense Link, US Department of Defense: www.defenselink.mil/news/Jan2002.d/20020109npr.pdf
"First Iran Meeting of Obama Presidency Planned," *Berlin: Associated Free Press*, January 29, 2009
"Implementation of the NPT Safeguards Agreement in the Islamic Republic of Iran," November 10, 2003.
"Iran Depicts Bush Plea as 'Arrogant,'" *The Washington Post*, January 28, 1989.
"Iran Profile: Nuclear Chronology, 1957–85," Nuclear Threat Initiative, (NTI), www.nti.org/e_research/profiles/Iran/1825_1826.html.
"Iran Reject NPT Unless all Nuclear Weapons are Scrapped," *Deutsche Presse-Agentur*, April 21, 1995; in Lexis-Nexis, http://www.lexis-nexis.com/
"Iran: Atomic Energy Program," A report by United States Energy Research and Development Administration, October 1976.
"Iran: Nuclear Intentions and Capabilities," *National Intelligence Estimate*, November 2007.
"Iran's Nuclear Program," *The Guardian*, April 28, 2006.
"Iranian Diplomats On Nuclear Warhead Purchases," *Proliferation Issues*, March 5, 1993.
"Iranian Nuclear Chief Ali Larijani:The West Should Learn the Lesson of North Korea," *IRINN TV*, September 20, 2005. Available online at http://memri.org/
"Iranians Defend Nuclear Rights," *Los Angeles Times*, March 7, 2006.
"Iranians To Learn In Russia How To Operate Nuclear Power Plant," *Middle East News Items*, February 4, 1999; in Lexis-Nexis, http://www.lexis-nexis.com/
"Iran's Chinese Shopping List," *Iran Brief*, October 1, 1996.
"Iranian Foreign ministry Spokesman's letter to UN Secretary General" *Agence France-Presse*, March 18, 2002.
"In the Club" *The Economist*, vol. 378, no 8473, London, April 15, 2006.
Khameini, Ayatollah Ali, Islamic Republic of Iran News Network, June 4, 2006, also on *BBC Online*, June 5, 2006.
"Khatami: Iran Entitled to Nuclear Energy," *Iran-UN Politics*, August 25, 2006.
"Middle East," *International Security Digest*, January 1995.
"Naseri Address UN Conference on NPT Issues," *IRNA* (Tehran), May 12, 1995; in FBIS Document FTS19950512000507, May 12, 1995.
"Nuclear Cooperation Agreement with Iran," Report of the National Security Study and Decision Memoranda (NSSM) 219 Working Group, April, 1975. http://www.gwu.edu./~nearchiv/nukevault/abb268/doc05a.pdf
"Nuclear Facilities," *Middle East Defense News*, June 8, 1992.
"Paper Reports Uranium Sales," *Worldwide Report*, July 13, 1987.

150 Bibliography

"President Inaugurates New Nuclear Research Facility," IRNA (Tehran) January 2, 1996; in FBIS Document FTS 19960102000243, January 2, 1996.

"President Mahmoud Ahmadinejad's UN Address," IRNA, September 17, 2005.

"President on Peaceful Use of Nuclear Power," IRNA (Tehran) January 2, 1996; in FBIS Document FTS 19960102000270, January 2, 1996.

Saddam Hussein's Cabinet Statement, June 23, 1981 (FBIS, June 24, 1981, p. E-3).

"The China-Iran Nuclear Cloud," *Middle East Defense News,* July 22, 1991; in Lexis-Nexis, http://www.lexis-nexis.com/.

"The Mystic Who Lit the Fires of Hatred," *Time Magazine*, January 7, 1980.

"US Report: Iran Stopped Nuclear Weapons Work in 2003," *CNN*, December 3, 2007.

"US Sent Data To Russia on Iran WMD," *Middle East Newsline*, vol. 4, no. 199, May 29, 2002, http://www.menl.com/.

"US, Iran Resume Atom Power Talks," *The Washington Post*, August 9, 1977.

"With Release of Terry Anderson, US Hostage Ordeal Ended in Lebanon," *Washington Report on Middle East Affairs*, December 1995.

A Report on the International Control of Atomic Energy. Prepared for the Secretary of State's Committee on Atomic Energy, Washington, D.C., U.S. Government Printing Office, March 16, 1946. Department of State Publication 2498. http://www.learnworld.com/ZNW/LWText.Acheson-Lilienthal.html.

Berman, Ilan, Interview by Dimitri Neos, Foreign Affairs Forum Interview, March 20, 2006.

Definition of hegemony provided by Wikipedia. See, http://en.wikipedia.org/wiki/ Hegemony.

Der Spiegel, February 8, 1975.

Excerpts from the Nuclear Posture Review, J. D. Crouch, Assistant Secretary of Defense for International Security Policy, Special Briefing on the Nuclear Posture Review, Department of Defense, January 9, 2002.

Faqihiyan, Dr Hossein, Director General of Nuclear Fuel Production Co., and Deputy of the Atomic Energy Organization (AEO), in Daily Newspaper, *Farhang-e-Ashti*, May 4, 2006; in BBC Online, May 10, 2006.

Ganji, Akbar, Talk on "Human Rights and Democracy," *Simon Centre*, The University of British Columbia, November 29, 2007.

http://bushlibrary.tamu.edu/research/papers/1990/90091101.html

http://disarmament.un.org/wmd/npt/1995dec2.htm; NPT/CONF.1995/32(Part I), Annex

http://disarmament.un.org/wmd/npt/1995dec2.htm; S/1995/263

http://newsweek.washingtonpost.com/postglobal/needtoknow/2008/09/iran_does_not_trust_the_west_a.html

http://www.antiwar.com/orig/porter.php?articleid=8982

http://www.arabicnews.com/ansub/Daily/Day/060825/2006082502.html

http://www.carnegieendowment.org/files/iran2006-01-18.pdf

http://www.carnegieendowment.org/files/iran2006-01-18.pdf

http://www.dni.gov/press_releases/20071203_release.pdf

http://www.globalsecurity.org/wmd/world/iran/khan-iran.htm

http://www.globalsecurity.org/wmd/world/iran/nuke2.htm

http://www.iaea.org/Publications/Documents/Board/2005/gov2005-67.pdf

http://www.iaea.org/Publications/Documents/Board/2003/gov2003-75.pdf

http://www.nti.org/e_research/profiles/Iran/1825_1826.html

http://www.pbs.org/wgbh/pages/frontline/shows/tehran/etc/cron.html

IAEA Director General's Report, "Implementation of the NPT Safeguards Agreement in the Islamic Republic of Iran," November 10, 2003.

IAEA reports at http://www.iaea.org/NewsCenter/Focus/IaeaIran/index.shtml.
IAEA, *Implementation*, GOV/2003/6, September 12, 2003.
IISS, *The Military Balance*, 1998–99.
"Iran Complains of Nuclear Bullying," CNN, February 23, 2007.
Papers presented at "Making Big Choices: Individual Opinion Formation and Societal Choice," conference at the Weatherhead Center for International Affairs, Harvard University, May 25–26, 2000.
PBS, *Frontline*, April 13, 1993.
Reuters, April 19, 2003.
Speech by Ali Akbar Hashemi Rafsanjani, Tehran Domestic Service, 19.35 GMT, October 6, 1988, Translation in FBIS-NES, October 7, 1988.
Speech by Hashemi Rafsanjani, Tehran Domestic Service, 19:35 GMT, October 6, 1988, Translation. In FBIS-NES, October 7, 1988.
Statement of Enders Wimbush on "Iran: Briefing and Hearing before the Committee on Foreign Affairs," *House of Representatives*, January 11 and 31, 2007, Serial no. 110–113.
Statement made by H. E. Mansuchehr Mottaki, Foreign Minister of the Islamic Republic of Iran before the United Nations Security Council, UN Press Release, March 23, 2007.
Statement of Ray Takeyh on "Iran: Briefing and Hearing before the Committee on Foreign Affairs," *House of Representatives*, January 11 and 31, 2007, Serial no. 110–113.
ThisNation.com, "State of the Union Address by Jimmy Carter 1980": www.thisnation.com/library/sotu/1980jc.html; American Government and Politics Online.
US Office of the President, National Strategy to Combat Weapons of Mass Destruction, The White House, December 2002, http://www.whitehouse.gov/news/releases/2002/12/WMDStrategy.pdf
William Rope, The State Department, Testimony before House Banking Committee, May 8, 1992, (Washington, DC: US Government Printing Office, 1992).
Woolsey, James, "Challenges to Peace," speech before the Washington Institute for Near East Policy 23 September 1994 (mimeo).

Index

9/11 6, 67, 89, 93, 94, 99, 103
9/11 attacks 6, 67, 89, 93
access 13, 19, 21, 40, 41, 74, 85, 110, 116
acquisition 2, 4, 16, 18, 19, 22, 28, 31, 34, 35, 36, 38, 39, 40, 42, 54, 62, 64, 81, 93, 96, 102, 111, 118
Additional Protocol 107
Ahmadinejad, Mahmoud 14, 50, 51, 91, 99
Al Qaeda 6, 93, 99, 101
Algiers Accords 66, 67
allies 5, 20, 40, 41, 42, 44, 47, 48, 51, 52, 53, 59, 68, 69, 70, 71, 72, 73, 82, 94, 99, 100, 111, 113, 115, 118
America 61, 64, 65, 67, 71, 72, 73, 80, 81, 82, 85, 86, 89, 90, 91, 93, 94, 97, 98, 101, 102, 103, 104, 106, 107
American Embassy 67, 82
American National Intelligence Estimate (NIE) 90
American values 81
Amirabad Research Center 49
anarchy 3, 27, 116, 117
Anti-Ballistic Missile (ABM) Treaty 95
Arab states 31, 39, 54, 58, 59, 72, 75, 114
Arab–Israeli conflict 39, 54, 58, 64, 72, 114
Arak 13, 87, 89
arms race 34, 35, 54, 96, 117
asymmetric/symmetric 27, 111
asymmetry 5, 34, 40, 63, 74, 77, 80, 83, 86, 88, 110, 113
Atomic Energy Organization of Iran (AEOI) 11
Axis of Evil 2, 6, 43, 94, 97, 98, 99, 103, 115
Axis of Evil speech 6, 94, 97, 103

Baghdad 50, 55, 70, 80, 114
ballistic missile 50, 79, 95, 97

bandwagoning 32
bargain 37, 50, 66, 105, 108, 112, 117
bargaining chip 17, 37, 105, 112
bargaining motivations 110
Bikaa Valley 67, 68
bomb 71, 84, 86, 89, 90, 91, 99, 102, 106, 111, 113, 116
bullying 71, 80, 86, 111, 112
Bush, George H. W.
Bush, George W. 78, 82, 92, 95, 97
Bush administration 2, 6, 23, 90, 92, 97, 98, 99, 102, 104, 115, 118
Bush Doctrine 101
Bushehr 12, 50, 56, 57, 85, 87, 88

Camp David Accords 59
Carter, Jimmy 49
causal connections 4
Chemical and Biological Weapons (CBW) 58
Chemical Weapons 12, 39, 53, 54, 55, 56, 70, 102, 114, 115
China 30, 43, 44, 50, 51, 53, 56, 57, 84, 87, 88, 95, 97
Christianity 81
CIA 79, 85, 86, 88
clandestine 5, 13, 19, 20, 21, 23, 31, 48, 71, 75, 79, 83, 84
clandestinely 11, 39, 47, 89, 99, 113
Clerics 5, 18, 50, 56, 57, 68
Clinton, Bill 67, 78, 80, 82
comprehensive nuclear program 48, 54, 56, 63, 71, 77, 89, 113
Comprehensive Test Ban Treaty (CTBT) 20
conflict engagement 27
conflict rival 34, 58, 72, 112
confrontational 34, 94, 106, 108, 112
congenial 118

constitution 97
constructivism 3, 116
controversy 1, 49, 65
co-optive behavioral power 31, 33
cordial 5, 47, 49, 72
cost-effectiveness 16, 40
Cuban Missile Crisis 31

defense 39, 40, 41, 53, 56, 79, 82, 83, 85, 87, 94, 95, 103, 104, 106, 113, 115
delivery systems 12, 50, 88, 90
democracy 6, 13, 59, 67, 72, 81, 90, 94, 99, 100, 104
democratic regimes 67
democratization 2, 79, 99
"Denial and Deception" Strategy 89
determination 14, 16, 52, 55, 67, 80, 87, 91
determined proliferators 2, 24, 27, 42, 43, 44, 111, 116
deterrent capability 2, 3, 6, 19, 30, 39, 57, 58, 64, 90, 111, 114
dialogue 13, 37, 67, 107
diaspora 73
diplomacy 30, 52, 99, 104
diplomatic relations 66
discriminatory policies 79
disparity 35, 40, 50, 116
domestic politics 16, 23, 110
double standard 14, 72, 102
dual-use nuclear technologies 84
dyadic 5, 27, 39, 41, 42, 47, 52, 54, 55, 58, 64, 111, 113, 114

Egypt 11, 58, 59, 60, 79, 100
El Baradei, Mohammad 13
enduring rivalry 35, 38, 39, 96, 101, 102, 112
enemy 1, 2, 6, 19, 38, 40, 41, 59, 69, 71, 74, 76, 82, 93, 94, 96, 97, 101, 106, 108, 113, 114
enriching 14, 48, 84, 89, 90, 102, 105, 107, 110
escalation 39, 41, 113
EU3 plan 13
EU3 proposals 14
European politics 32
European states 91
expertise 23, 51, 59, 84

facilitate 30, 83
facilities 13, 15, 47, 48, 51, 85, 88, 97, 98, 100
Ford 49
fungibility 36

Gates, Robert 79, 85
generalization 116
German 50, 56
global power 3, 32, 33, 34, 35, 36, 37, 38, 40, 41, 42, 43, 63, 74, 86, 96, 111, 112, 115, 116, 119
global reach 5, 35, 115
Great Satan 23, 65, 78
grievances 107
Gulf War of 1990–91

Hamas 60, 69, 114
hegemon 36, 37, 80
hegemonic power 4, 6, 32, 33, 44, 51, 63, 111
Hezbollah 2, 58, 60, 67, 68, 69, 72, 93, 98, 104, 113, 114
hierarchy 58, 74, 104, 106
higher-than-normal probability 29
hostage crisis 65, 66, 67, 68
hostility 1, 30, 37, 38, 63, 65, 66, 73, 76, 93, 97, 104, 108, 112
human rights 16, 67, 81, 99
human rights violations 81
Hussein, Saddam 1, 32, 53, 55, 58, 70, 75, 80, 81, 100, 101, 104, 110, 114

ideology 18, 33, 40, 55, 58, 65, 66, 68, 81, 82
inclination 5, 6, 12, 14, 15, 28, 94
incompatibility 66, 67, 74
indefinite extension 83, 86, 88, 100
intentions 11, 12, 17, 20, 33, 37, 38, 41, 51, 52, 54, 57, 60, 79, 80, 83, 98, 99, 103, 108, 109, 112, 113, 119
International Atomic Energy Agency (IAEA) 13
international community 1, 14, 15, 17, 41, 44, 48, 49, 51, 52, 54, 55, 60, 61, 63, 70, 78, 82, 89, 90, 92, 99, 107, 110, 114, 116, 119
International Crisis Behavior (ICB) 29
international environment 33
international laws 21
international norms 70, 78, 95
International Relations 3, 56, 116, 117
international system 3, 15, 27, 28, 29, 32, 33, 35, 37, 38, 42, 77, 78, 81, 102, 111, 112, 115, 116, 119
intractable conflict 1, 3, 4, 7, 23, 27, 47, 63, 64, 66, 78, 79, 97, 108, 111, 113, 117
Iranian assets 2, 66
Iranian nationalists 21
Iranian opposition group 84, 89

154   Index

Iranian Revolutionary Guard Corps 85
Iran–Iraq protracted conflict 63
Iran–Iraq War 1, 5, 12, 13, 50, 53, 58, 69, 70, 76, 100, 108
Iran–US protracted conflict 6, 66, 77, 115
Isfahan 14, 75, 85, 88
Isfahan Nuclear Technology Center (INTC) 75
Islam 12, 18, 81
Islamic culture 81
Islamic ideology 55, 58, 65, 68
Islamic Jihad 60
Islamic Leadership 2
Islamic Republic 2, 13, 18, 22, 23, 61, 64, 72, 74, 81, 92, 95, 97, 104, 108, 110, 118
Islamic Revolution 1, 5, 12, 13, 20, 50, 53, 56, 60, 62, 64, 65, 66, 67, 68, 72, 75, 81, 90, 92, 106, 113
Islamic world 52, 59, 60, 61, 86

Khameini, Ali 5, 50, 56, 68, 84
Khan, A. Q. 12, 52, 82, 91, 115
Khatami, Mohammad 13, 50, 51
Khomeini 12, 13, 18, 50, 64, 65, 67, 76, 84, 113
Kurdistan 52
Kuwait 69, 77, 79, 80, 81, 83, 103

Lebanon 2, 58, 60, 67, 68, 69, 71, 72, 93, 98, 113, 114
Libya 43, 50, 65, 78, 97
light-water research reactor 47
long-range missiles 95, 115

maturation 16, 22
Memorandum of Understanding (MOU) 72
Middle East 1, 2, 6, 12, 19, 20, 40, 41, 44, 48, 50, 51, 55, 57, 58, 59, 60, 61, 63, 64, 66, 67, 69, 72, 75, 79, 80, 81, 82, 83
Middle East peace 69, 104
military applications 48, 84, 86, 110, 115
military confrontation 32, 91, 92, 97, 112
Ministry of Defense 85
minor power 112
miscalculating 33
miscalculations 41, 113
misperceptions 37, 38, 112
missile programs 6, 86
misunderstanding 33
modernization 2
Mojahedin 84
Mordechai Vanunu's testimony 59
Mossadeq, Mohammad 47

motivation 3, 4, 11, 15, 19, 21, 22, 23, 33, 37, 49, 64, 90, 98, 110, 112, 116
multiple conflicts 4, 24, 39, 40, 41, 42. 44, 111, 116, 117
Mutual Assured Destruction (MAD) 31

Natanz 13, 60, 89, 90, 106
National Council of Resistance of Iran (NCRI) 89
National Missile Defense System 95, 115
National Security Strategy (NSS) 97
National Strategy to Combat Weapons of Mass Destruction (NSWMD) 97
Negotiation 14, 38, 41, 61, 90, 91, 100, 105, 107, 108
Neorealism 116
new world order 77
No-Dong missile 95
Non-Aligned Movement (NAM) 85
Non-Nuclear-Weapon State (NNWS) 20
non-proliferation 2, 3, 12, 21, 27, 49, 86, 88, 90, 94, 98, 100, 104, 118
non-state actors 94, 98
North Korea 6, 21, 22, 30, 31, 34, 43, 44, 50, 51, 56, 75, 78, 80, 84, 85, 88, 89, 92, 95, 97, 104, 119
NPT Review and Extension Conference 85
nuclear ambition 1, 4, 5, 23, 24, 47, 49, 75, 77, 82, 95, 110, 113
nuclear capabilities 5, 21, 36, 59
nuclear fuel cycle 17, 19, 22, 48, 51, 99
nuclear Iran 21, 40, 61
nuclear issue 2, 16, 17, 18, 19, 60, 67, 82, 87, 88, 89, 91, 103, 105, 108
Nuclear Non-proliferation Treaty (NPT) 12
nuclear posture 97, 98, 99, 115
Nuclear Posture Review 97, 115
nuclear power plant 57, 85, 87, 88
nuclear rivals 3, 5
nuclear scientist 12, 56, 57, 87
nuclear sites 110
nuclear technology 11, 14, 23, 48, 50, 75, 83, 84, 85, 87, 88
nuclear weapons program 1, 2, 4, 5, 6, 11
Nuclear Weapons-Free Zone (NWFZ) 12

Opaque 5, 22, 23, 59, 60, 64, 72, 75, 110, 114
Operation Desert Storm 81
opponent 2, 5, 22, 23, 27, 30, 32, 33, 35, 36, 37, 38, 71, 111, 112
Osiraq 21, 57, 114

Index

pace 2, 3, 5, 6, 50, 89, 91, 95, 96, 103, 110, 113, 116
Pakistan's assistance 84
parallel nuclear programs 85
parity 34, 35, 40, 50, 75, 81, 112, 116, 117
peace 1, 2, 6, 14, 20, 22, 28, 33, 35, 36, 38, 41, 43, 47, 48, 49, 51, 52, 57, 61, 69, 73, 77, 85, 86, 87, 88, 94, 96, 97, 99, 100, 102, 104, 107, 110
Pentagon 79, 94
perception 15, 22, 29, 37, 38, 84, 87, 112, 115, 117, 118
Persian Gulf 6, 20, 51, 78, 103
pivotal 30, 53, 66, 73
political instability 53, 55
possession 2, 3, 21, 22, 30, 31, 34, 35, 37, 39, 40, 49, 60, 74, 98, 111, 112
powerful 6, 18, 20, 33, 35, 74, 92
prestige 4, 15, 18, 19, 20, 21, 34, 35, 36, 37, 40, 74, 81, 83, 110, 111, 112, 117
proliferators 1, 2, 3, 4, 5, 11, 15, 17, 23, 24, 27, 42, 43, 44, 50, 61, 73, 83, 89, 96, 110, 111, 116
propensity 3, 4, 5, 29, 30, 33, 36, 42, 63, 96, 100, 112, 114, 116
protracted war 2, 17, 19, 50, 53, 63, 74, 114
protracted/non-protracted 27, 111
proximate/non-proximate 27, 111
proxy wars 2, 31
psychological 15, 16, 37, 40
public 16, 17, 18, 69, 78, 82, 90

radicals 98
Rafsanjani, Ali Akbar Hashemi 5, 50, 84, 98
Reagan, Ronald 68
Realism 3, 116
reforms 30
regional peace 2, 6, 107
regional proliferators 1, 43, 89
regional superpower 75, 81
relentless 2, 6, 16, 41, 83, 90, 102, 110, 113
renouncing 59, 118
reprocess 48, 49
Republican Guards 84
resolution 3, 14, 27, 50, 55, 67, 105, 106, 117
retaliate 23, 30, 93
revelations 18, 58, 82, 90, 106, 107
rhetoric 6, 77, 80, 91, 97, 108
rivalry 2, 31, 32, 35, 36, 38, 39, 41, 64, 74, 75, 96, 101, 102, 106, 111, 112

Rogue Doctrine 79
rogue state 2, 21, 77, 78, 79, 83, 92, 115
Russian assistance 87

Samson Option 60
sanctions 21, 22, 52, 55, 58, 65, 66, 72, 75, 77, 80, 82, 86, 88, 89, 91, 96, 99, 105, 106, 107, 117
scientific/technological momentum 16
security challenges 5, 50
security guarantees 21, 41
Shah 1, 5, 11, 12, 16, 19, 47, 48, 49, 53, 54, 64, 65, 74
Shatt-al-Arab 52, 53
Shehab 1 51
Shehab 2 51
Shehab 3 51
Shehab 4 79
Shiite clerics 68
South Africa 43, 48, 56, 57, 84, 87
stability 2, 6, 22, 33, 61, 77, 80, 82, 94, 107
status inconsistency 37, 112
strategic capabilities 6, 50
strategic imbalance 44, 114
structurally-determined rivalry 32, 111
Supreme Leader 5, 13, 50, 75, 84, 87, 91
Supreme National Security Council 87
suspension agreement 91
swaggering 40, 80, 81
Syria 11, 39, 51, 58, 59, 78, 94, 97, 104
systemic power structure 112

technical assistance 84
technology 11, 14, 15, 19, 21, 23, 28, 41, 48, 49, 50, 75, 79, 83, 84, 85, 87, 88
Tehran Nuclear Research Center (TNRC) 47
Tel Aviv 65, 72, 93
tendency 28, 34, 35, 37, 41, 112
territorial/non-territorial 27, 111
terrorism 33, 56, 60, 61, 65, 68, 69, 70, 76, 77, 78, 79, 82, 93, 94, 107
terrorist organization 60, 93
Track II meetings 67
triple protracted conflicts 5, 62, 63, 75
trust 23, 33, 41, 76, 100, 103, 107, 108, 113, 118
twin protracted conflicts 5, 47, 54, 113

unconventional 22, 23
unipolar world 2, 6, 32
United Nations 2, 13, 54, 66, 98, 100, 101, 105, 107

156   *Index*

United Nations Security Council (UNSC) 105
uranium 1, 2, 13, 14, 48, 50, 51, 56, 57, 60, 75, 84, 85, 87, 88, 89, 90, 91, 99, 102, 105, 106, 107, 110
uranium conversion 14, 75, 88
uranium enrichment program 1, 85, 90, 91, 99
US foreign policies 6, 7, 76
US marine barracks 68
US National Security Council Memo 49
US State Department 84, 88

variables 4, 11, 13, 15, 23, 24, 27, 43, 117, 119

war avoidance mechanisms 28, 30
war probability 29, 30, 34, 39, 42, 111
Washington 2, 22, 47, 59, 65, 69, 70, 72, 79, 80, 81, 82, 88, 93, 94, 95, 97, 101, 102, 106, 116, 118
weaker challenger 33
weaker power 5, 31, 32, 34, 35, 36, 37, 38, 111, 112
weaponization 90
weapons of mass destruction 2, 6, 18, 70, 78, 88, 97, 102
West, the 12, 17, 21, 22, 23, 31, 65, 69, 77, 81, 85, 86, 87, 90, 92, 93, 95, 96
westernization 2, 81
window of opportunity 55, 109, 114
World Trade Center (WTC) 94

yellowcake 48, 91

zero-sum mentality 30, 34
Zionist 23, 57, 59, 64
Zionist regime 23, 59, 64

For Product Safety Concerns and Information please contact our EU
representative GPSR@taylorandfrancis.com
Taylor & Francis Verlag GmbH, Kaufingerstraße 24, 80331 München, Germany

www.ingramcontent.com/pod-product-compliance
Lightning Source LLC
Chambersburg PA
CBHW051747230426
43670CB00012B/2194